AROUND MIDDLESBROUGH

PAUL MENZIES

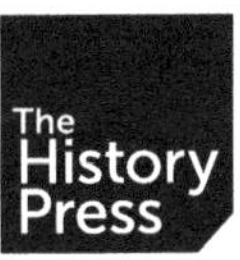

*I would like to dedicate this book to my wife Jackie Menzies,
Lauren Kirtley, the late John Lindberg, Lavinia Simpson and the workers
at Corus, now seemingly consigned to history*

First published 2010

The History Press
The Mill, Brimscombe Port
Stroud, Gloucestershire, GL5 2QG
www.thehistorypress.co.uk

Reprinted 2017

ISBN 978 0 7524 5730 7

Typesetting and origination by The History Press
Printed in Great Britain by TJ International Ltd, Padstow, Cornwall

CONTENTS

ACKNOWLEDGEMENTS

I give grateful thanks to all those individuals and organisations that have allowed me to copy and use their material, given of their time and generally helped in my research. I have taken a great deal of time in tracing and establishing ownership of all material and ensuring that permission for reproduction in this work has been given, whether in copyright or not.

My thanks must go to the late John Lindberg; the late Wilf Mannion; Len Whitehouse; Revd W. Wright; Steve Wild at Stockton Reference Library; the now defunct Cleveland County Council Planning Department; Mark Rowland-Jones and Jo Faulkner at Stockton Museum Service; the staff at Middlesbrough Reference Library, particularly Larry Bruce back in the 1980s; David Tyrell, Janet Baker, Stuart Pacitto, Anne Thirsk and Debbi Dale at Teesside Archives; Louise Harris at i/c Collections at Dorman Museum; Alan Sims at the *Evening Gazette* Teesside; Jeff and Vera Wilkinson; Bill Bandeira; Steve Hearn at the Ordnance Survey; NRM York; and of course Matilda Richards, my editor at The History Press, who has offered such good support during the writing of this work. Other material is from the author's own collection. If there are any unmentioned sources here I offer my grateful thanks as well as my apologies for failing to mention them by name.

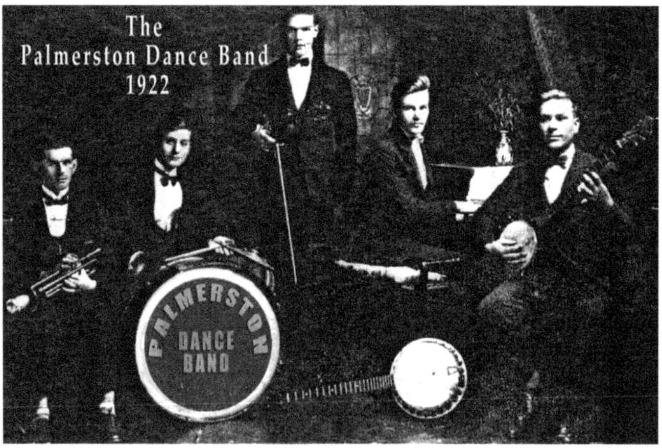

The Palmerstone Dance Band featuring John Lindberg on piano.
They were one of the leading jazz bands in Middlesbrough
during the 1920s.

INTRODUCTION

It is almost fifteen years since I first wrote a book looking at the history of Middlesbrough and it is pleasing to note that there has been a consistent interest in this area in the years that have passed since then. A great deal more evidence has come to light since then, enabling the history of Middlesbrough to be increasingly well documented. Suffice to say, when I first began to research the history of the area evidence was scattered. This was particularly the case with photographic evidence, where the need to preserve the past in a visual sense was not necessarily regarded as a priority for those who held such material. However, awareness of the past has grown immensely in the past quarter of a century and in the process a lot of new material has come to light. Excellent organisations like Teesside Archives provide an invaluable service for people with an interest in the past. Added to this, many wonderful new images have come to light which, while not always providing new discoveries about the past, can always endorse our current knowledge.

There have also been immense strides forward with computer technology, an invaluable aid in improving not only the quality but also the range of images available. Many of the images in this book have been digitally restored using Photoshop. In doing so the sole aim has been to restore each image as closely as possible to its original state. Occasionally, in performing digital restoration, decisions have to be taken to include something which does not exist – for example, a missing part of an image. It is hoped that where this is the case you will agree the image has been sensitively restored. Indeed I hope you will not even be able to tell!

Research for this book has involved many hours of looking through material and making decisions about what to include and, much more difficult, what to leave out. This has been a labour of love for me as I have always been a historian 'by trade' through a university degree and the more specialised post-graduate study leading to my Master of Arts in history. My academic speciality – twentieth-century political history – ran parallel to an insatiable appetite for local history, and in particular, the history of Middlesbrough, home to my maternal grandparents. I was very fortunate in having a father who took me to Middlesbrough Reference Library from an early age and was prepared to wait patiently while I looked with fascination through huge volumes of old newspapers (no microfiche machines then). To read about events in my area a century before fired within me an endless desire to know everything that had happened. There was also the added edge called 'change'. To think that there was once a farm next to the clear, flowing waters of a river on land which was by then row after row of terraced houses, gas-lit streets next to a heavily polluted stretch of water was just amazing. And that was it – a historian was born and that longing to find out about the past is still there today.

Two centuries ago, a small farmhouse would be just visible standing on a slightly elevated site above the river; today it is the urban development of Middlesbrough. History allows us to make that time come alive again; an example is the diary of Ralph Jackson

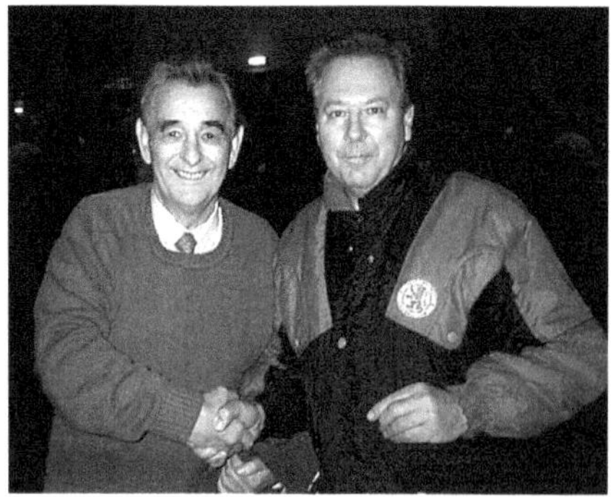

The author with Brian Clough. I was privileged to know one of Middlesbrough's heroes, Brian Clough. Brian, born and bred in the town of Middlesbrough and a star of the Middlesbrough football team in the late 1950s. This photograph was taken on a visit during his final years to see Middlesbrough against Sunderland on 10 September 2002. A statue in Albert Park Middlesbrough ensures Brian's links with the town will not be forgotten.

when he writes in 1783 of riding down from Normanby Hall across the fields to the River Tees and seeing Middlesbrough Farm across the fields. The scenario of contrast between the rural past and today's urban world could be repeated many times. Eventually it borders on the edge of romance and the fanciful as the temptation looms for many of us to regard it as a better world then. It wasn't of course (reading of some of the difficulties of dealing with illness alone should convince anyone of this) – but it was very different.

That is where this work comes in. I have not attempted to produce a complete history of Middlesbrough – lack of space prevents this. It is hoped, however, that this book will make the reader stop and think for a moment of aspects of the world as it was in our area. Whether this is the pre-industrial world of the eighteenth and early nineteenth century or of more recent times is not really important. I think of this book as a signpost to aspects of the history of Middlesbrough with the images acting as a visual stimulus to that journey into the past.

While I have attempted to ensure that there are no obvious mistakes in this work, I would like to apologise in advance for any errors that have been made, factual or otherwise. Please let me know of any errors and I will update my records. In the same vein, if anyone has any more information or evidence about any aspect of the history of Middlesbrough that they would like to share with me please get in touch, especially if you have any images that you will allow me to copy. With computer technology they can be copied in minutes and, in the case of damaged material, they can even be restored to a state which may even be an improvement on the original print! I have been pleased to provide digitally-restored images for a number of people. Also, in digitally preserving these images they are being saved in a form where they will not deteriorate.

Writing of any nature always impacts on those people closest to you and this is the case here. I would like to offer an enormous thank you to my dear wife Jackie, who not only proofread this work but has had to put up with many months of my rising at five o'clock in the morning to write before going off to my other job, as well as many rainy afternoons spent at either Teesside Archives or the Reference Library in Middlesbrough.

Paul Menzies, 2010
m.menzies1@ntlworld.com

1

FROM GREEN FIELDS

The town of Middlesbrough is comparatively young – less than 200 years ago the site was an isolated farm built close to the ruins of a medieval Benedictine Priory.

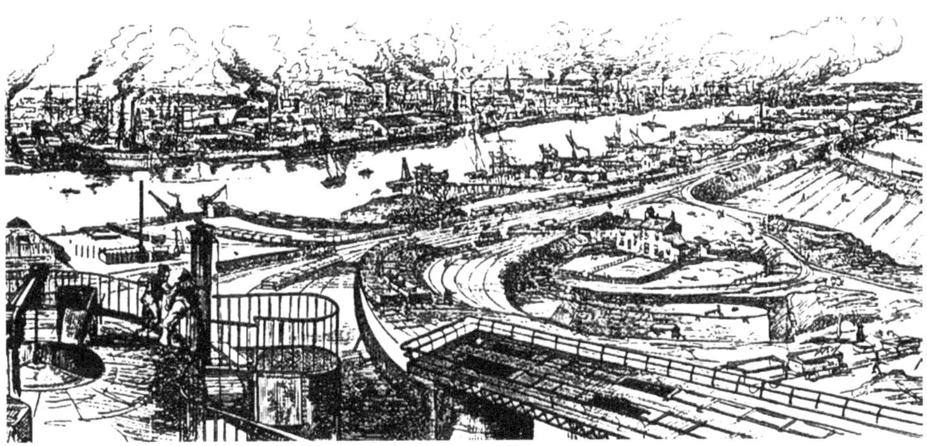

A view of Middlesbrough printed in the *Illustrated London News* of October 1881 to mark the town's jubilee. Looking across from the top of a blast furnace, it portrays Middlesbrough as a place of enterprise and industry – a far cry from the green fields of 1830.

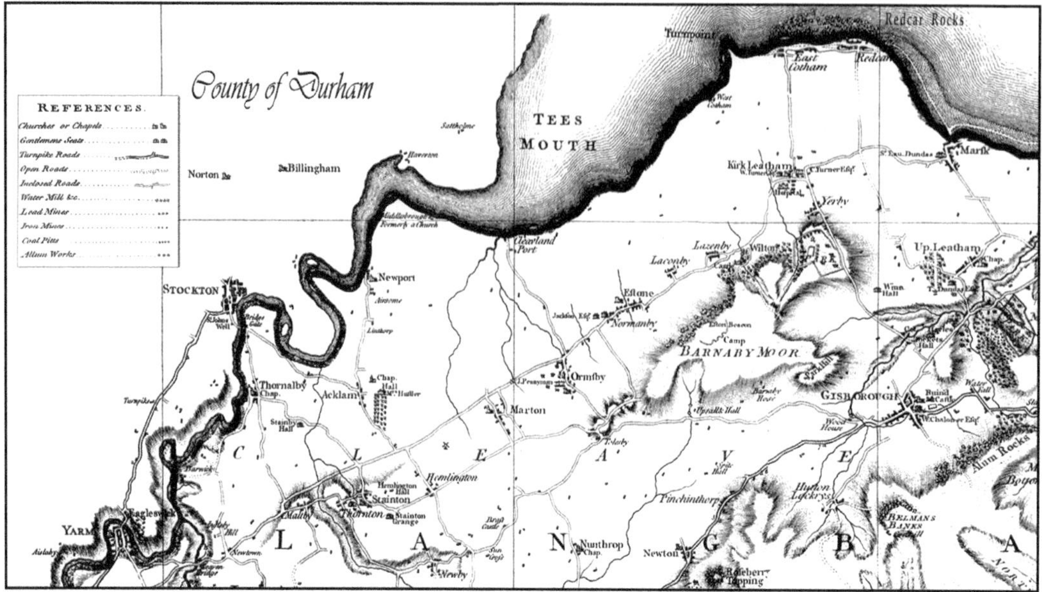

Middlesbrough is one of several small communities shown on Thomas Jeffery's map of 1772 of the lower reaches of the Tees. Others include Cleveland Port (later Cargo Fleet), Newport, Airesome and Linthorpe, while Marton, Ormesby, Normanby and Eston were on the route from Yarm to Redcar. The local economy was mainly dependent on agriculture although a number of mining concerns, mainly alum, are shown. The main route in the region, the ancient road from Durham to Whitby, passed through Stockton and Gisborough [*sic*]. It had been considerably improved for travellers in 1769 with the new toll-bridge at Stockton, a venture which helped in the expansion of port activities at Stockton at this time, despite its navigational limitations. These included being some distance from the sea due to the meanders at Mandale and Portrack, as well as hazardous, narrow, shallow channels and shifting sandbanks. Ships of more than 100 tons were unable to leave Stockton fully laden, while those heading up river to the port often had to unload down river at either Cleveland Port or Newport for transhipment. Ultimately these factors would limit development of trade at the port. Elsewhere the coastal area is remote, populated only by small fishing communities including East Coatham, Redcar, Marske and Saltburn. The 'seats' of several landowning families are also shown, including Acklam Hall (the Hustler family), Ormesby Hall (the Pennyman family), Normanby Hall (the Jackson family) and Kirkleatham Hall (the Turner family).

Opposite: These two images of Wilton Castle in 1829 (above) and in the 1840s (below) are interesting because they provide a prospect of almost the whole of the lower reaches of the Tees in the early stages of local industrial development. The image from 1829 shows boats sailing in Teesmouth – which is extremely wide compared with the modern-day estuary. The shores of south-east Durham are some distance away, while close to Wilton lies the estuarine floodplain, where flooding regularly washed away the best efforts of those attempting to farm the land. Almost twenty years later, the 1840s view of Wilton Castle shows the river up to Middlesbrough. In the foreground is the windmill at Cleveland Port while the early development at Middlesbrough is visible in the distance. Much of the land in this view would later become part of the urban development, as from the mid-nineteenth century subsequent reclamation along the lower reaches of the Tees artificially constrained the river and provided areas of land vital for the expansion of local industry.

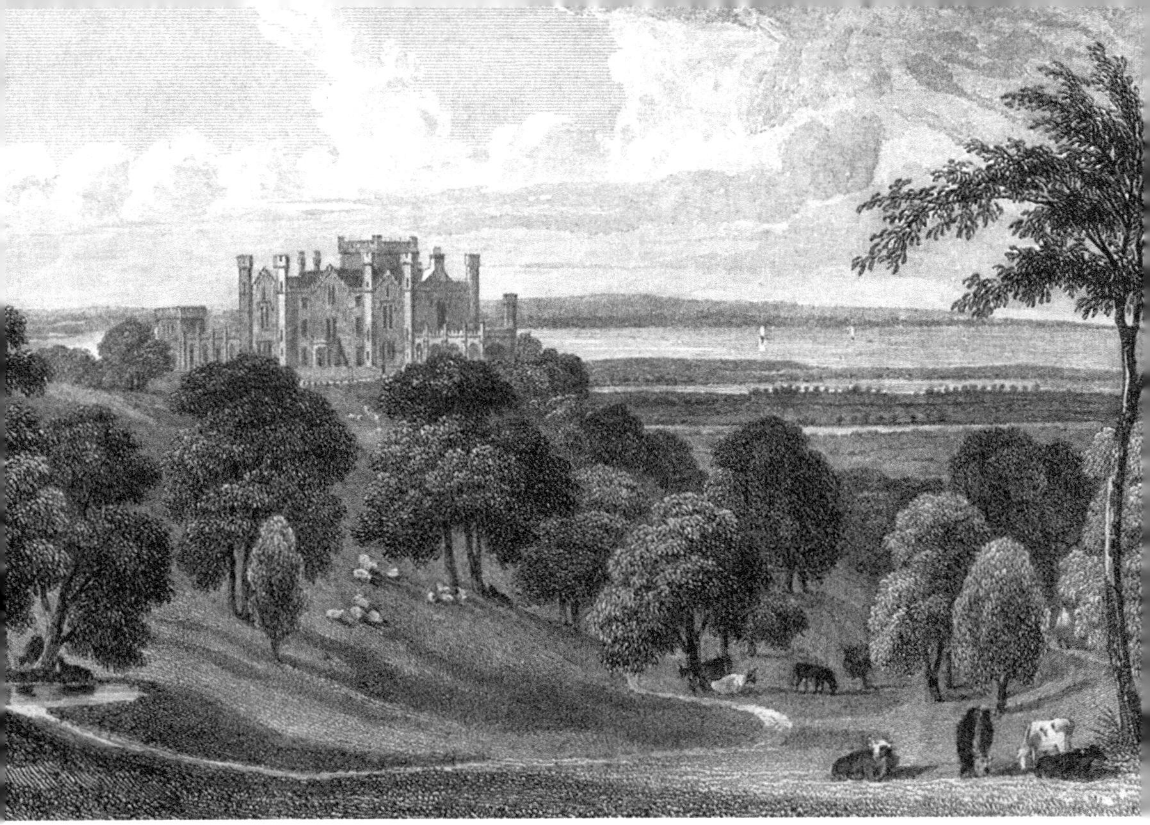

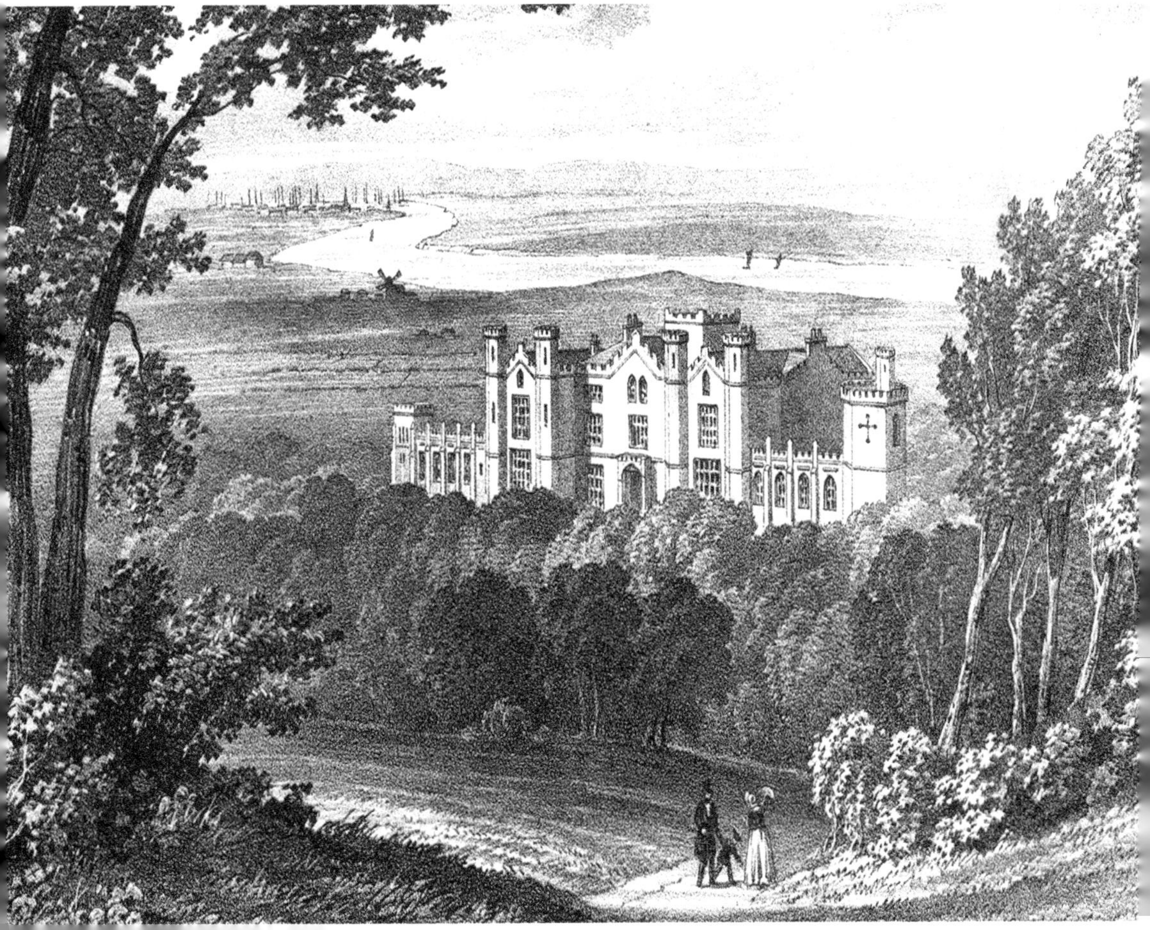

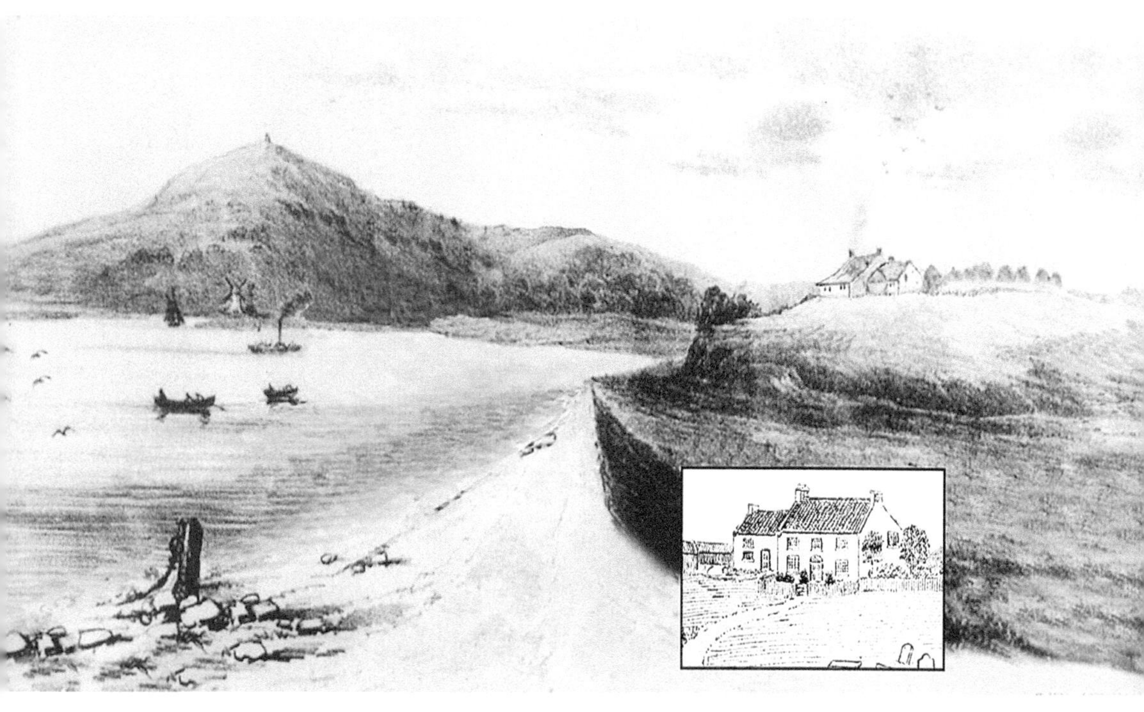

A Benedictine Priory, founded in the twelfth century, existed in peaceful solitude for several centuries on the site of modern Middlesbrough. After the Dissolution, the priory fell into disuse and its lands were leased out. John Gibbon's map of 1618 still shows church buildings at the site, but much of the stone had been taken for use elsewhere, leaving only ruins, some of which were later incorporated into the buildings of Middlesbrough Farm. Although a small community at the priory site survived, this view, based on a drawing of around 1830, shows little more than Middlesbrough Farm on an elevated site close to the river Tees. The inset image, dating from around 1808, shows how close the ancient burial ground – still used then – was to the house. One of the last inhabitants of the farm, Tom Parrington, spoke of the enchanting view across the fields towards the Cleveland Hills and the beacon erected on Eston Nab during the Napoleonic Wars. In the shadow of the hills are the windmill and granary at Cleveland Port (later Cargo Fleet). Large ships, unable to navigate any further up river, unloaded their cargo here to be taken by smaller boats up to Stockton. New cargo was then taken on board; diarist Ralph Jackson writes of spending time aboard ships 'moored at the Quay [*sic*]' while on 4 December 1787 he saw 'the Sloop Fox haul from the Granery [*sic*] at Cargo Fleet: loaded with corn ... bound for London.' It is interesting to note how wide the river is as it is not yet contained within the narrow channels created artificially in later years.

Opposite below: To those who recall the heavy industry, dreadful pollution and the endless terraced housing that covered this area, it stretches the imagination now to think of Newport, Linthorpe and Ayresome as hamlets amidst the green fields and hedgerows shown here in these map extracts of 1856. Only the Middlesbrough Branch of the Stockton & Darlington Railway hints at future industrial development. Today names like Linthorpe Green, the Ferry Boat Inn at Newport, Ayresome Grange and Old Gate Farm (later the site of Ayresome Park football ground) are the only reminders of a more rural age. (Reproduced from 1856 Ordnance Survey map, 25-inch series, with the kind permission of Ordnance Survey)

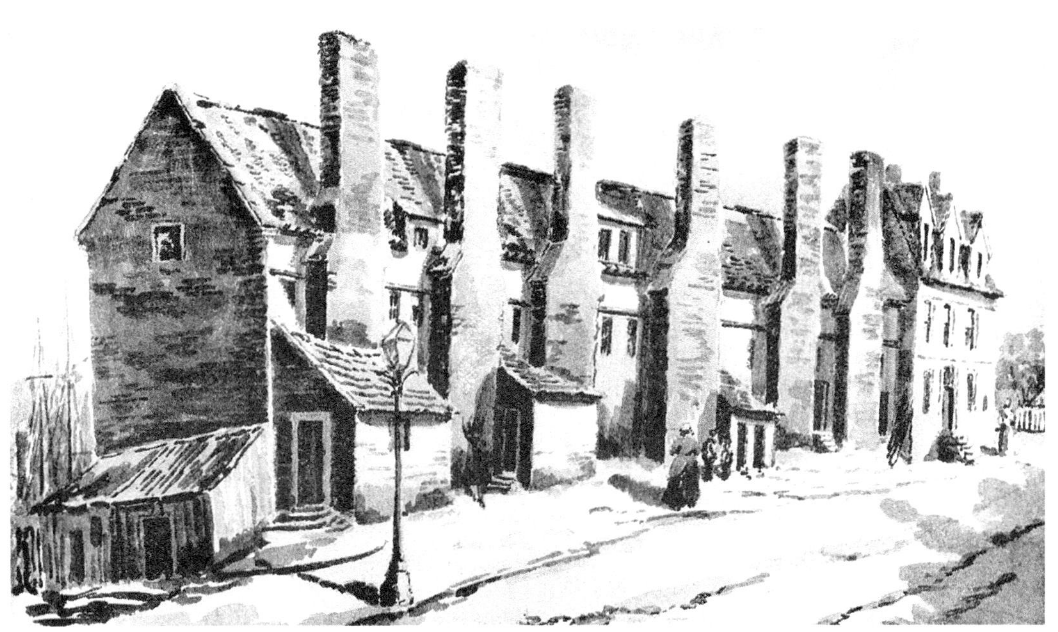

Above: After purchasing Acklam Estate in 1637, the Hustler family erected a quay and a granary close to an ancient ferry point across the Tees. This commercial venture was aimed at attracting river trade, particularly that linked to the transhipment of cargo. Newport, however, remained a small hamlet of some cottages, a farm and an inn, eventually being absorbed into Middlesbrough. The warehouse facilities later became part of Newport House, seen in this image from a sketch by J.S. Calvert, *c.* 1898. Comprising of a number of connected dwellings with a larger property at the eastern end of the building, Newport House was demolished in the 1930s.

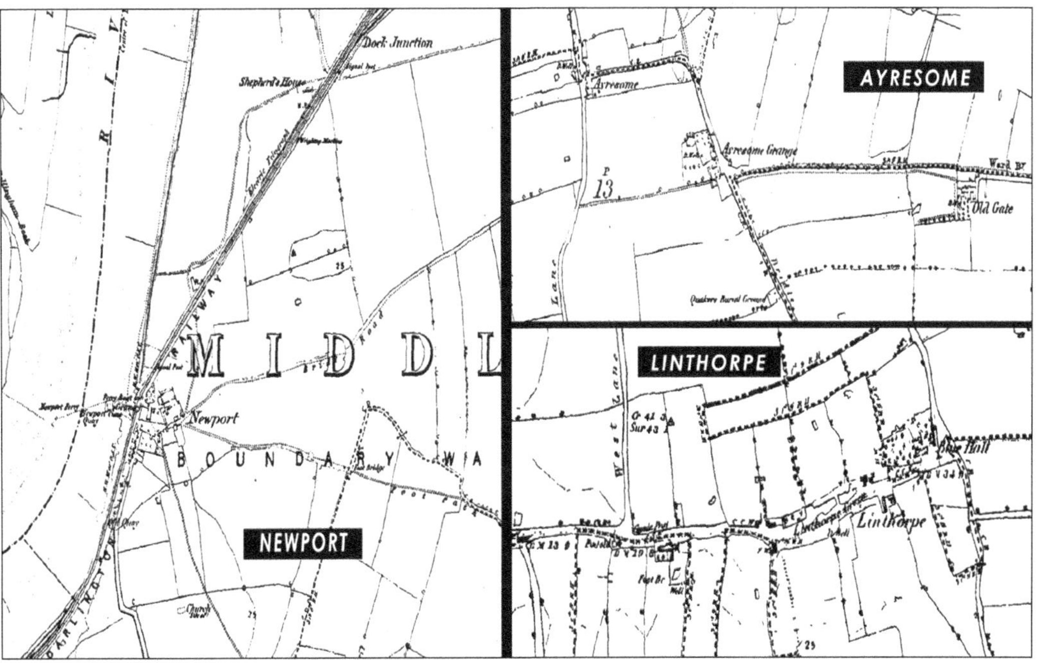

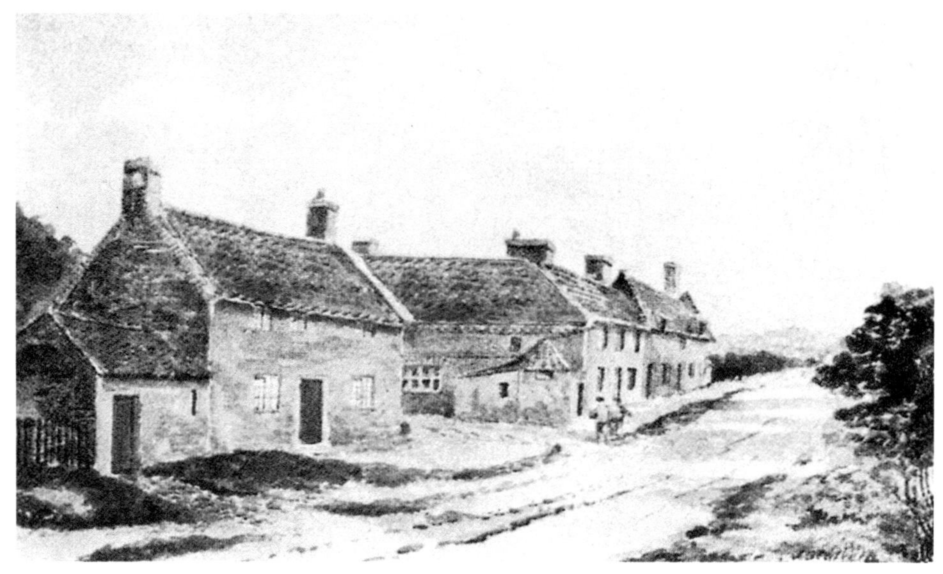

Less than a mile to the south of Newport was Airesome (Ayresome), part of the township of Linthorpe. This painting of around 1898 by J.S. Calvert shows the diminutive collection of seventeenth-century cottages which made up the village. The view looks south towards West Lane, with the turning beyond the first cottage being close to the modern junction of Ayresome Green Lane and Ayresome Lane.

Walking along this lane in 1898 led to Airesome Grange, shown here in about 1900. The farm was located close to the modern-day main vehicle entrance to the former Middlesbrough General Hospital. Both the farm and the old cottages survived into the twentieth century, being demolished just before the start of the First World War.

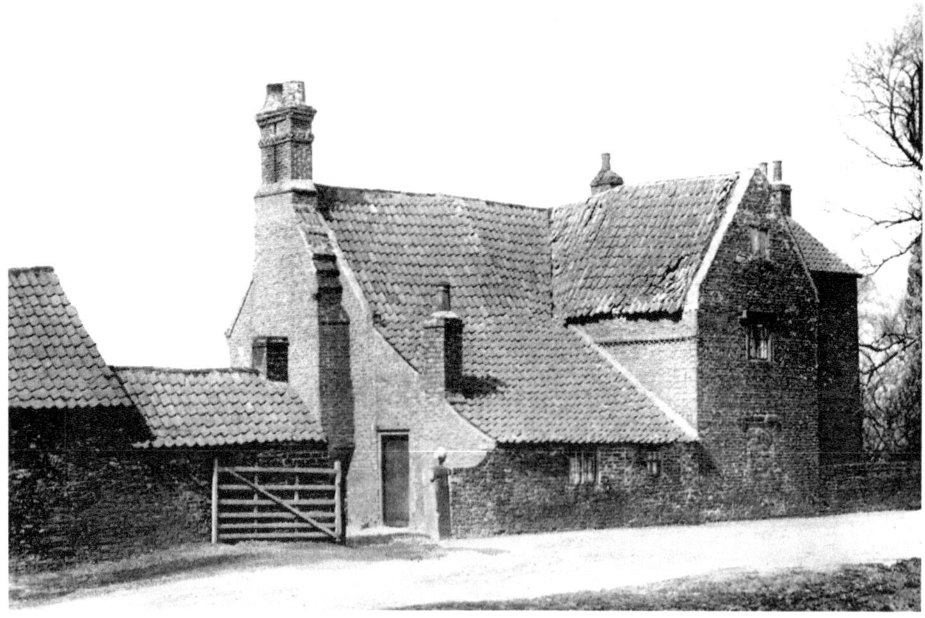

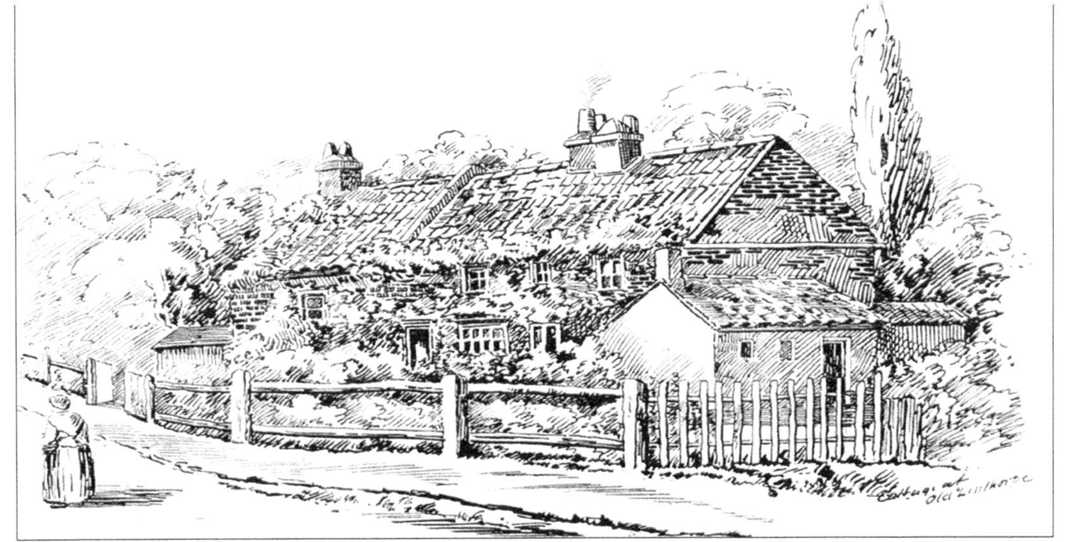

Another long-established community was Linthorpe. Probably of Saxon or Viking origin, two derivatives of the modern place name 'Levingthorpe' and 'Levynthrop' exist in church records of the post-Conquest era. Gibbon's 1618 plan of Middlesbrough shows Linthorpe as a community situated along the modern Burlam Road, with Linthorpe Green being a long strip of land close to where the cemetery is today. The Hustler estate plan of 1716 shows Linthorpe as consisting of two rows of houses, each dwelling standing in its own 'garth' or enclosed plot. This late nineteenth-century drawing, again by J.S. Calvert, shows some of the cottages in 'Old Linthorpe', a name used by then to distinguish the ancient community from the newer nineteenth-century development.

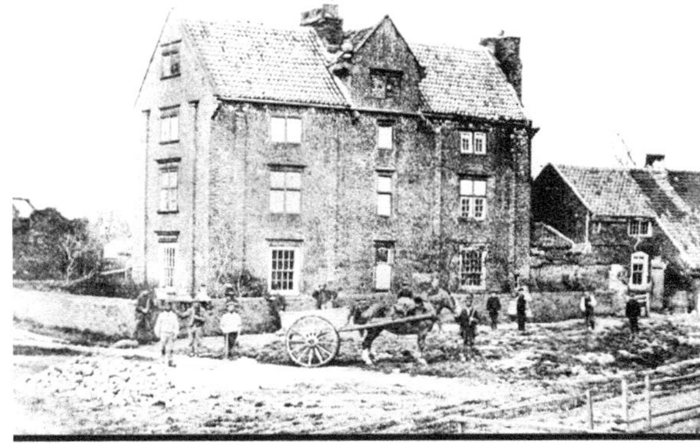

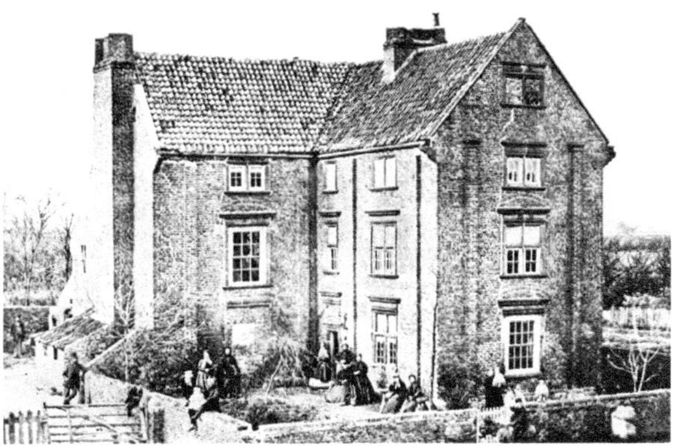

Blue Hall, Linthorpe stood east of old Linthorpe village at the corner of Burlam Road and Roman Road. The L-shaped building with its mullion and transom windows was probably built in the late seventeenth century – it features in Samuel Buck's sketchbook of 1720. Different aspects of Blue Hall are seen here in about 1865. It was demolished in 1870 and replaced by a new brick residence. On 18 December 1887 it opened as a rescue-home for women under the auspices of the Salvation Army. This appears to have lasted only until 1893, when it became again a private residence. By 1925 it was unoccupied and for sale and it was was eventually demolished in July 1927.

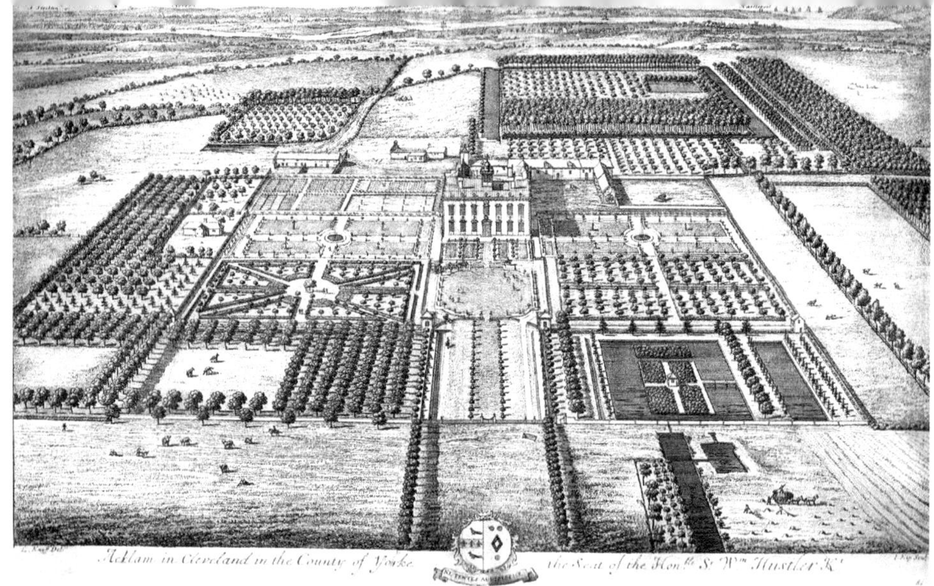

The Acklam Estate, bought by William Hustler of Bridlington in 1637, is shown in this Kyff/ Kypp engraving of 1703. The estate, which included the hamlets of Newport and Middlesbrough, reached down to the river and was dominated by Acklam Hall, erected by Hustler's grandson, also William Hustler, between 1680 and 1683. An elaborate building, it was surrounded by well-planted formal gardens, very much the fashion of the time for wealthy landowners. North of the Hall is Acklam Church, which, when rebuilt in 1770, contained some fittings from an unconsecrated chapel at Airesome some of which were originally from Middlesbrough Priory. In the far distance the mouth of the Tees and Hartlepool are both visible.

Acklam Hall after substantial alterations had been made following a fire in December 1845. Restoration formality was replaced by a new 'Gothic' architectural style, featuring gables and turrets. Attic rooms and a new porch were added, decorated with Gothic gables. The gardens were altered too, with large lawns laid and woods planted close to the Hall.

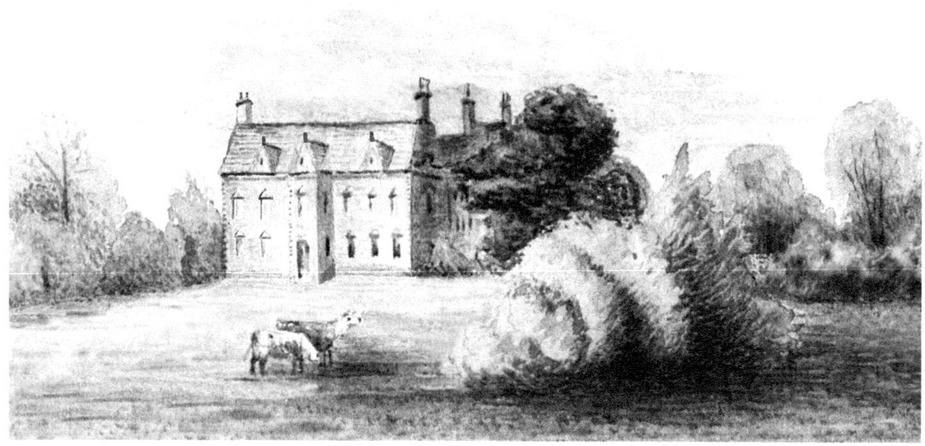

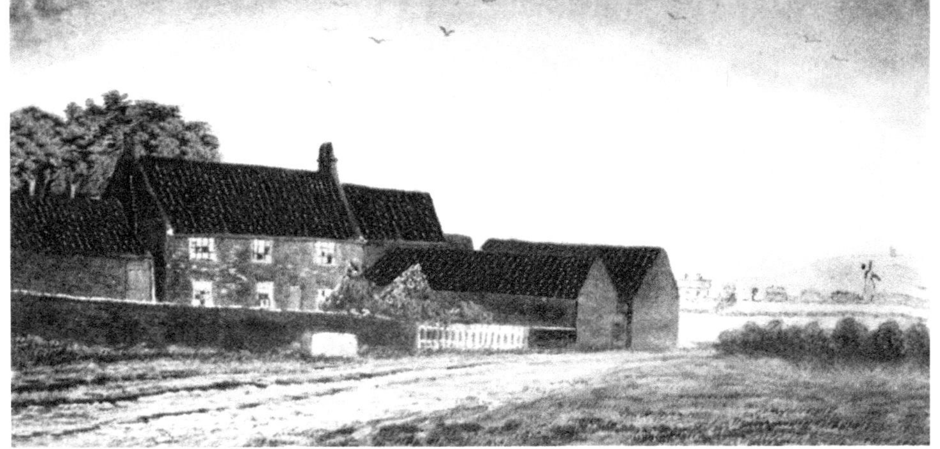

Another farm in the area was Swathers Carr (or Swatters Carr) which stood at the corner of Linthorpe Road and Southfield Road, shown here around 1870. Mentioned as early as 1618 on John Gibbon's plan of Middlesbrough, by the mid-nineteenth century areas of the farm were gradually being sold off to the developers, as Middlesbrough expanded southwards. Middlesbrough Cricket Club used part of the land between 1857 and 1874 and the Cleveland Agricultural Society held their annual show there in 1879, but by 1900 the farm was no more. This image shows the farmhouse looking south towards the mill on Acklam Green Lane.

White House Farm on the Pennyman Estate is another of the many farms worked in this area in the pre-industrial era. Situated close to where King's Road and Westbourne Grove today merge as Ormesby Road, the farm was for many years tenanted by George Wilkinson and his family, some of whom are seen posing here in about 1900. They were the last tenants of the farm before it was demolished to make way for local development, including the building of the Majestic Cinema, which opened on 17 December 1938. (Reproduced from 1893 Ordnance Survey map, 25 inch series, with the kind permission of the Ordnance Survey)

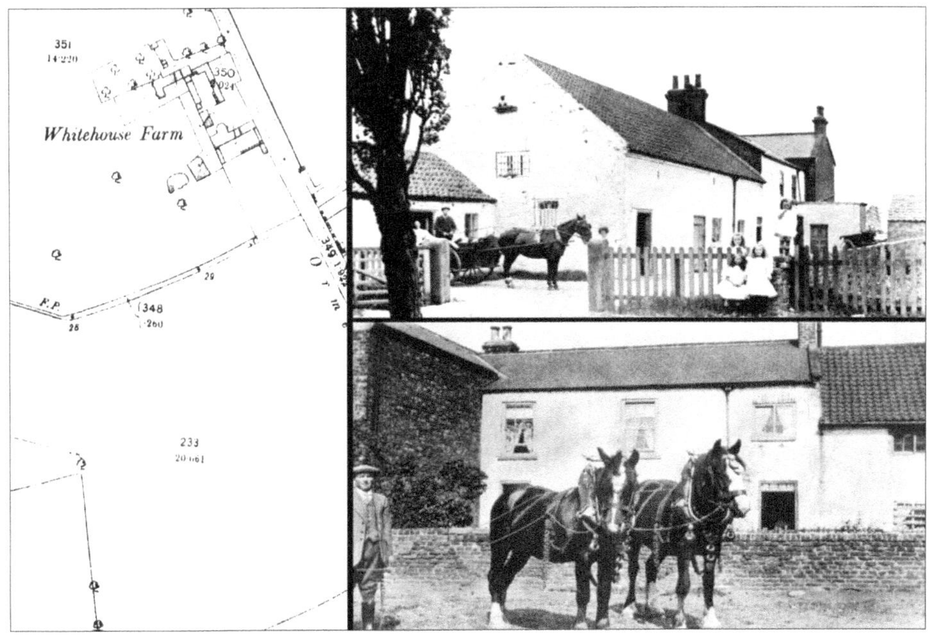

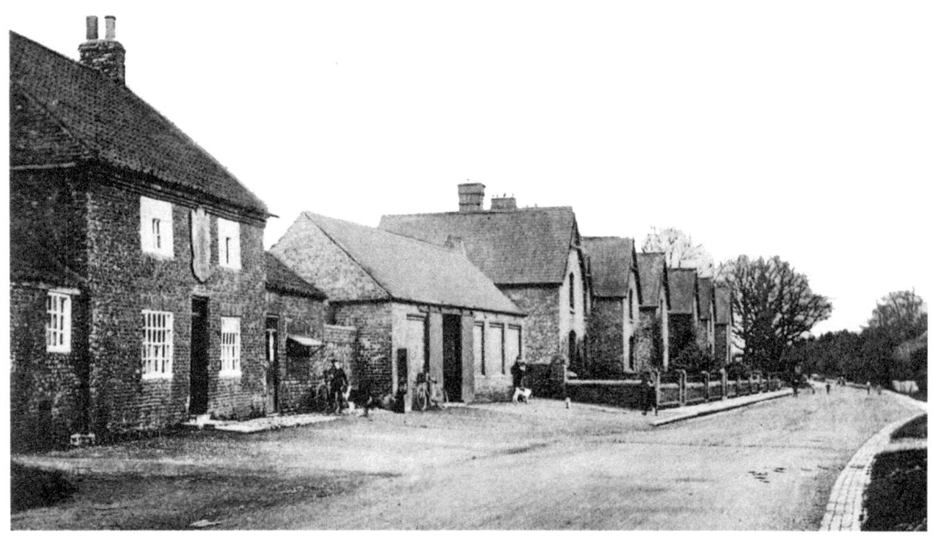

Other long-established agricultural communities in the area included Marton and Ormesby, small hamlets near to the ancient route from Yarm to Guisbrough. Marton, thought to come from the word 'mere' (marsh) and 'ton' (town), is mentioned in the Domesday Survey. Owned for several centuries by the Lowther family, it was sold in 1786 to Bartholomew Rudd of Marske, whose family owned the land when Middlesbrough was built in 1830.

Although the name 'Rudd' has a long association with Marton the community is better known for its connection with Captain Cook, who was born here and whose baptism on 3 November 1778 is recorded in the parish registers of St Cuthbert's Church, shown here around 1905. Cook lived here with his family until the age of eight during a time when Middlesbrough was nothing more than a farm with a few buildings close by. The land between Marton and Middlesbrough slopes generally down towards the river and Cook probably cast an eye towards the ships sailing on the River Tees as he played or worked in the fields.

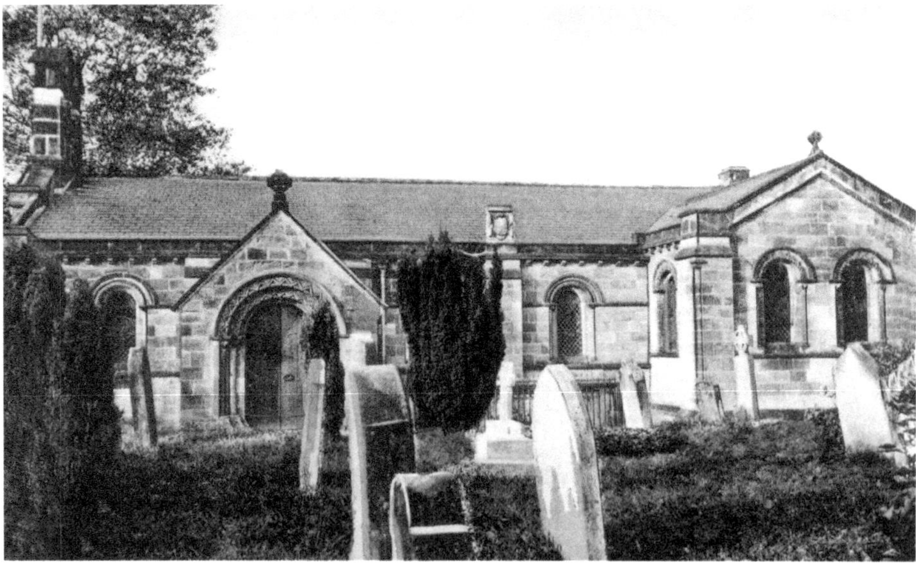

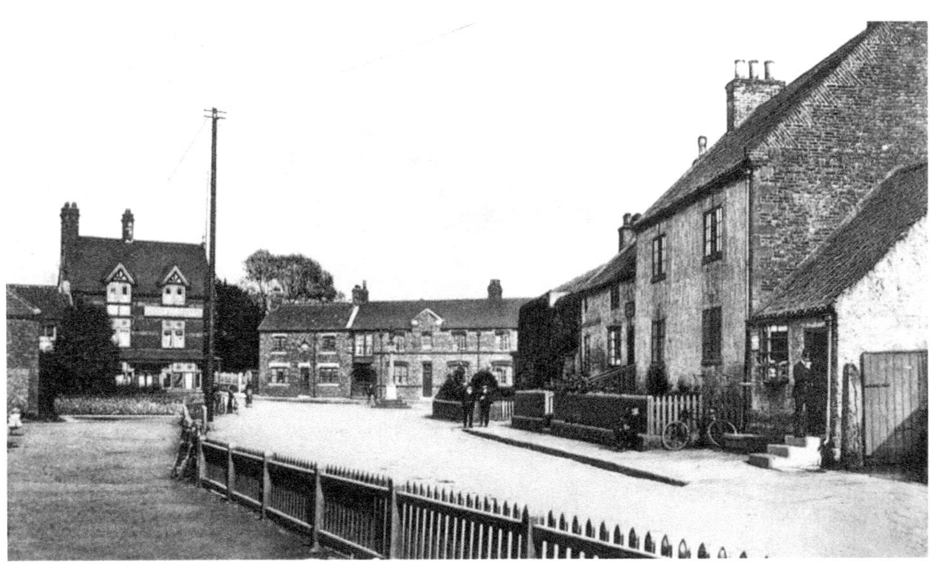

Another village mentioned in the Domesday Survey was Ormesby. Various families owned land here including Robert de Brus, the Percys of Northumberland, the Conyers and the Strangeways, before the long-standing association with the Pennyman family began in the late sixteenth century. This view shows the village from the west in about 1900, with the eighteenth-century almshouses on the left. Despite the rapid expansion of nearby Middlesbrough, Ormesby retained many of its village features well into the twentieth century due mainly to the conservative stewardship of the Pennyman family.

James Pennyman first acquired the Manor of Ormesby in 1600, an association which was to last for almost 400 years. James Pennyman (grandson of the original owner of Ormesby) was granted a baronetcy by Charles II for fighting on the side of the royalists in the English Civil War. The baronetcy died out, but the Pennyman family remained living at the Hall until 1983. The oldest parts of Ormesby Hall date from the seventeenth century, but the main residential part is of eighteenth-century origin. This view is from the gardens south of the building, *c.* 1900.

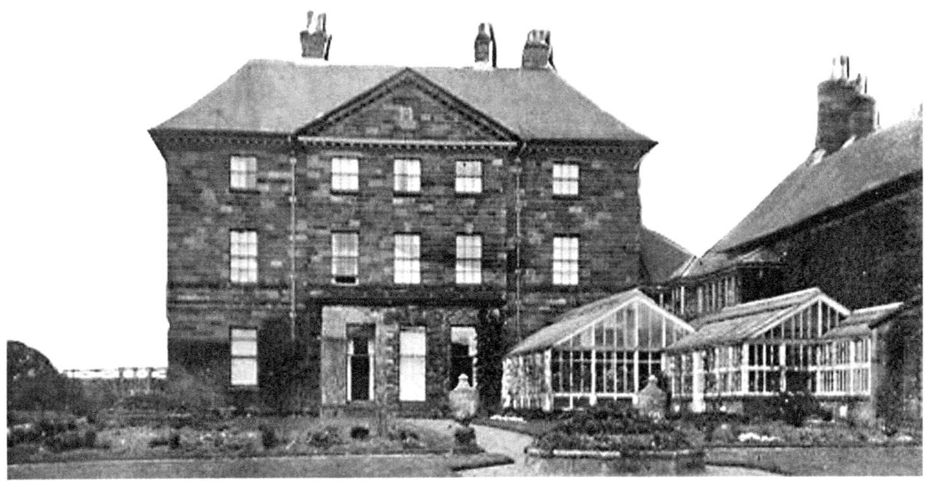

Joseph Pease and his
diary entry for
18 August 1828

Whether you regard him as a man of exceptional vision or a shrewd entrepreneur, Joseph Pease is a key figure in the founding of Middlesbrough.

It was Pease who, despite the immediate success of the Stockton to Darlington Railway (S & D), voiced his concerns about the role of Stockton as a port in developing the coal export trade. Writing in October 1827, he pointed out the need for an extension of the railway 'lower down the Tees so as to obtain deeper water and a better place … than the present place affords'. Pease, the first Secretary of the S & D, carried a lot of influence; despite their initial opposition, S & D directors were persuaded to agree to development downriver. Two sites, Haverton Hill and Middlesbrough, were considered as a terminus for the proposed extension; both were closer than Stockton to the sea, they offered deeper water access and could be reached with fewer navigation problems. Middlesbrough was chosen – it was closer, thus construction costs would be less.

The Bill received Royal Assent in May 1828. Later, on 18 August 1828, while holidaying at Seaton, Pease took a boat trip up the Tees to view the site. He records in his diary his immense pleasure with the site, adding that one day he envisioned that the 'bare fields we were traversing would be covered with a busy multitude and numerous vessels crowding to these banks denoting a busy seaport'.

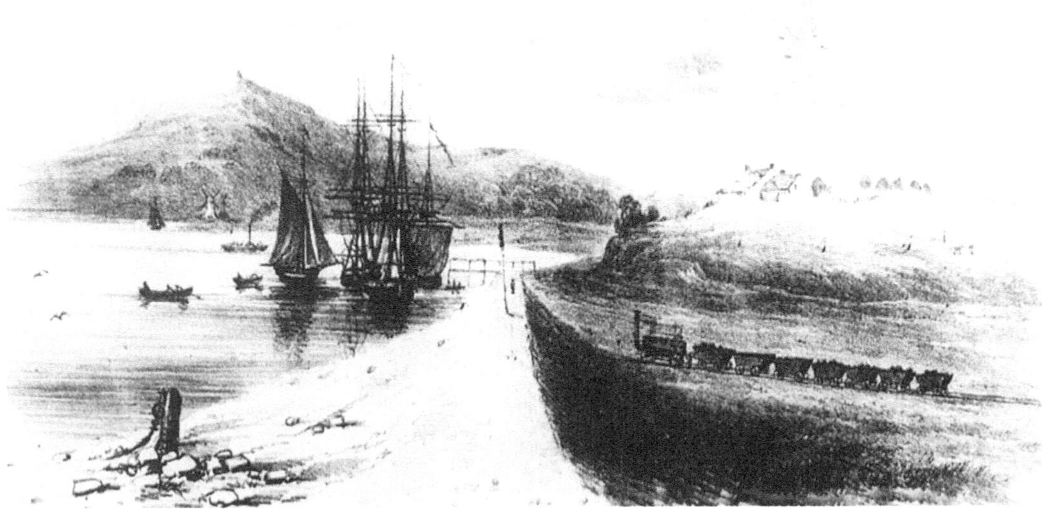

The new shipping point was named Port Darlington, clearly a reference to the role played by businessmen of that town. This contemporary drawing shows the site as it appeared in those early days. The extension of the railway, completed on 27 December 1830, was marked by a day of celebration. On a fine frosty day a train carrying many dignitaries travelled from Darlington to the new terminus, where its arrival was the signal for the firing of guns from vessels in the river echoed by others on the shore. The first coal was unloaded onto a ship at one of the newly erected shipping staithes. A dinner followed; a cold collation set out in one of the adjoining staithes.

This extract from a contemporary drawing shows a number of ships lining up to collect coal at the new staithes in Port Darlington. These staithes, designed by Timothy Hackworth, were a great improvement on previous designs as they not only allowed coal to be unloaded more quickly – thus avoiding the queues of fully laden coal wagons waiting to unload, as had happened at Stockton, but the coal was also able to be unloaded with less breakage, an important factor in the buying and selling of coal.

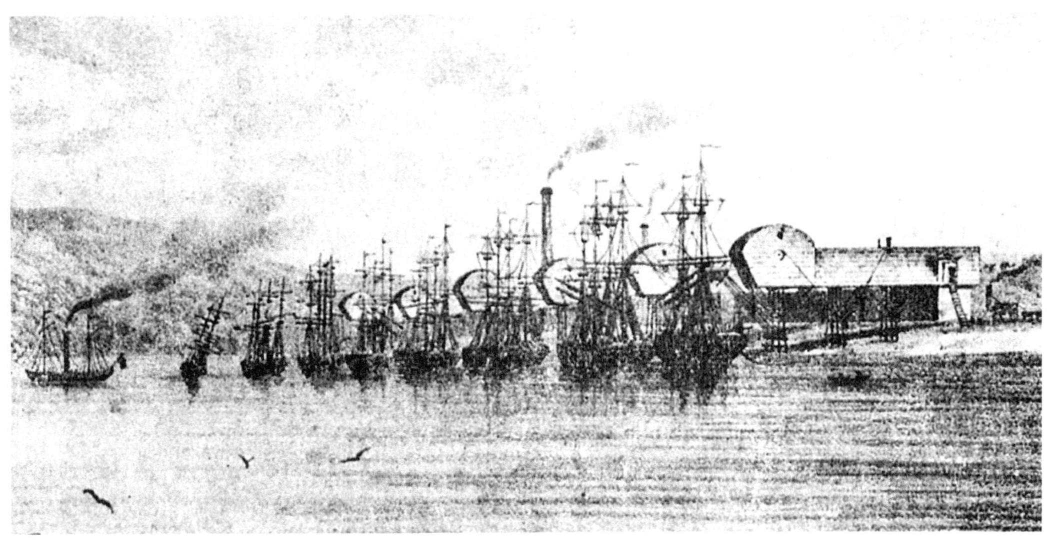

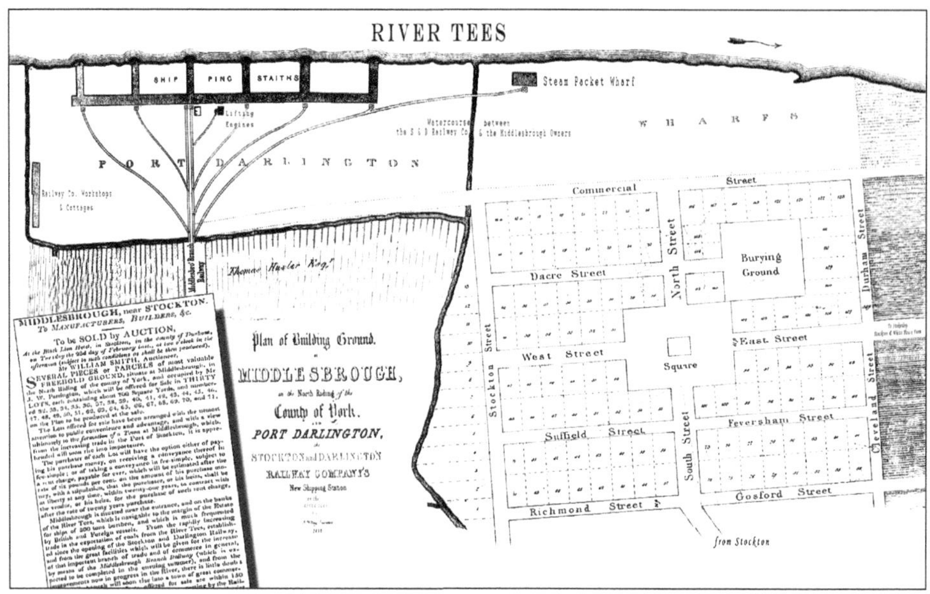

As well as the S & D, Joseph Pease had other business interests, including mining. His business acumen was demonstrated further in December 1828; he was instrumental in the decision of a consortium of six Quaker businessmen to purchase 521 acres of land comprising Middlesbrough Farm and some adjacent lands including Breckon Hill from owner William Chilton of Billingham. Following completion of the sale in May 1829 for £30,000, the Owners of the Middlesbrough Estate (OME) commissioned Richard Otley, a land surveyor, to prepare a town plan. Otley's proposed layout can be seen here – a simple grid pattern around a central square. The land was divided into 125 building plots with street widths varying between 30 and 60ft. The faint outline of the Middlesbrough Farm buildings can also be seen.

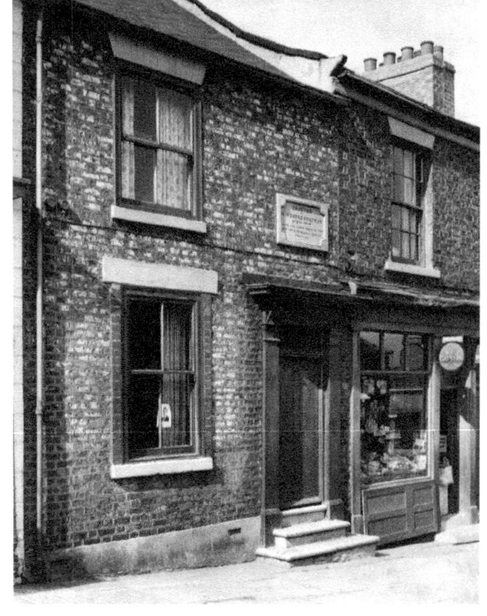

The plots were sold off by public auction. Plot 46 at 26 West Street, bought by carpenter George Chapman, became the site of the first house to be built in Middlesbrough, in April 1830. The house, sold on 29 August 1831 to Robert Morrow, survived until 1959 when it was demolished when the area was redeveloped. The role of the OME in further development was retained through a 'Deed of Covenants', a series of contractual obligations which purchasers were legally obliged to abide by.

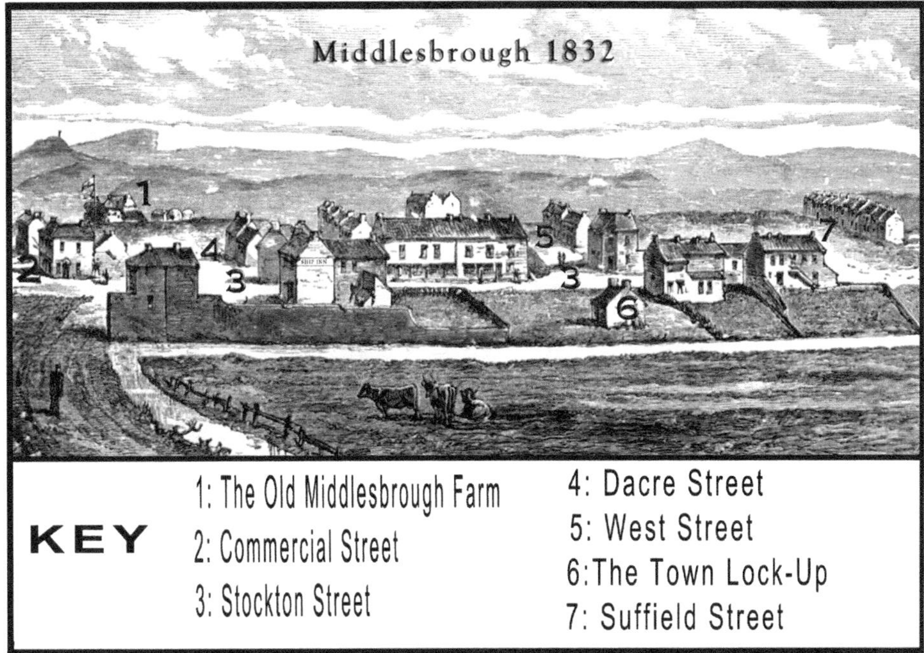

The enormity of constructing a new town can be grasped by looking at this drawing of Middlesbrough in 1832, based on a picture by Joseph Dodshon. The town, seen from a point close to modern-day Snowdon Road, is still little more than a few houses, built close to the Middlesbrough Farm seen in the distance on elevated ground. Unmade streets and a lack of the most basic amenities show the development still to be done. Most houses were small, consisting of a combined kitchen and living room plus a bedroom downstairs with another two rooms above. A numerical annotation provides a topographical guide to the new town.

This close-up provides a more detailed look at the area close to the Ship Inn. Located on Stockton Street, the Ship Inn, which then faced north not east as it does today, was close to the stell (or small stream) which marked the western extent of the new town at that time. Today the Ship Inn is the oldest surviving building from the old town of Middlesbrough. Further down from the Ship Inn are the recently constructed houses on Stockton Street as well as the Steam Packet, which, like the Ship Inn, was another public house which opened in 1831.

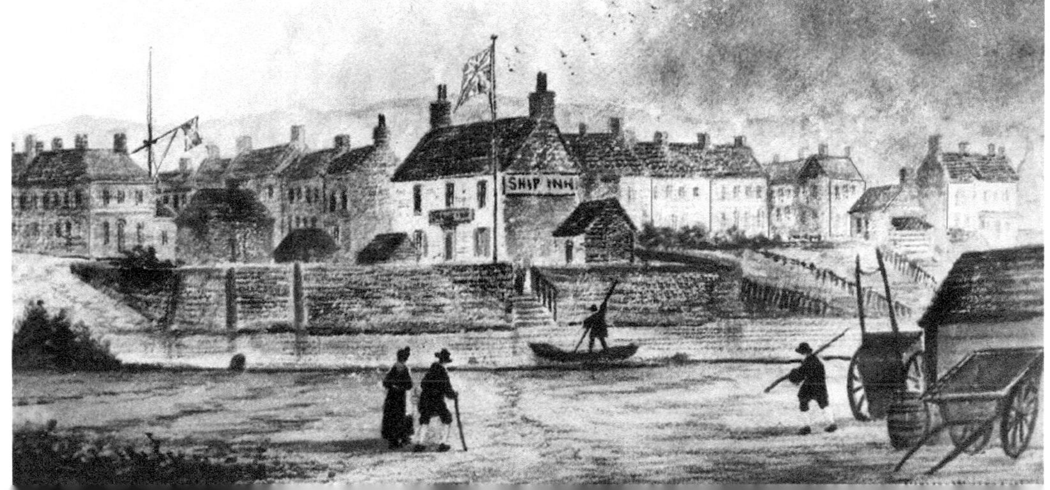

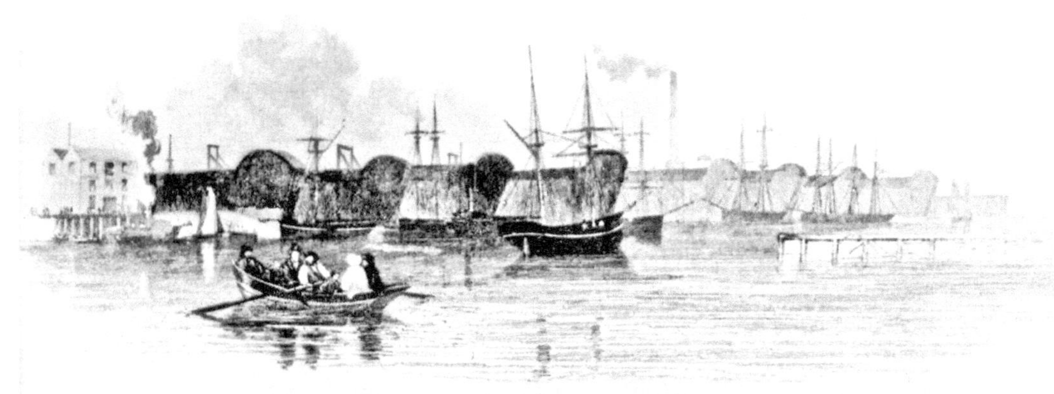

A group of ships are unloading at the coal staithes in this drawing of the town, *c.* 1841. The staithes had been in use for ten years but the depth of water was gradually being reduced owing to river-borne silt being steadily deposited around them. This eventually led to the opening of Middlesbrough Dock. Behind can be seen one of the chimneys which were part of the first ironworks in the town, opened by Bolckow and Vaughan in 1841.

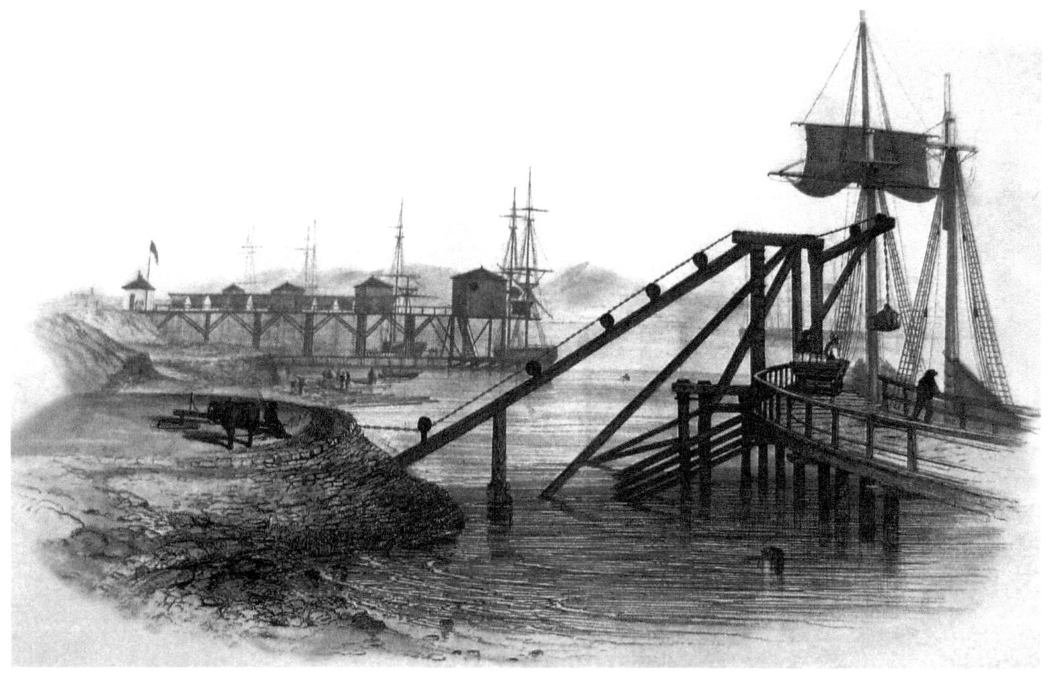

This illustration is from *A History of Coal, Coke, Coalfields and Iron Manufacture in Northern England* first published in 1860. Originally the Stockton & Darlington Railway intended to use Haverton Hill as a shipping point for coal but abandoned this in favour of using Middlesbrough. When the Clarence Railway took over the scheme they extended the line to Samphire Batts – renamed Port Clarence, a point where deep water allowed access for shipping. The coal drops are shown operating in this drawing which is dated 1841.

2

FROM VISION TO REALITY

Joseph Pease saw his vision become reality within his lifetime when Middlesbrough became a town of some renown ...

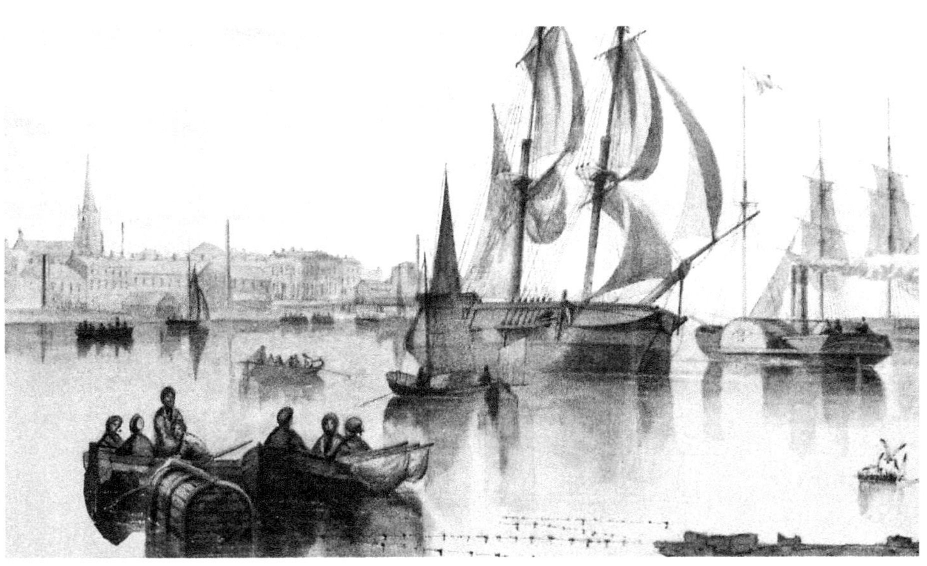

This extract is from Joseph Bloom's painting of the town in 1868. A site which only forty years earlier had been marshland, green fields and country lanes was now a bustling port with a growing reputation throughout the kingdom, in the minds of many a fitting tribute to 'one man's vision'. Despite its problems, it was an incredible feat to construct a new town so quickly.

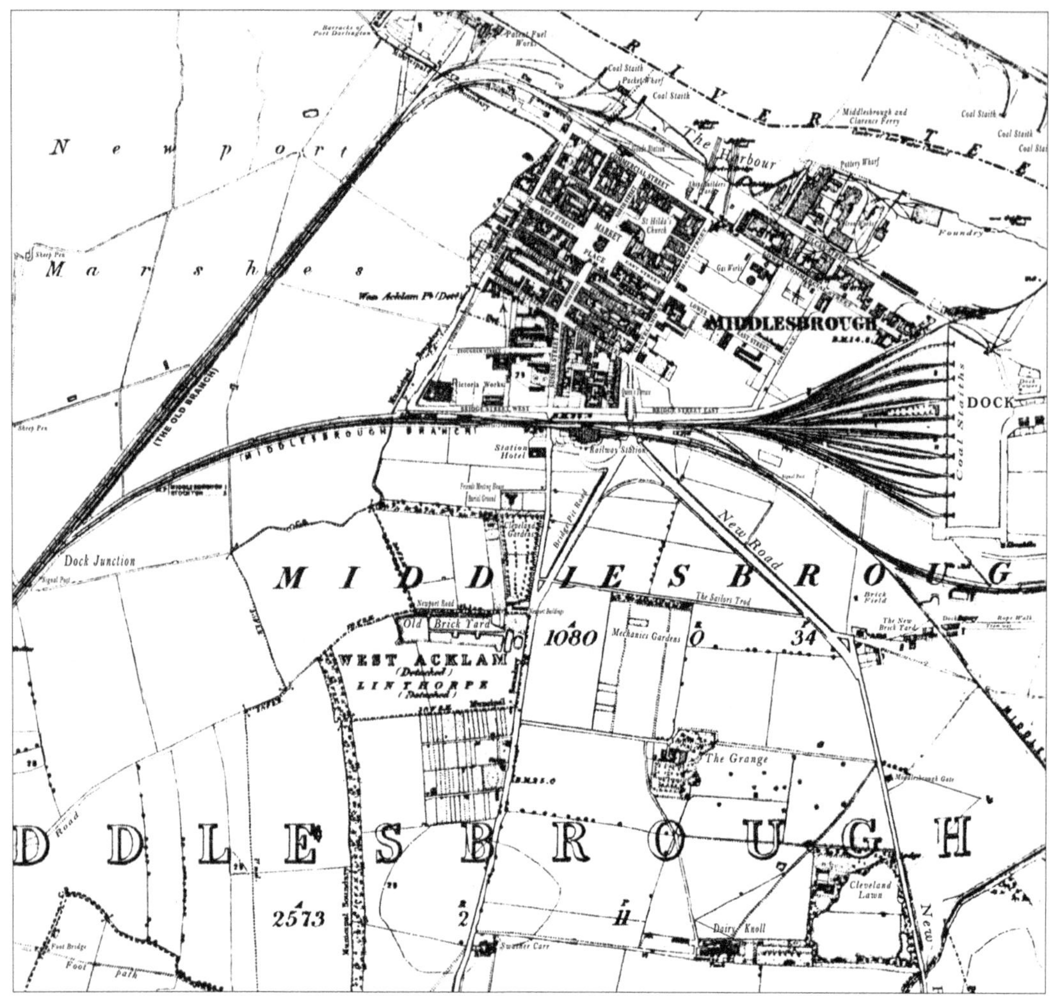

Middlesbrough in 1856 was still mainly contained within its original site. To accommodate the rapidly increasing population infilling occurred with the building of the infamous yards. Middlesbrough Dock, which opened in 1842, and a number of new industrial sites close to the river are now operating. The first coal staithes, erected in 1829, are still visible at Port Darlington close to a row of terraced houses – the 'Barracks'. The railway serving the staithes has been renamed 'The Old Branch', distinguishing it from the new branch line to the Dock and to Redcar. It's interesting to see that the area south of the railway is still fields, with farms and market gardens. (Reproduced from 1857 Ordnance Survey map, 6 inch series, with the kind permission of the Ordnance Survey)

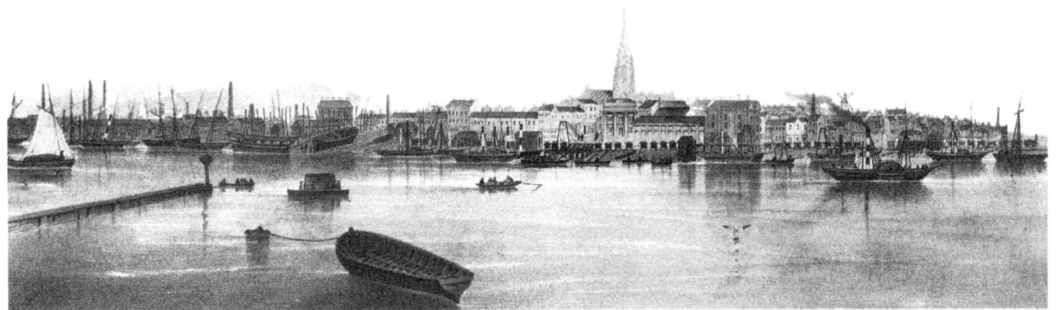

Middlesbrough as seen from Port Clarence in 1846. Fronting the river is Commercial Street with coal wagons nearby waiting to be unloaded at the coal staithes. Further east are the ship yards and Middlesbrough Pottery. North Street is mid-centre with the original Exchange with its Grecian portico visible. The 120ft-high spire of St Hilda's Church dominates the sky-line, while to the west is Stockton Street, the perimeter of Middlesbrough at that time. A steam ship sails down the river – regular services operated to Newport and Stockton. In the distance the corn mill that once stood in Mill Street, then close to the southern perimeter of the town, is just visible.

In 1841 the OME formally handed development of the town over to twelve Improvement Commissioners. In 1846 they erected a Town Hall in the centre of the Market Place. Made of stone and white brick, the building contained a communal hall with a gallery, a lock-up (with two cells) and a house for the Superintendent of Police. An octagonal market was built around the base of the prominent clock tower. In 1862 W.E. Gladstone was received at the Town Hall at a banquet to celebrate his visit. This view of South Street shows the Town Hall and the Talbot Hotel, which was also known as 'Sackers' or 'The Dog' – familiar landmarks in Victorian Middlesbrough.

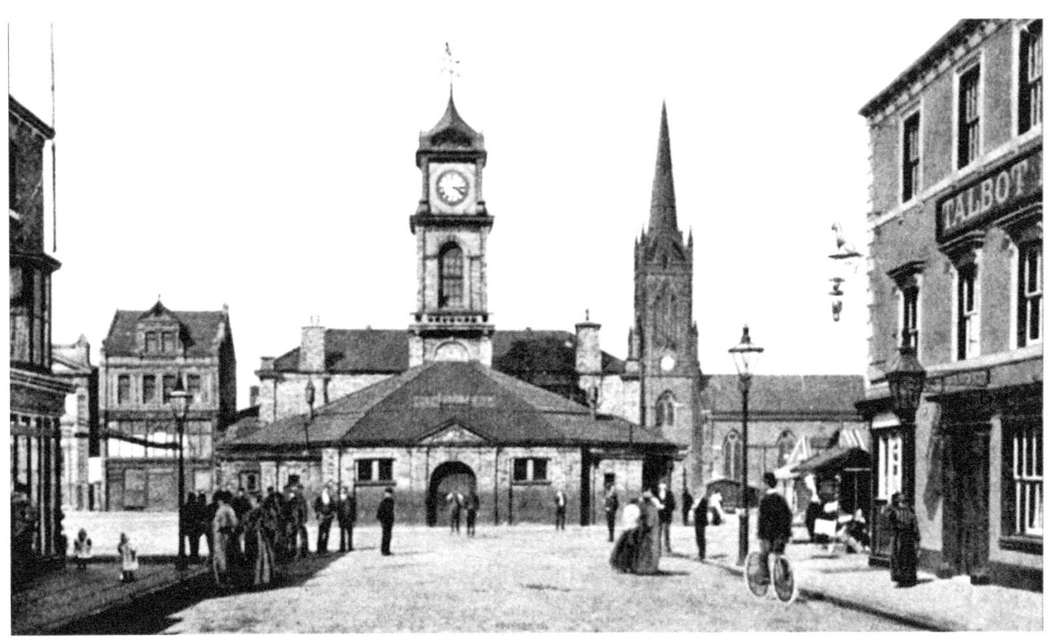

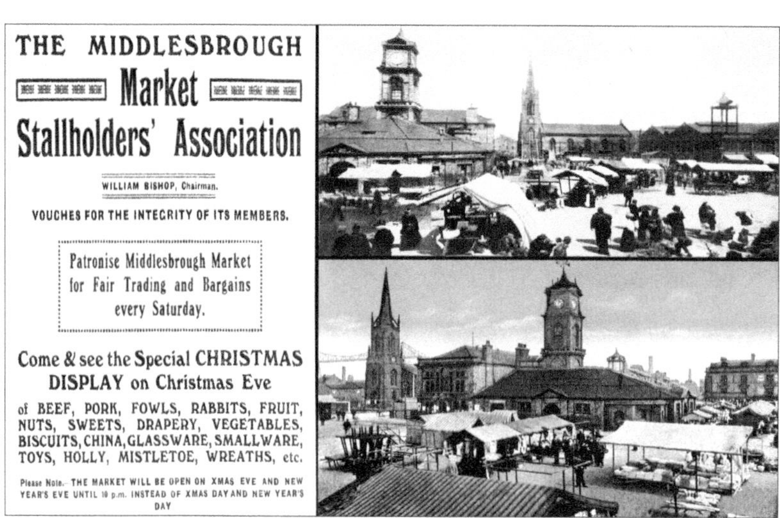

At the centre of the town was the Market Square, home to Middlesbrough Market for more than a hundred years, despite attempts to move it elsewhere, especially after the town spilled across the railway line. In 1883 a petition signed by over 2,000 people asked for it to be moved close to Newport Road, while in the late 1930s there were calls to move it close to Grange Road. The opening of the market on 12 December 1840 had been marked by a large dinner. The market proved so popular that it was expanded in 1856 followed by a vegetable market opening on the corner of East Street in 1861, visible in the upper image behind the unusual bell-tower which stood outside.

Beyond the Town Hall and Market Hall, North Street slopes down to the river. A number of market stalls are shown: many traders became familiar names including Walter Bishop, Richardson's, J.D. Lane, Whitfield's, Garbutt's, Bella Miller and Hartley's. Behind the canvas stalls, the butchers' market, which opened on the corner of West Street in 1865, is visible. People queued to buy a wide variety of locally grown produce. There were also many amusements such as shooting-galleries, roundabouts and street entertainers, including Sequah the famous medicine man. The market was so popular it often remained open until midnight.

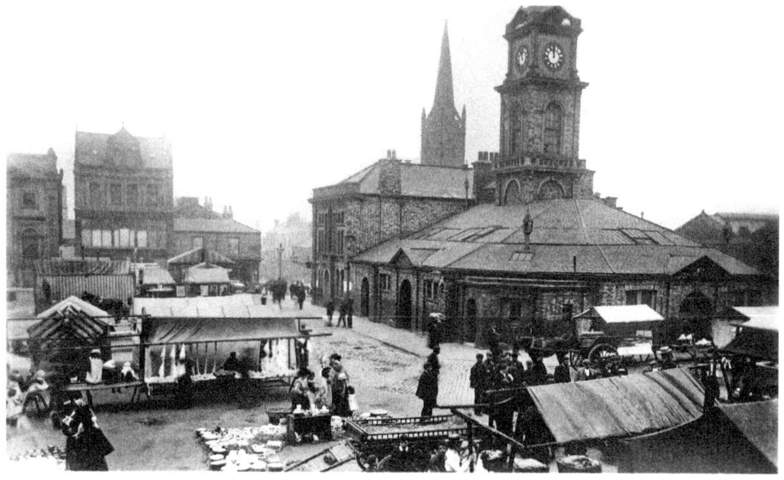

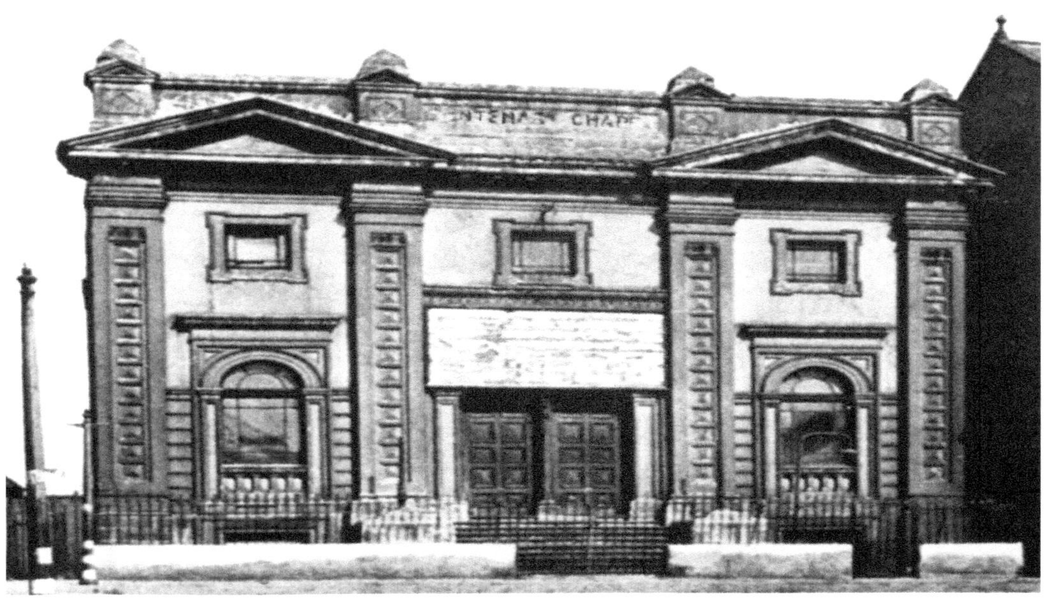

With no permanent church buildings in Middlesbrough, some inhabitants sailed up to Stockton for Sunday services, others made the long walk across the fields to St Mary's Church at Acklam. In 1833 the town's first permanent church building opened, the Centenary Chapel in the north-west corner of the Market Square. This survived as a religious building until 1949, when it became commercial premises until it was demolished a decade later.

Another church, also now demolished, was St Hilda's Church. The OME, keen to have the calming influence of religion in the town, even donated land close to the Market Square on which to build the church. A large amount of money from public subscriptions helped to meet construction costs and the church was consecrated on 25 September 1840. The surrounding burial ground closed in 1854 with burials being transferred to Ayresome Gardens.

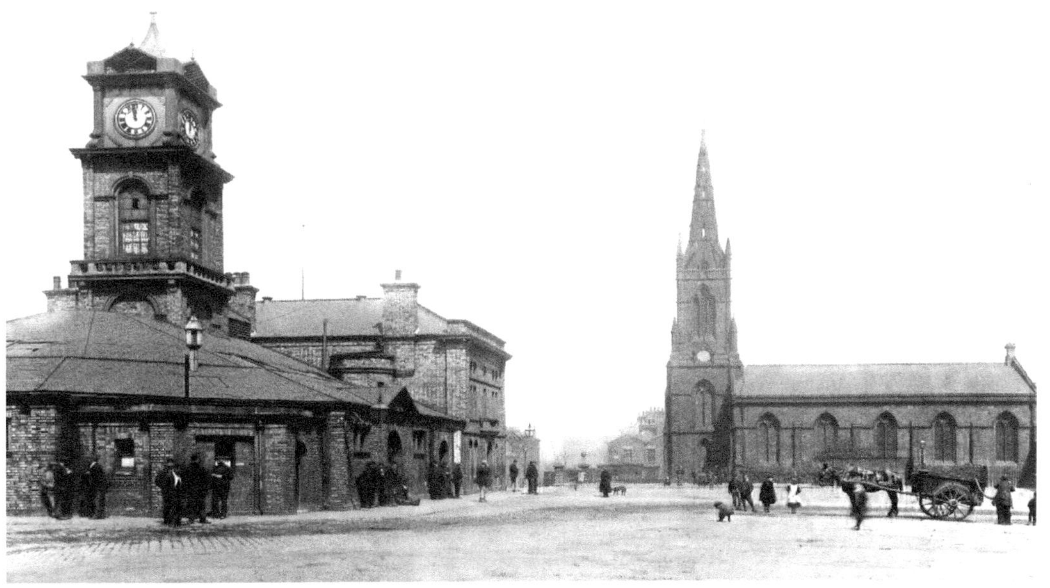

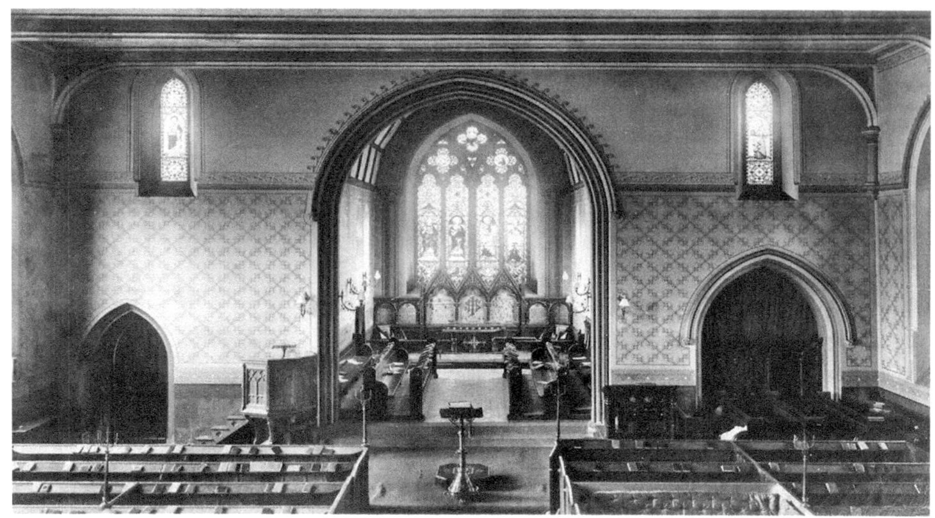

The interior of St Hilda's, *c.* 1896. A gallery, which was added in 1861, increased the capacity from 600 to 900 people. During its 130-year history the church was very much a focal point of life in the town, a point of religious sobriety in an often rowdy environment. As was common then, the church was closely involved with local education through nearby St Hilda's School.

South Street was a busy southern exit from the town, ideal for the retail trade. Some well-known names in the history of Middlesbrough's retail trade, including Amos Hinton, Matthew Collingwood and Wilson Newbould, began here. This busy scene from around 1908 shows some of the many shops as well as the overflow of stalls from the market place. The Market Hall is also visible, while the 'Foreign Money Exchange' building on the corner of Henry Street reminds us of the town's role as a port. Suffield Street, beyond the Exchange, had the public houses, The Fleece and The Globe, on each corner. The draper's, Pottages, close to the corner of Garbutt Street, is obviously very popular with shoppers.

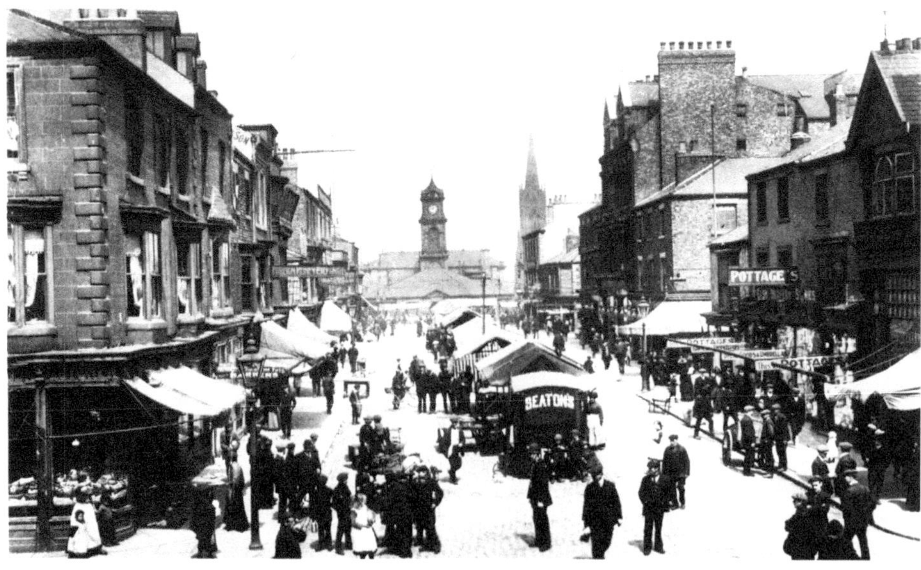

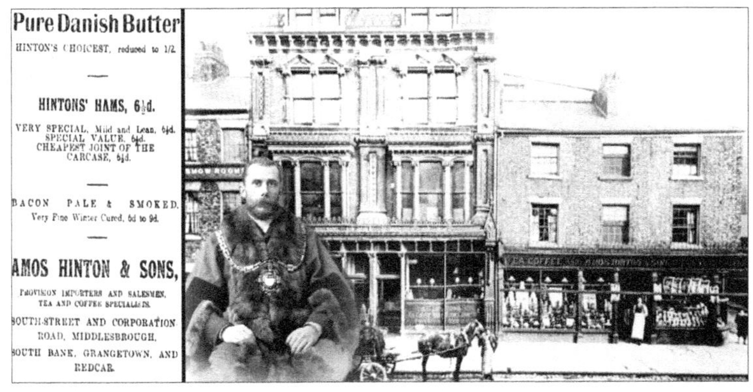

Amos Hinton arrived in Middlesbrough in 1862 as an apprentice to greengrocer John Birks at his shop in South Street, seen here. In 1868 Hinton became Birks' partner, eventually buying the shop outright in 1888. When Dr William Grieves' died in 1890, Hinton bought the Cleveland Academy site on the corner of Albert Road and Corporation Road and opened the Oriental Cafe. With the addition of adjoining premises he opened a large Hinton's store in 1906, which became one of the town's best known shops, and a flagship store among the chain of stores which later stretched across the region until the late twentieth century. Amos played a not inconsiderable part in the civic life of Middlesbrough, becoming mayor in 1886. Seen here in his mayoral robes, Hinton remained an important local figure until his death in 1919. The advertisement is from February 1906.

The Middlesbrough Exchange Association was formed on 9 September 1835. Inspired by the town's growing commercial success, they built a Coal Exchange with offices, public rooms and a residential hotel. The two-storied building on the corner of Commercial Street and North Street was constructed in the Greek revival style. It opened in 1837 and was named the Exchange Hotel (seen here in a contemporary drawing). On 29 October 1838 the first royal visit to the town took place when the Duke of Sussex, uncle of Queen Victoria, was entertained here amidst great scenes of celebration. When the hotel was later found to be unprofitable it was sold in 1853 for £2,750 to the newly formed Middlesbrough Council. It was renamed Corporation Hall, replacing the Town Hall building which had become too small.

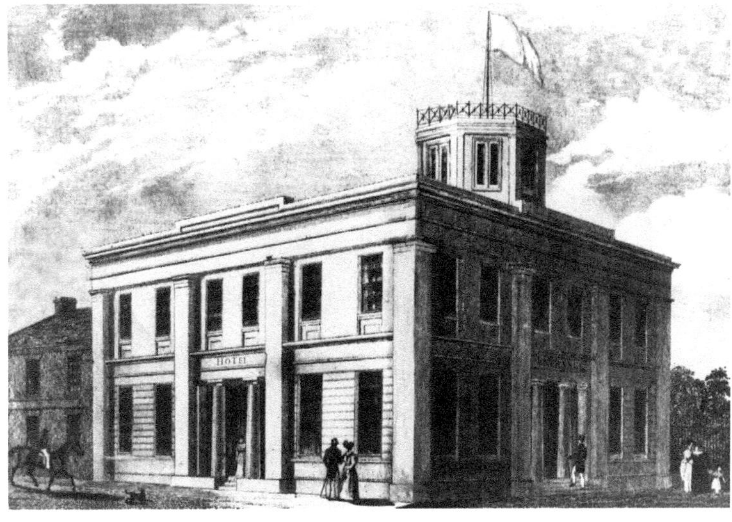

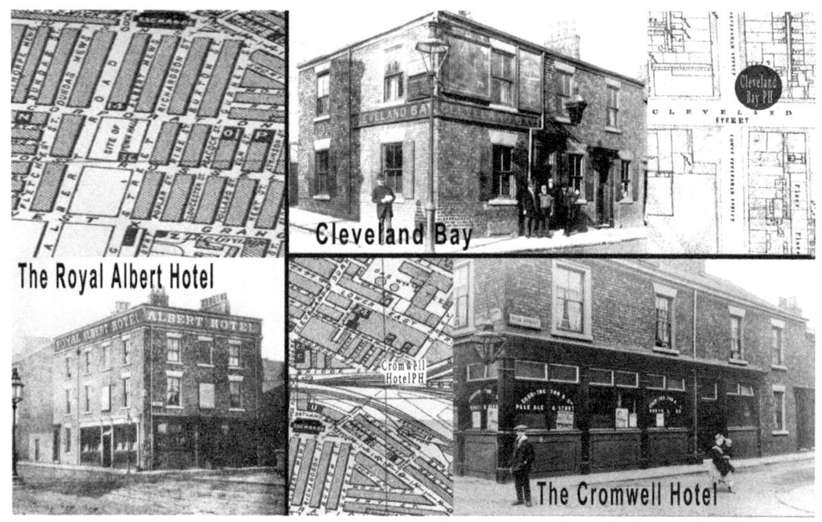

Three of the large number of public houses, inns, taverns and alehouses which were in Middlesbrough are shown here. The predominantly male population often with little to do after a day's heavy manual labour, patronised the pubs in large numbers. At one time, over a hundred institutions were selling alcohol in the old town north of the railway. Drunkenness was rife and concerns about the image of the town were frequently voiced in local newspapers.

Travelling entertainers came to Middlesbrough, setting up in the Market Square or on the flatts in Lower East Street. Billy Purvis was an early favourite, playing to full houses for twenty years until his final season in 1852. The first regular theatre, the Royal Alhambra, opened on 5 November 1859, followed by several more, including the Theatre Royal in Durham Street (opened 1861) and the Royal Albert in Albert Street (1866). They merged as the Theatre Royal in 1868, which remained open for more than sixty years. Also well known was the Oxford Palace of Varieties (seen here) opened on 9 August 1867. Many famous entertainers appeared there including Dan Leno, Vesta Tilley, Marie Lloyd, Harry Lauder, Harry Houdini and a young Charlie Chaplin before it closed in 1907. After being used for several different purposes it was destroyed by a bomb in 1940.

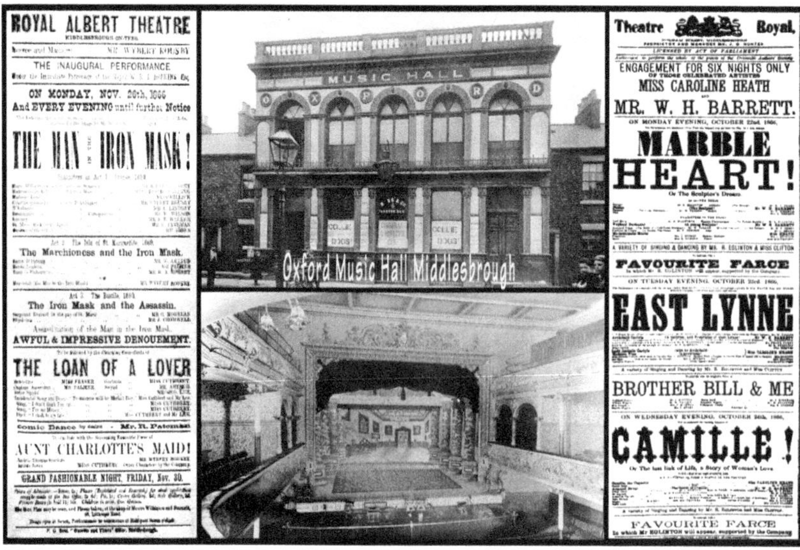

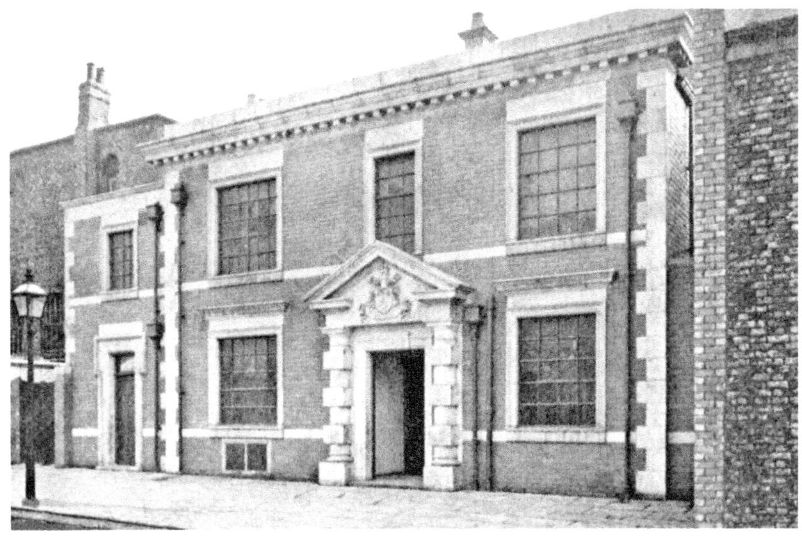

To ensure law and order was maintained there were several police stations in Middlesbrough, including this one in Dacre Street. It opened in September 1914, replacing the Old Market police station, which closed on 8 June 1915 having been in use since 1846. A reorganisation of policing in the 1920s saw the closing of the Binks Street (Linthorpe), Cannon Street and Dacre Street stations in 1927. The latter two were reopened as slipper baths in May 1931.

Middlesbrough's first school, the British School, opened in Stockton Street in 1838 with accommodation for 220 pupils, having cost £377 to build. Other schools also opened including Dr William Grieves' Cleveland Academy, a grammar school, and St John's School. Cleveland Academy stood on a country site on the corner of Corporation Road and Albert Road. Fees were thirty guineas for boarders over eleven; a broad curriculum included Greek and Italian. In 1858 a Sergeant Bowes was on the staff – as a Drill Master. Remains of St John's School House were discovered during the demolition of buildings in Marton Road in 1938 following the site being taken over by Jordison's the printers. The adjoining school had opened on 16 January 1860, taking up to 500 pupils at *2d* per week. The school is still remembered today by the street named School Croft.

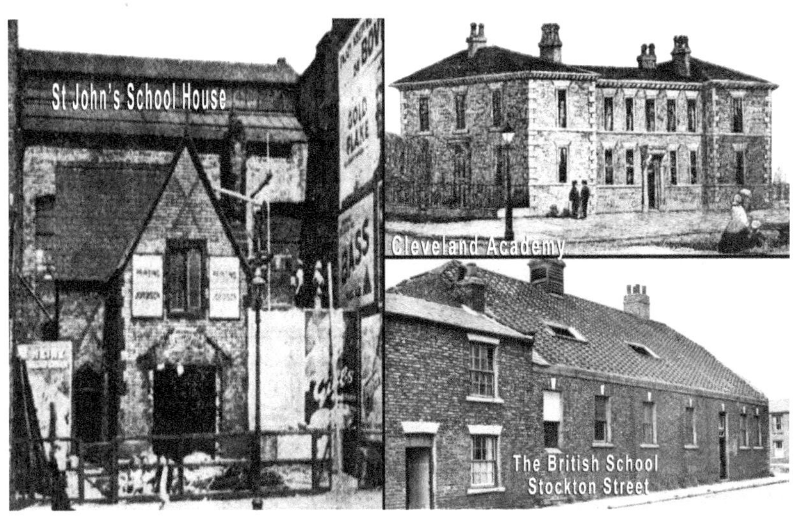

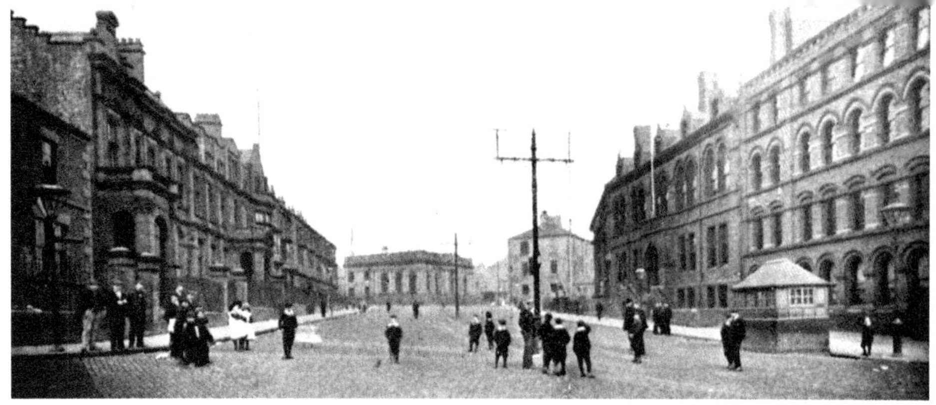

The town quickly expanded southwards as the OME sold off various pieces of their land. Developers laid down new streets, including the architecturally pleasing area around Queens Square, shown here in about 1903. Wealthy individuals lived here, including Henry Bolckow (1841-1854) and John Vaughan (1841-1858) at the Cleveland Buildings, marked today by a blue plaque. To the rear were well laid out gardens looking onto the nearby hills. Opposite, a large, elegant, two-storied red-brick house was owned by local shipbuilder John Gilbert Holmes. Here the sloping lawns reached almost as far as Albert Bridge. Bought by the National Provincial Bank in 1864 as business premises, it was demolished in 1872 when the current building was erected. On the left is Queens Terrace, a stylish terrace of eight houses built in 1850, which today are also commercial premises.

A second royal visit took place in 1868 when HRH Prince Arthur came to open Albert Park, named after the late Prince Consort and built on land donated to the town by Henry Bolckow. This was a significant event for the town, an endorsement of its importance. After the Prince arrived on Monday 10 August at Middlesbrough railway station, the royal procession went to Marton Hall. Dinner was followed by an orchestral concert with music including Weber, Beethoven and Haydn. Next day, after a morning visit by the Prince to Eston Mines, the royal procession set off at 11.45 a.m., proceeding to town via Marton Road. These remarkable images provide a record of the day. Look beyond the decorative arch in the Marton Grove image to see how Middlesbrough was then still fields and hedgerows.

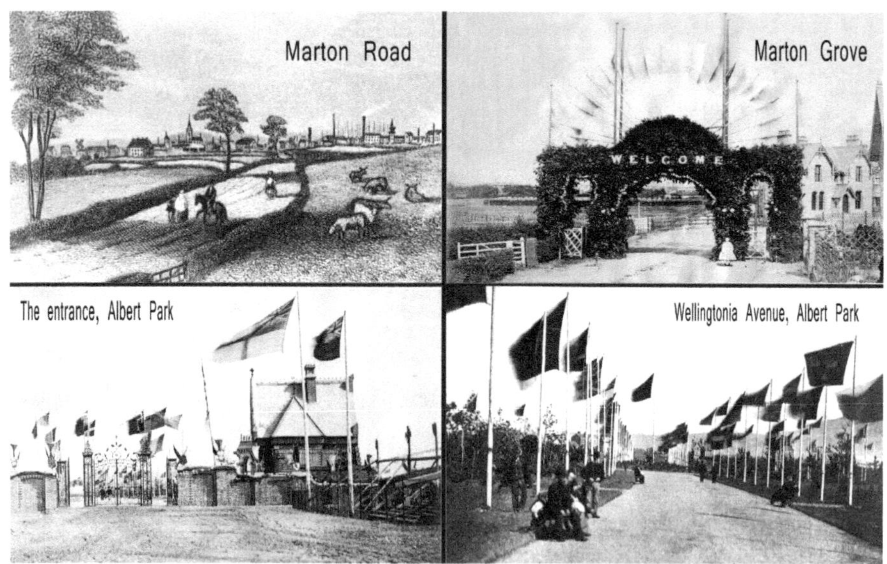

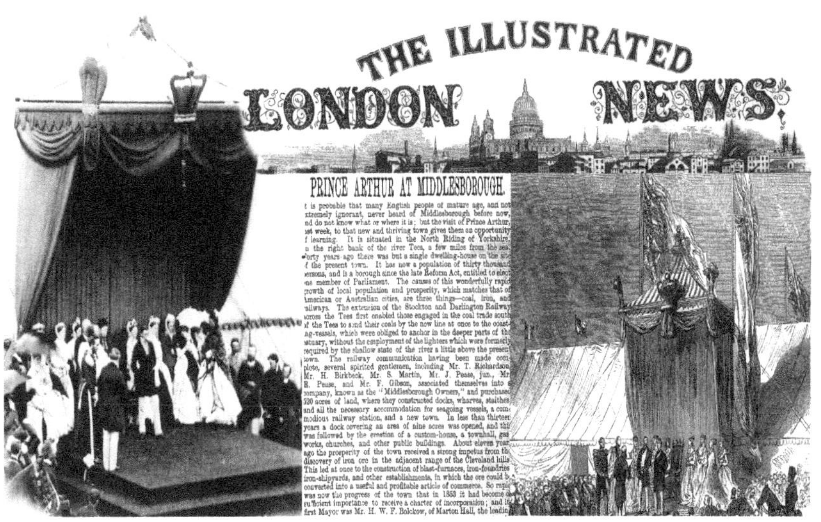

THE ILLUSTRATED LONDON NEWS

PRINCE ARTHUR AT MIDDLESBOROUGH.

t is probable that many English people of mature age, and not xtremely ignorant, never heard of Middlesborough before now, nd do not know what or where it is; but the visit of Prince Arthur, ast week, to that new and thriving town gives them an opportunity f learning. It is situated in the North Riding of Yorkshire, n the right bank of the river Tees, a few miles from the sea. Forty years ago there was but a single dwelling-house on the site f the present town. It has now a population of thirty thousand persons, and is a borough since the late Reform Act, entitled to elect ne member of Parliament. The causes of this wonderfully rapid growth of local population and prosperity, which matches that of American or Australian cities, are three things—coal, iron, and railways. The extension of the Stockton and Darlington Railway across the Tees first enabled those engaged in the coal trade south of the Tees to send their coals by the new line at once to the coast-ng-vessels, which were obliged to anchor in the deeper parts of the estuary, without the employment of the lighters which were formerly required by the shallow state of the river a little above the present town. The railway communication having been made complete, several spirited gentlemen, including Mr. T. Richardson, Mr. H. Birkbeck, Mr. S. Martin, Mr. J. Pease, jun., Mr. R. Pease, and Mr. F. Gibson, associated themselves into a company, known as the "Middlesborough Owners," and purchased 520 acres of land, where they constructed docks, wharves, staithes, and all the necessary accommodation for seagoing vessels, a commodious railway station, and a new town. In less than thirteen years a dock covering an area of nine acres was opened, and this was followed by the erection of a custom-house, a townhall, gas works, churches, and other public buildings. About eleven years ago the prosperity of the town received a strong impetus from the discovery of iron ore in the adjacent range of the Cleveland hills. This led at once to the construction of blast-furnaces, iron-foundries, iron-shipyards, and other establishments, in which the ore could be converted into a useful and profitable article of commerce. So rapid was now the progress of the town that in 1853 it had become of sufficient importance to receive a charter of incorporation; and its first Mayor was Mr. H. W. F. Bolckow, of Marton Hall, the leading

From the arch at Grove Hill, the route travelled through Queens Square, Commercial Street, North Street and Market Square, where 3,653 children were assembled to sing the National Anthem. Cheered by large crowds, they proceeded via Linthorpe Road to Albert Park, where artillery fired a royal salute on their arrival. Following the opening ceremony, seen here, the Prince planted a commemorative tree. After a luncheon, a visit was made to the ironworks of Hopkins, Gilkes & Co. Ltd before a banquet in the Exchange Hall, followed by a ball at Marton Hall. There was great civic pride in this visit, marked by a public address made to Henry Bolckow in October 1868 expressing the grateful thanks of the town.

St Mary's Roman Catholic Cathedral was opened on 21 August 1878 on a site close to where the old mill had stood in Sussex Street. The cost of construction was £20,000 and the architects were Goldie and Child from Kensington, London. The wonderful ornate interior, seen here, had seven arches on either side between the nave and the altar. The Congregational Church, built in Queens Square in 1856-7, was sold to The Seamen's Mission in 1892 for £2,000. The Mission provided an invaluable service until 1964, when it moved to Wilton. Several carriages wait for fares outside the adjacent building, the Erimus Club, which opened in 1873 and was frequented by local businessmen.

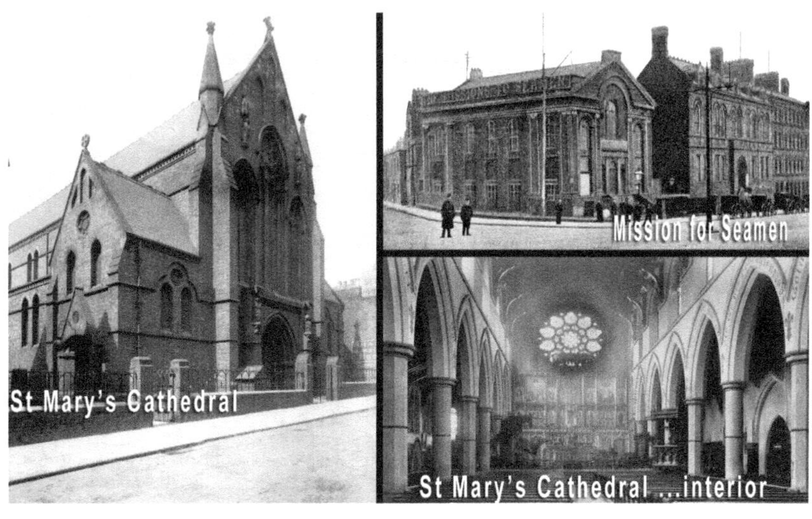

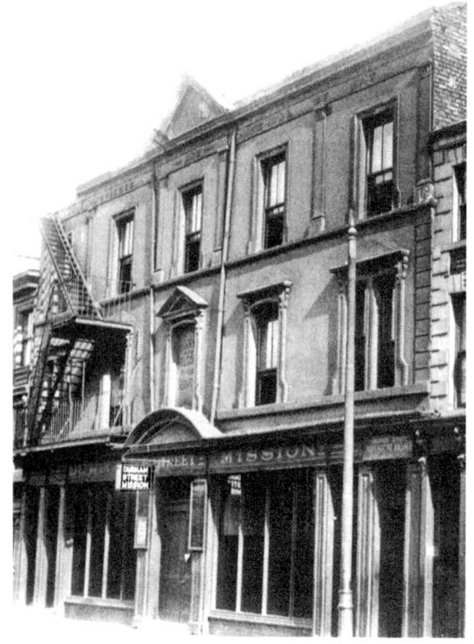

The Mechanics Institute, founded in 1840, was another organisation devoted to the provision of culture and education for the working man. The premises shown here, on Durham Street, were opened in 1860. The Durham Street Mission was later established by St Peter's Church and used the old Institute premises. The Mission had a reading room and also a lodging-house for those with literally nowhere else to go.

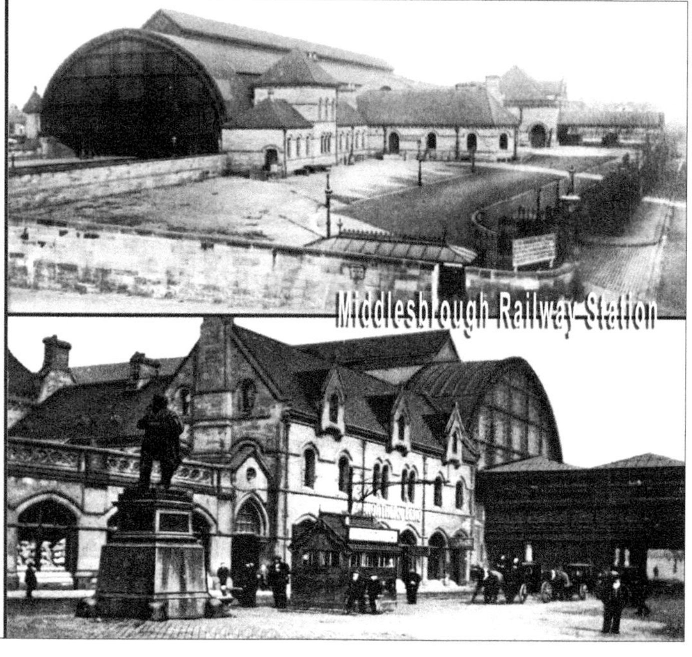

The *Majestic*, a horse-drawn carriage using the branch line, provided a daily service to Stockton until being replaced in 1834 by a locomotive-drawn service run by the S & D. Three times daily the loco left the first station, a bleak wooden hut near the original coal staithes. A more substantial building in Commercial Street opposite the Exchange Hotel replaced the hut until a new station at the end of Sussex Street opened in 1847, serving the new line to Redcar. The location of the new station caused unrest – a petition protested that the site was too far from the town. A new station was opened on the same site in 1877, by which time the town had spread beyond the location. Reflecting the importance of the town, it had a 300-yard arch with a glass roof which was later destroyed when the station was bombed on 3 August 1942.

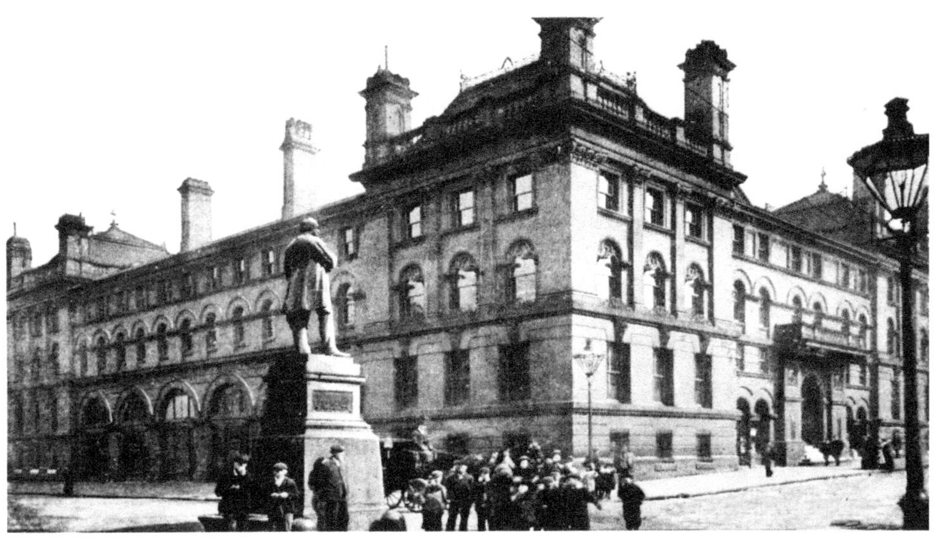

To meet the needs of the town's rise as an industrial centre, 'The Middlesbrough Exchange Company Ltd' (formed in 1864) inspired the building of the Exchange, seen here from Albert Place close to the railway bridge. Opening on 28 July 1868, construction cost £28,000, despite a 130ft tower being omitted due to a lack of money. The statue of ironmaster John Vaughan dominates the scene; it was unveiled by Sir J.W. Pease on 29 September 1884, a fitting tribute to a leading figure in Middlesbrough's industrial history. The statue was later moved to Victoria Square on 23 October 1914.

Seen here from the junction of Wilson Street and Albert Road in around 1896, the Exchange had now become the commercial centre for the iron trade, its close location to the railway station making it very accessible for businessmen visiting the town. This impressive building reflected the commercial importance of the iron industry to the town as well as to the regional and national economy. The fine stone carvings which adorned the red-brick Exchange are clearly visible here.

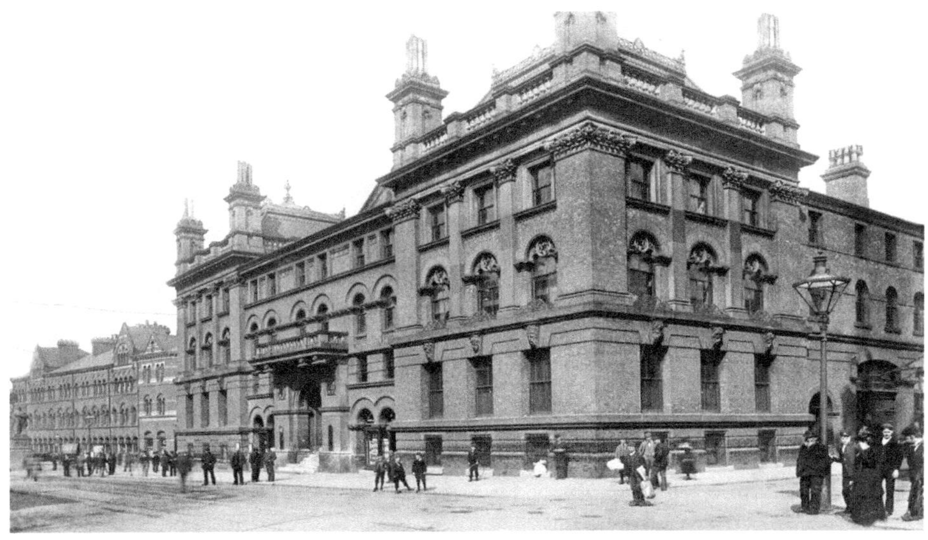

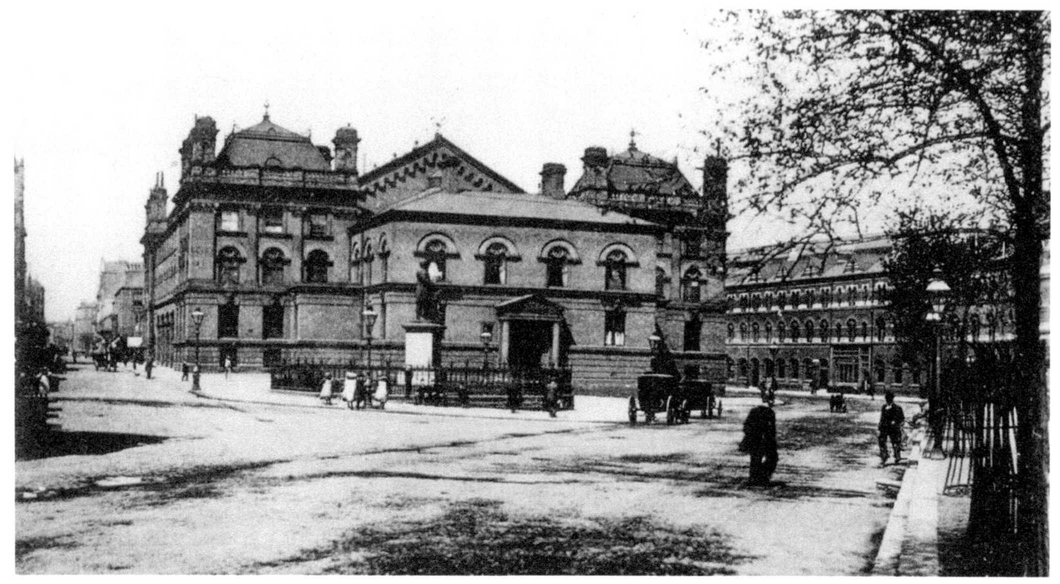

The entrance to the Exchange Building from Exchange Place with Wilson Street on the left and Marton Road opposite. The main internal feature was a large room over 50m long, with a vaulted roof where the Iron Market was held each Tuesday and Friday to fix price levels to facilitate the trade in iron as well as other commodities. In addition to offices there were shops and a licensed restaurant in the Exchange. The well-known Cleveland Club met here too.

Until Middlesbrough got its own post office in the 1840s, letters were brought from Stockton to the town in the Tees Coal Company's letter bag, where they were displayed in their office window for claiming. In the early days of the town, postal facilities were based in North Street and Dacre Street, eventually moving on 17 September 1879 to the impressive Post Office Chambers site on Marton Road under the management of John Jordison. The premises are seen here in about 1912.

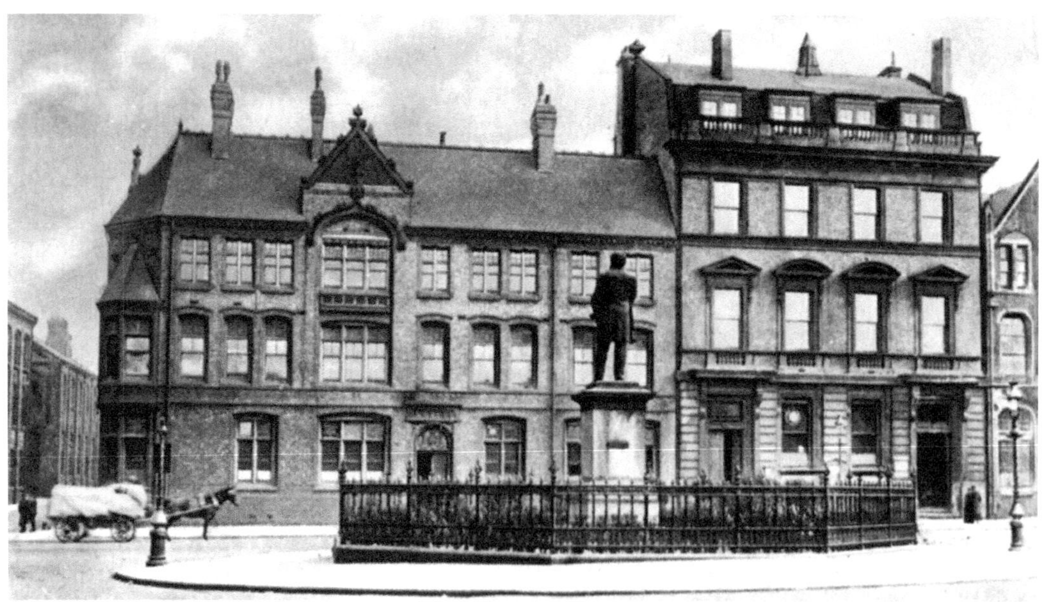

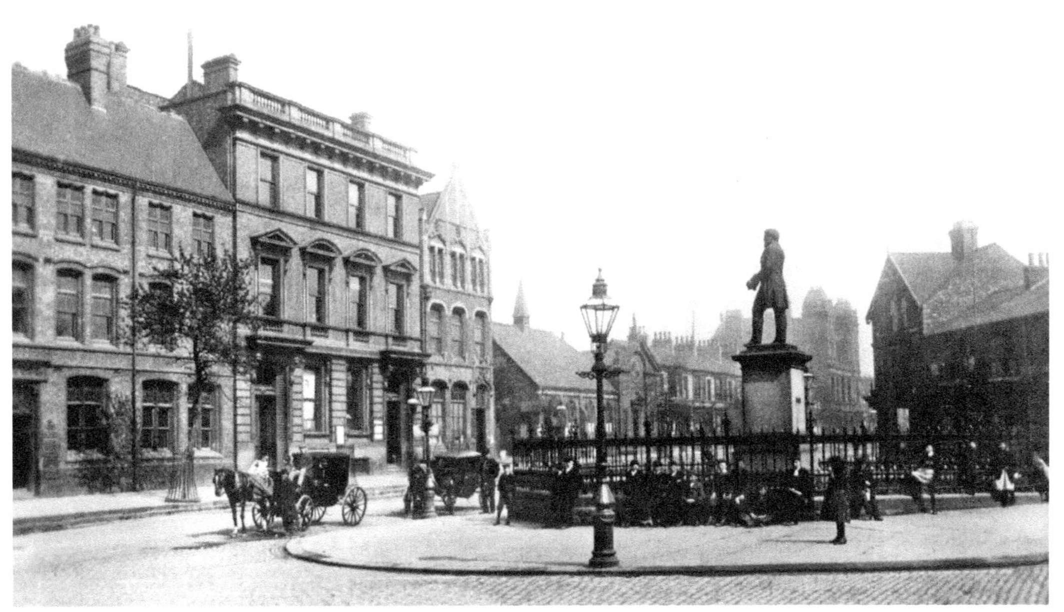

Also in Exchange Place was the statue of ironmaster Henry Bolckow, who, along with John Vaughan, played an important role in the history of Middlesbrough. The statue, enclosed by an octagonal fence, was unveiled by Lord Cavendish on 6 October 1881 during the town's 50th Jubilee celebrations. Also in view is the Freemason's Hall which opened on 12 January 1861. The site for the Hall cost £159 and the building and furniture cost £838.

Sussex Street was once the southern perimeter of the town, petering out into a lane to Linthorpe. When a new branch line opened to Middlesbrough Dock a small halt and platform were built in 1841 close to where the lane crossed the railway. The railway crossing was built later when the railway opened to Redcar in 1846. Seen here in 1908, this rare view from the corner of Station Street looks across to the Crown Hotel in Bridge Street West.

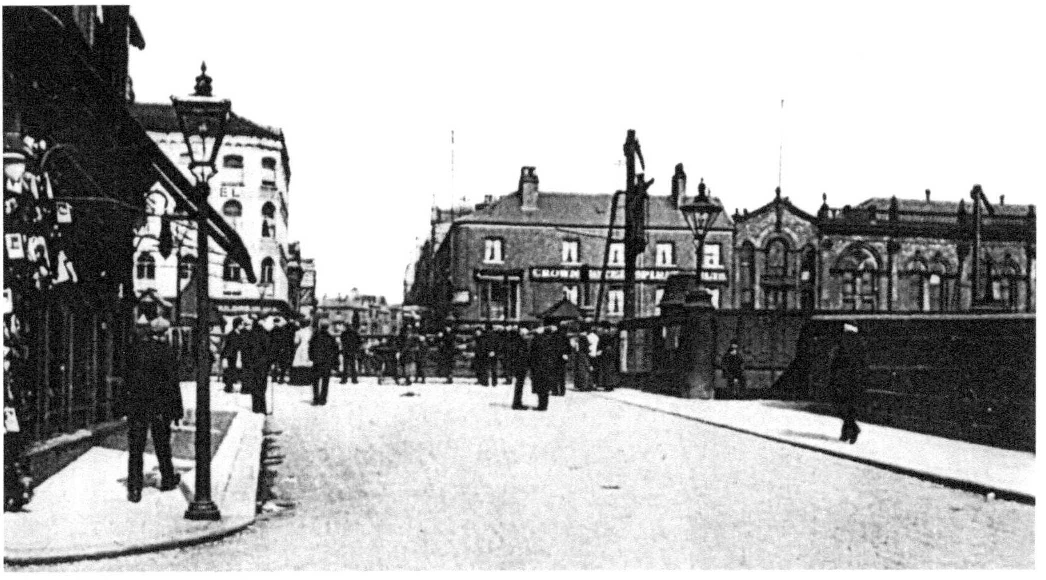

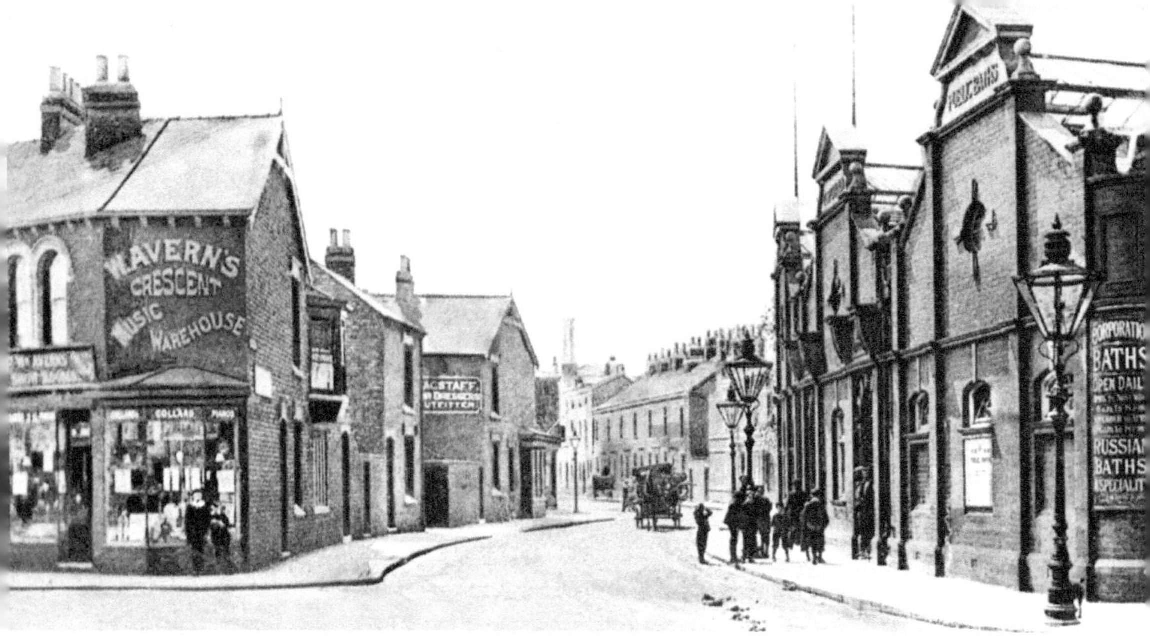

As the town gradually spilled across the railway many roads familiar in modern Middlesbrough were laid out. One, Newport Road, was constructed in two stages – Linthorpe Road to Boundary Road, the original boundary, and from there across the marshes to Newport village. Newport Crescent, shown here around 1904, was part of this building programme, becoming well known because the Corporation Baths were built here in 1884 on the site of an old brick pond. The baths were well used and as a result facilities were extended in 1901.

Newport Road looking towards Linthorpe Road from the corner of Dale Street, *c.* 1910. The old Cleveland Hall on the right was opened in 1872 as an auction and display rooms, although it soon became a social club. It later became Middlesbrough's first cinema, in 1908, after Thomas Thompson rented the Hall. Closing in April 1930, the Hall was demolished in 1936 to make way for the new United Bus Station. The tall building opposite opened as a Presbyterian Church in 1865 and became the Scala Cinema from 1919 to 1961.

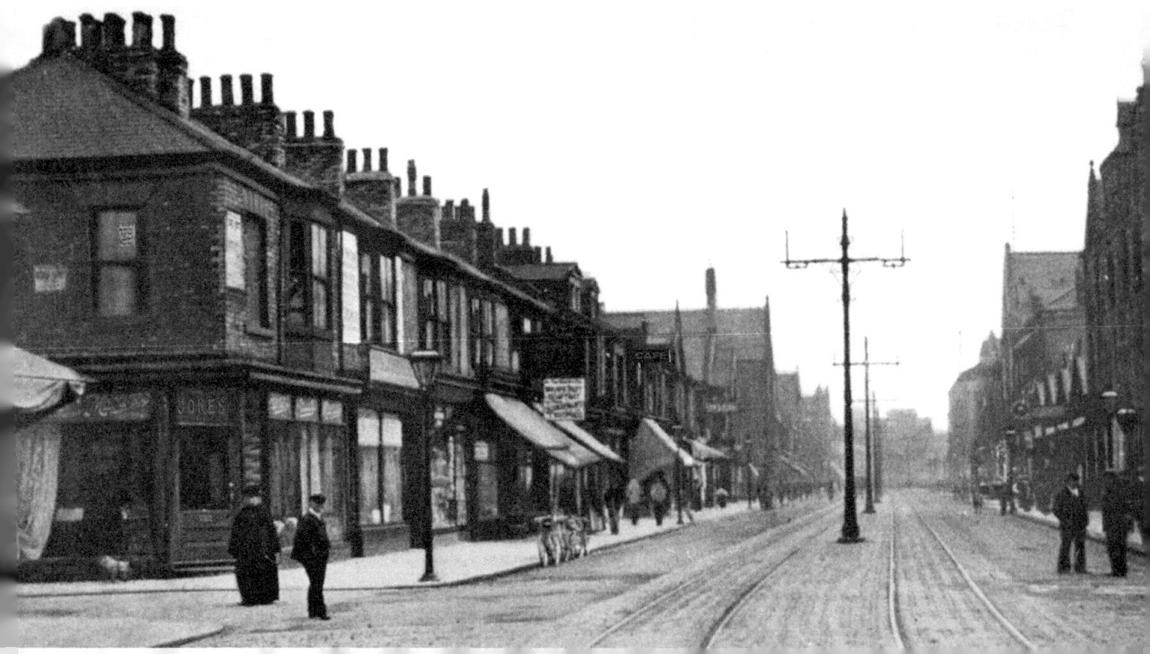

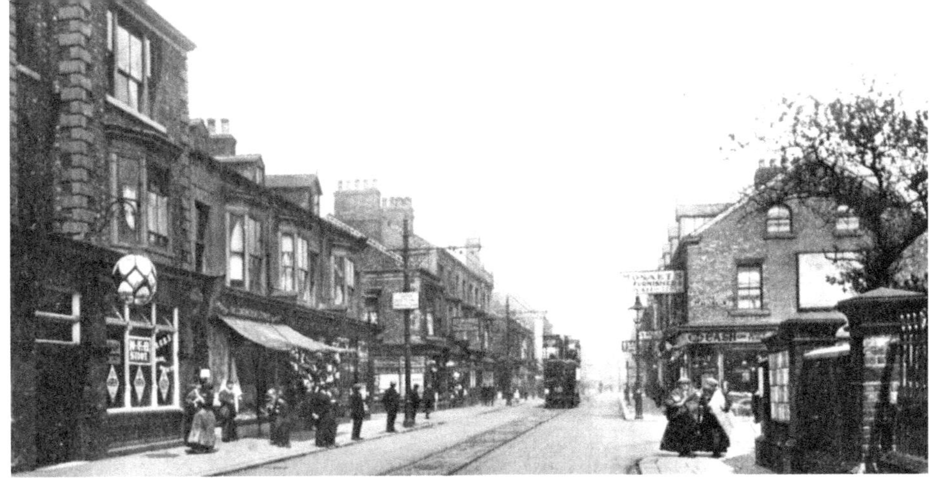

For many years the only road between Middlesbrough and Stockton was the lengthy route through Linthorpe and Acklam. In 1858 a turnpike was opened across marshland and the old river Tees to Newport, where it went no further until Newport Road was built to Boundary Road across North Acklam, farmland owned by the Hustlers. The road is seen here close to the junction with Hartington Road, where a toll bar stood until Middlesbrough's boundary extension in 1866 brought the road under the control of the town. The road became one of the main routes into the town, a centre of local retail trade with a variety of shops offering many different products.

Cannon Street has almost assumed a legendary status in the social history of old Middlesbrough. Built in the later nineteenth century on land adjacent to the Ironmasters District as Middlesbrough extended south, Cannon Street ran parallel to Newport Road. Almost a 'community within a community', Cannon Street inspired many tales about life there and is still strongly identified in many people's minds with the tight-knit communities of old Middlesbrough. This image shows one of the many shops which existed in the area at the time – although the owners are unidentified.

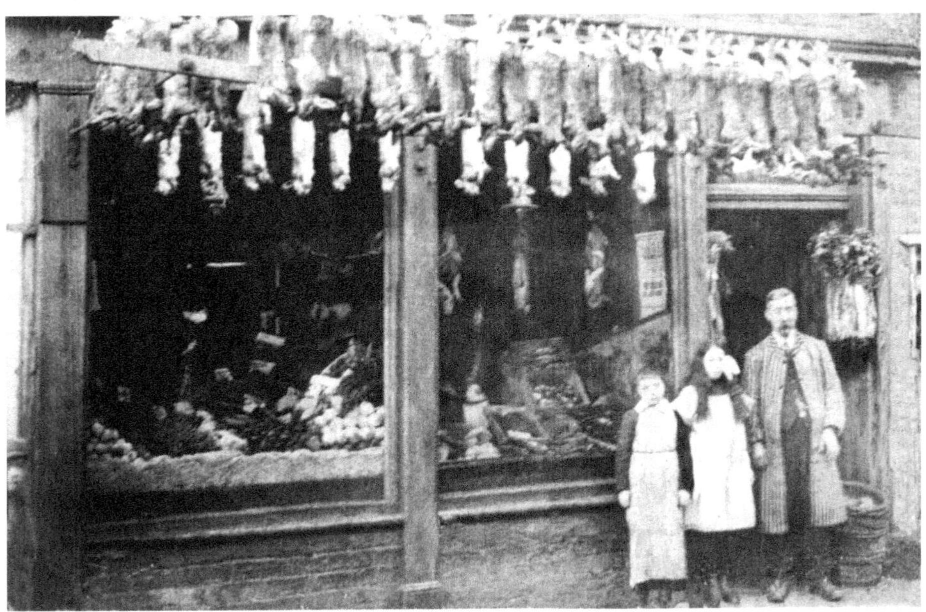

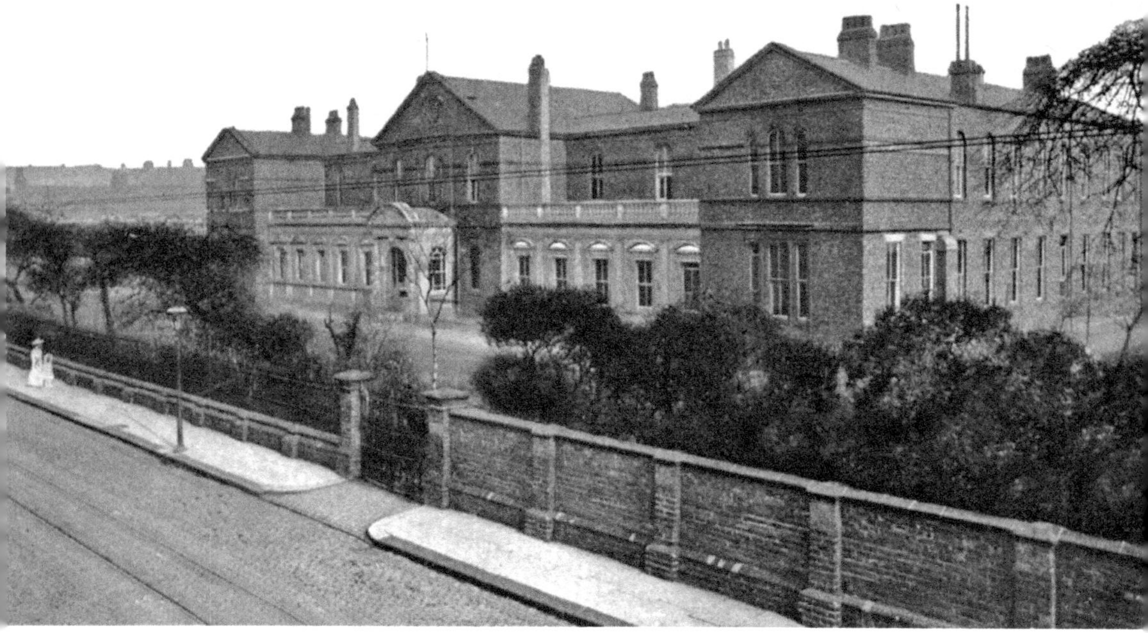

'Long Plantation', an acre of land adjacent to Newport Road, was donated by the Hustler family, along with a financial contribution to the £7,865 construction costs, for the purpose of building Middlesbrough Infirmary. The new hospital which replaced the town's Cottage Hospital which had opened in 1859 and was opened by Henry Bolckow on 5 June 1864. Many of its patients were casualties from the nearby Ironmasters District. The hospital remained one of the most familiar sites in Middlesbrough until its closure in 2004. Despite a public outcry, the hospital was bulldozed in 2006.

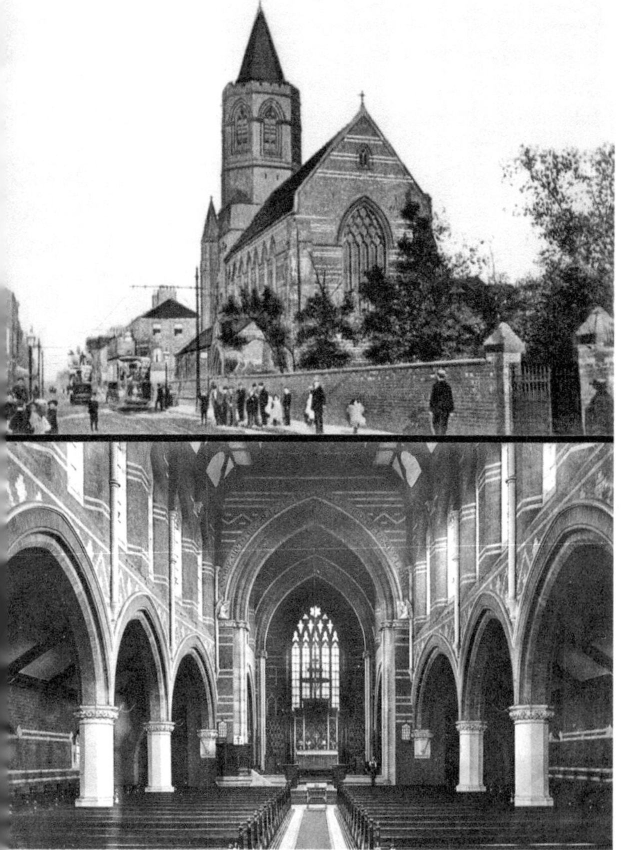

St Paul's Church, a huge, red-brick structure which stood on the corner of St Paul's Road, was for many years a familiar feature along lower Newport Road. The Revd George Austin, who arrived in Middlesbrough in 1867, obtained a donation of £1,000 from the Hustler family towards the church. When it was consecrated in 1871, it was called 'St Paul's, North Acklam' – then being outside the town boundaries. Having survived bombing during the Second World War, it was demolished in 1967. The interior of St Paul's is shown here around 1896 looking towards the elegant arched window at the east end. St Paul's, like many of the churches in Middlesbrough, played an important part in helping to set up Missions in the local area.

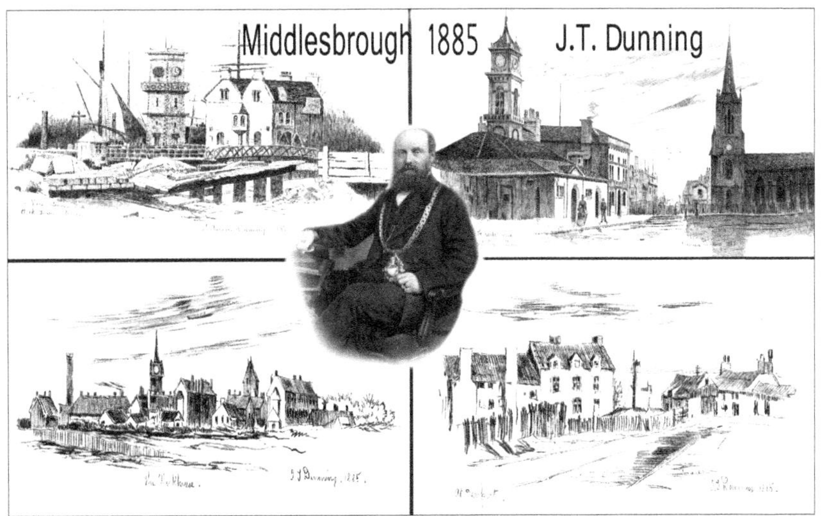

John Dunning, once an agent to the OME, held a number of important posts in local government, including being a councillor, an alderman from 1877 to 1895 and mayor in 1875. He helped to design Linthorpe Road as well as the turnpike road to Stockton, which became part of Newport Road. Dunning was an excellent artist and his sketchbook, published in 1885, contained a number of pencil sketches of the town, some of which are reproduced here. As well as being artistically pleasing, they provide an interesting 'snapshot' of late-Victorian Middlesbrough.

Following the visit of Prince Arthur, it was over thirty years before the next royal visit, when the Prince and Princess of Wales opened the new Town Hall on 23 January 1889. The royal train arrived at lunchtime and then a long procession travelled through streets decorated with flags and other regalia to the Market Square. They then went via Linthorpe Road and Grange Road into Albert Road, where 'God Save the Queen' rang out from children accommodated in a huge grandstand. Following the official opening, the royal party were treated to a banquet before they departed by train at 3.40 p.m., an event marked by a salute of guns from Albert Park. That evening the townspeople were treated to a huge firework display on waste ground which is now Victoria Square.

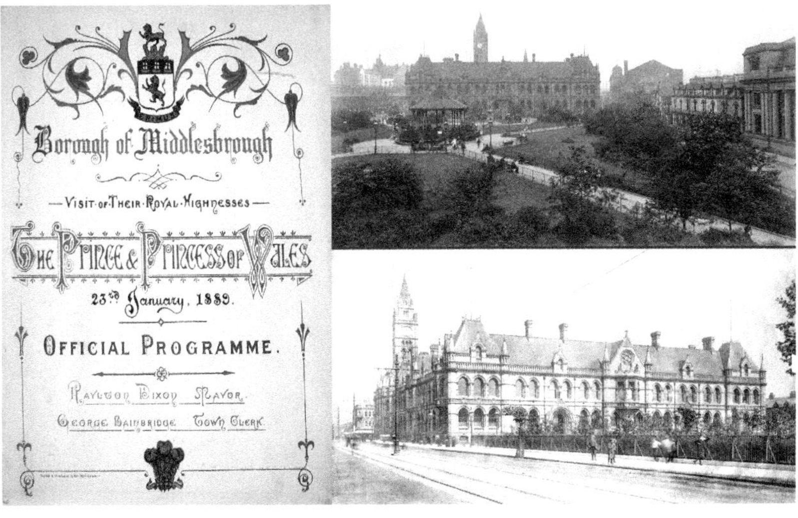

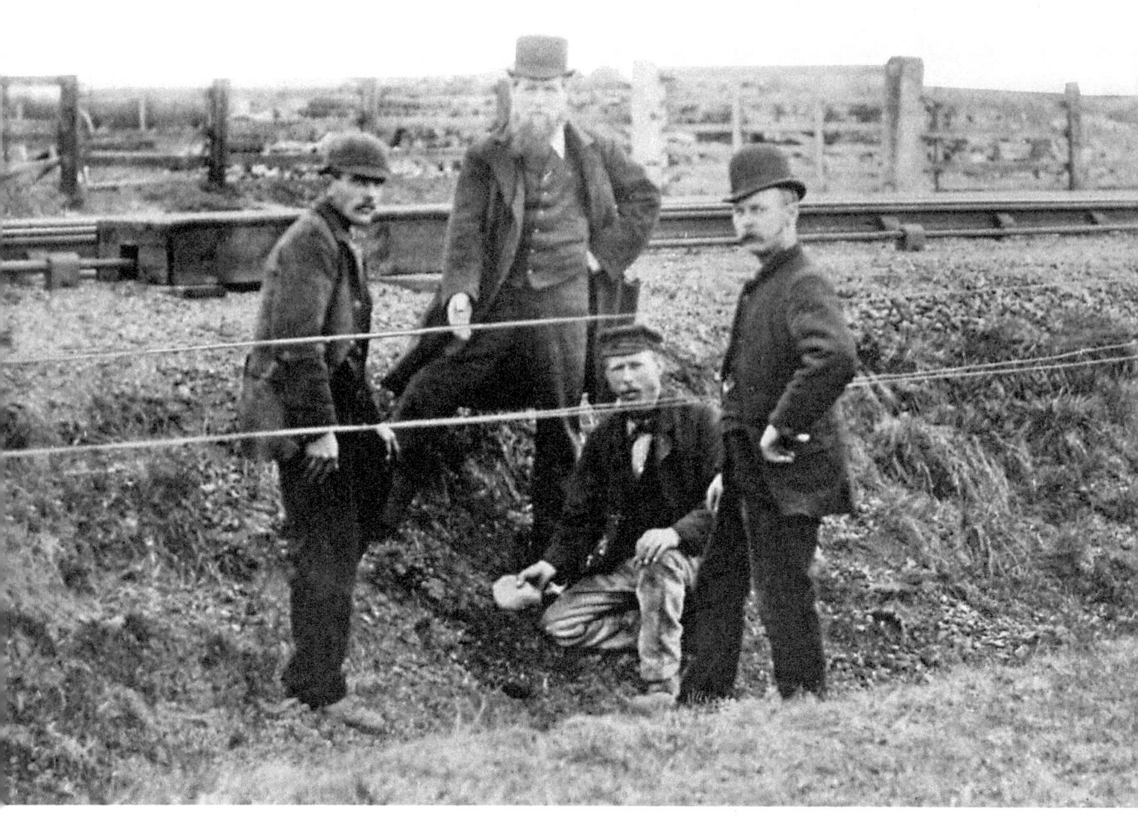

An unusual event which occurred in March 1881 was the arrival of a small meteor falling close to the Pennyman Siding near Berwick Hills, part of the Guisborough Branch railway. Railway workers are seen here holding the object. The 'Middlesbrough Meteorite' has again featured in the news in 2010 when experts from NASA asked to examine the object – which is over 4,500 million years old – so they can load details onto their mission to Mars to enable the probe to spot any similar objects on the surface of the planet.

3

'THE INFANT HERCULES'

William Gladstone uttered this phrase in 1862 – a succinct description of Middlesbrough ...

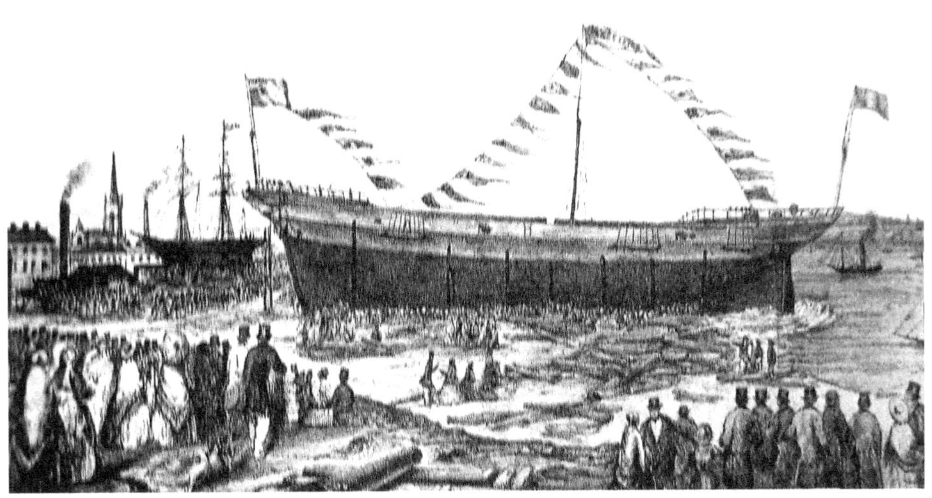

Crowds watch the launch of the *Excelsior* on 14 July 1855. Built by J.G. Holmes & Sons at their yard close to Commercial Street, for use in the Australia and China trade, it was then the largest ship ever built on the Tees. A full rigged ship with an Elliptic stern, 850 tons register and 1,500 tons burthen; length of keel and foretake 171ft and extreme breadth 30.5ft.

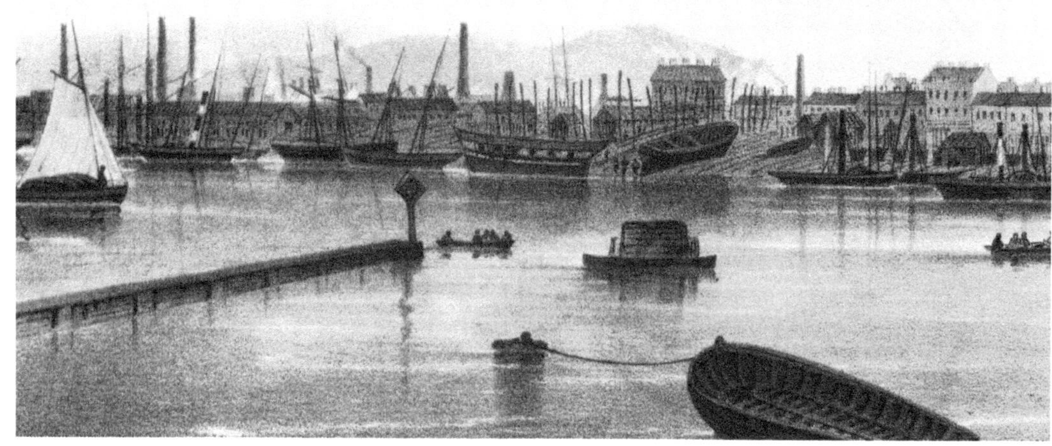

The OME encouraged other industries to develop in Middlesbrough. From the early 1830s a number of small shipyards were operating including J.D. Laing, J.G. Holmes and the North Yorkshire & Durham Ship Co. The yards mainly built collier brigs, wooden vessels with full sail, although by 1840 William Cudworth had built the first steamship, *Fortitude*, while in March 1858 the first iron ship, *De Brus*, was launched at Rake, Kimber & Co. Other ship-building companies operating at this time included J. Langdale (1845) and J.H. Leach (1862).

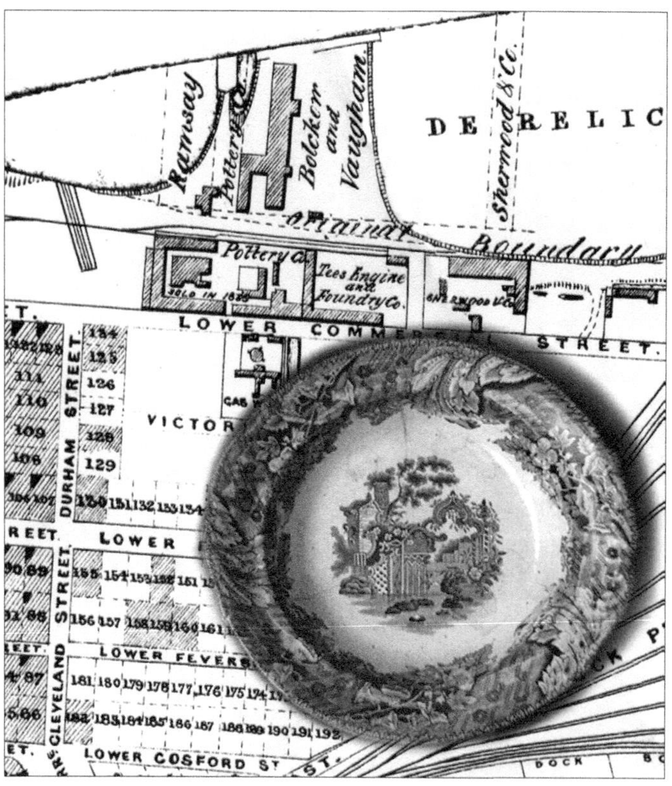

Middlesbrough Pottery, which was located north of Commercial Street, was owned by Richard Otley and opened in 1834. The pottery had its own wharf for importing china clay which was brought by colliers from Cornwall. Goods were also exported from here. Between 1844 and 1852 it was known as the Middlesbrough Earthenware Co. and then became Isaac Wilson & Co. The pottery closed in 1887, being replaced by metal works. This image shows the layout of the pottery factory in 1882 and a piece of pottery made in the factory's later years.

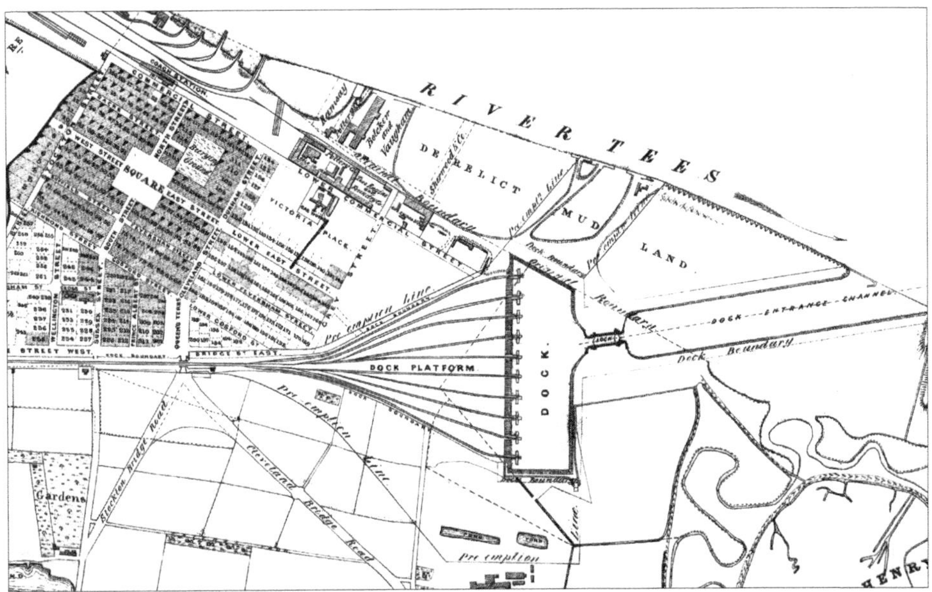

Middlesbrough Dock was built on marshland east of the original town as an answer to the problems caused by silting-up at the original coal staithes at Port Darlington. The enclosed dock, which had a constant water level to prevent silting-up, was designed by Sir William Cubitt and opened on 12 May 1842. Facilities were much improved and included ten coal drops served by a fan of railway lines from the Dock Branch, an extension from the original line to Port Darlington.

The old Clock Tower, erected in 1842. The tower contained a reservoir for maintaining hydraulic pressure to dockside cranes. One peculiarity about the clock is that the side which faced the Bolckow & Vaughan iron works had no clock face, a snipe at the company when they refused to subscribe to the clock because they didn't want their workers constantly aware of the time. Another tower was built in 1870, replacing the old Clock Tower and it was eventually demolished in 1903.

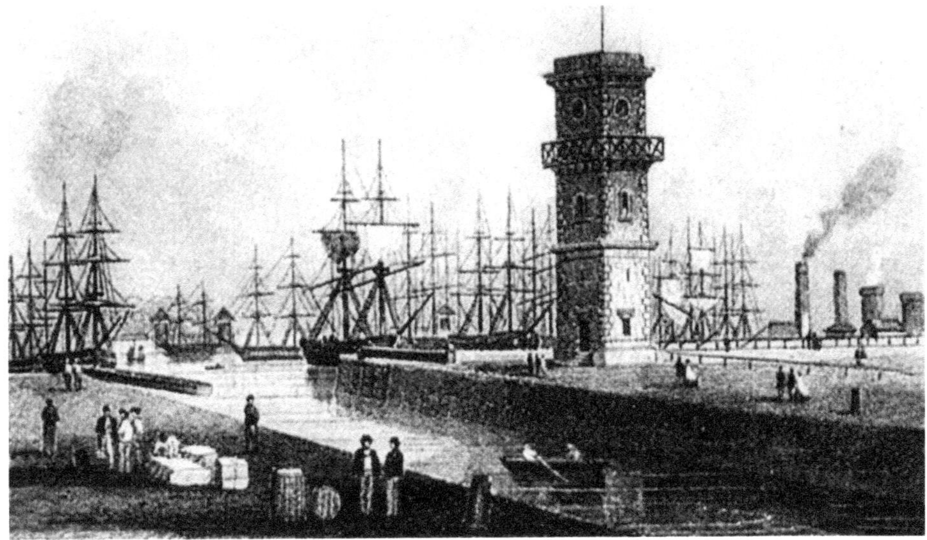

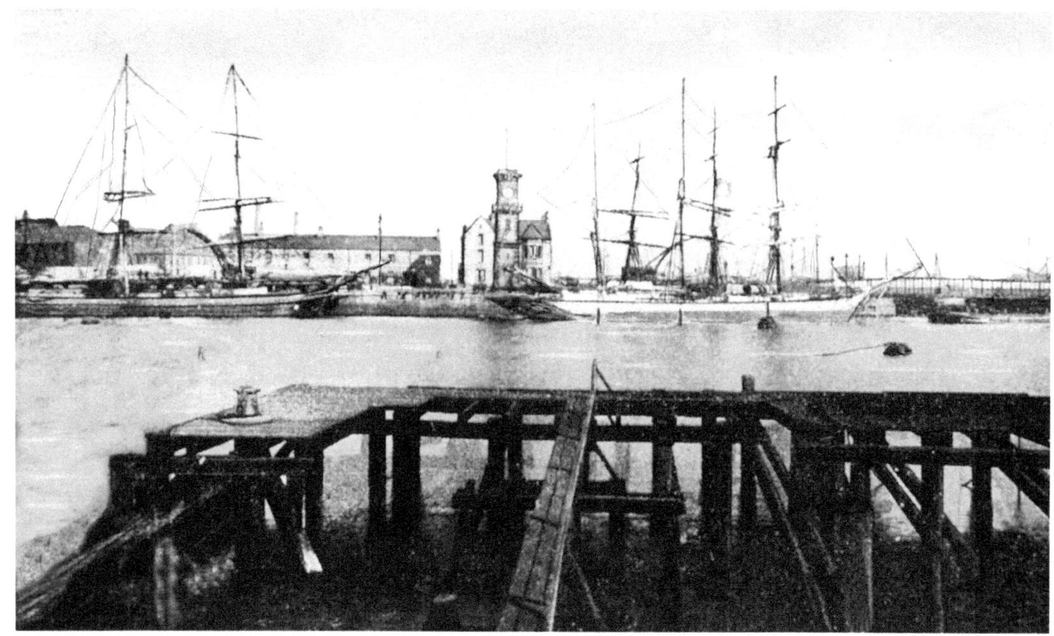

Several sailing vessels are berthed in front of the old Clock Tower and the row of terraced houses which stood along Dock Street, *c.* 1902. In the foreground is part of the dock. Ships travelled to the port of Middlesbrough from many different places, bringing cargoes essential for local industry.

This view looks from the dock towards the river with the old Clock Tower on the left. The new tower which replaced this stone edifice was said to act as a navigational aid to river pilots when bringing ships up river, as they could line up the tower with the old Town Hall to find the right line of entry to the dock.

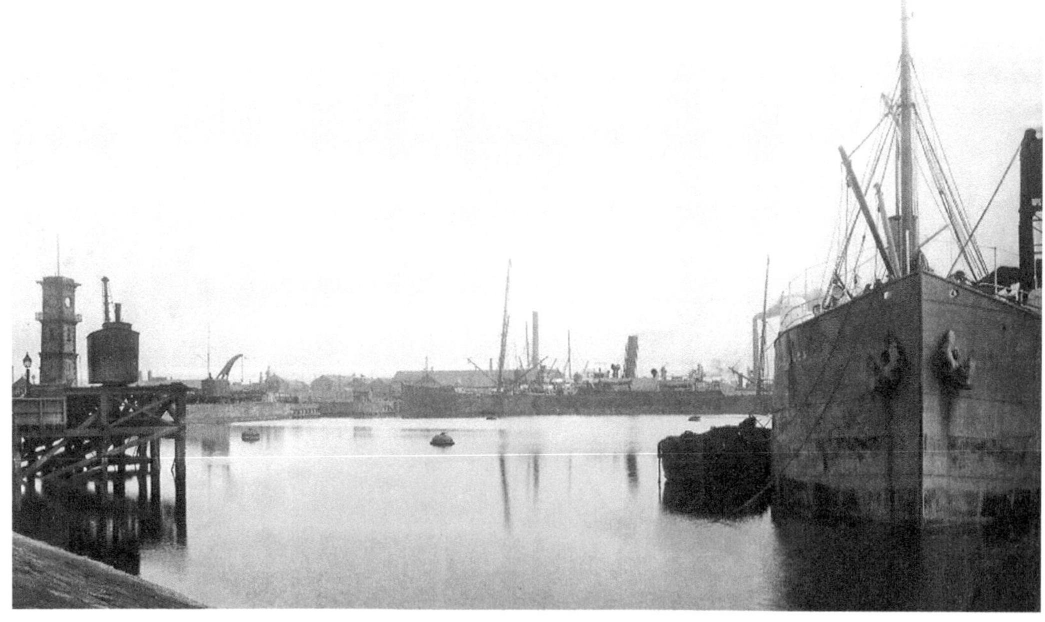

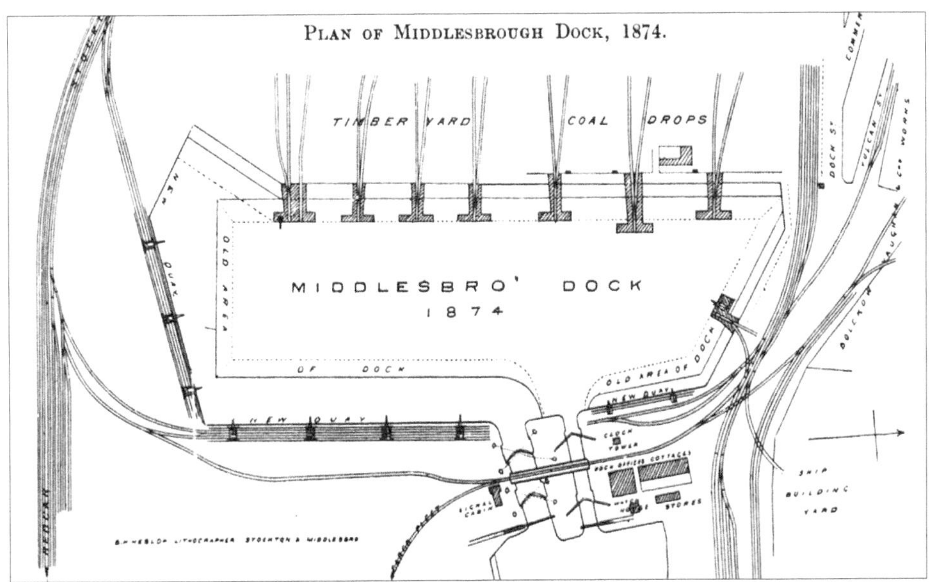

The increasing size of ships and a need to handle other cargoes after the decline in the shipment of coal led to several changes in Middlesbrough Dock. When the dock opened the enclosed water level was 3.6 hectares, but further extensions in 1869, 1885 and 1898 expanded this to 10.1 hectares and 2,134m of quayage. The extent of the new quayage, which was part of the enlargement of the dock in 1869, is clearly shown in this detailed drawing.

The sailing ship *Caradoc* docked in Middlesbrough, *c.* 1908. The number of sailing ships using the river fell steadily throughout the nineteenth century. By 1890 only 33 per cent of ships cleared on the Tees were sailing ships, a figure which had declined to only 14 per cent by 1913.

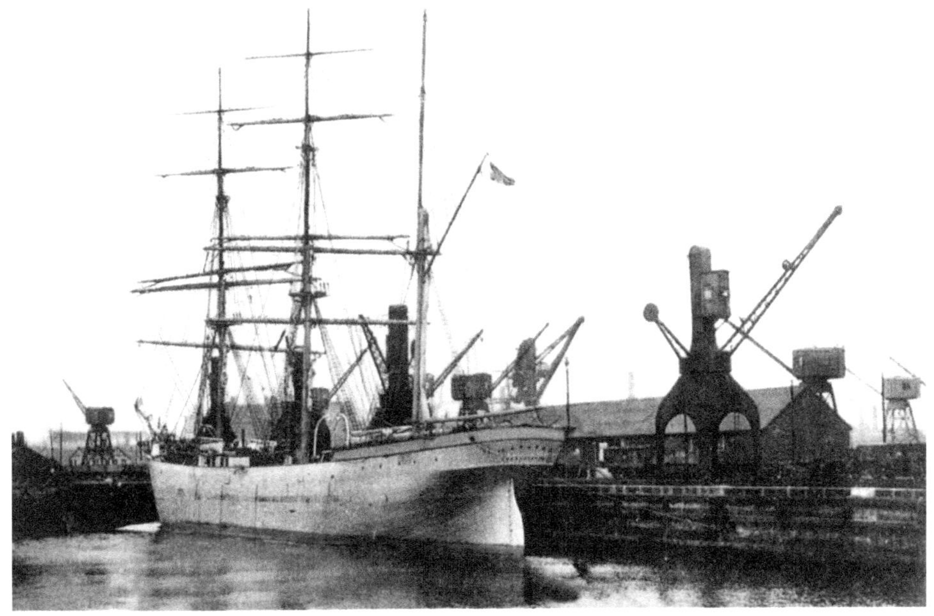

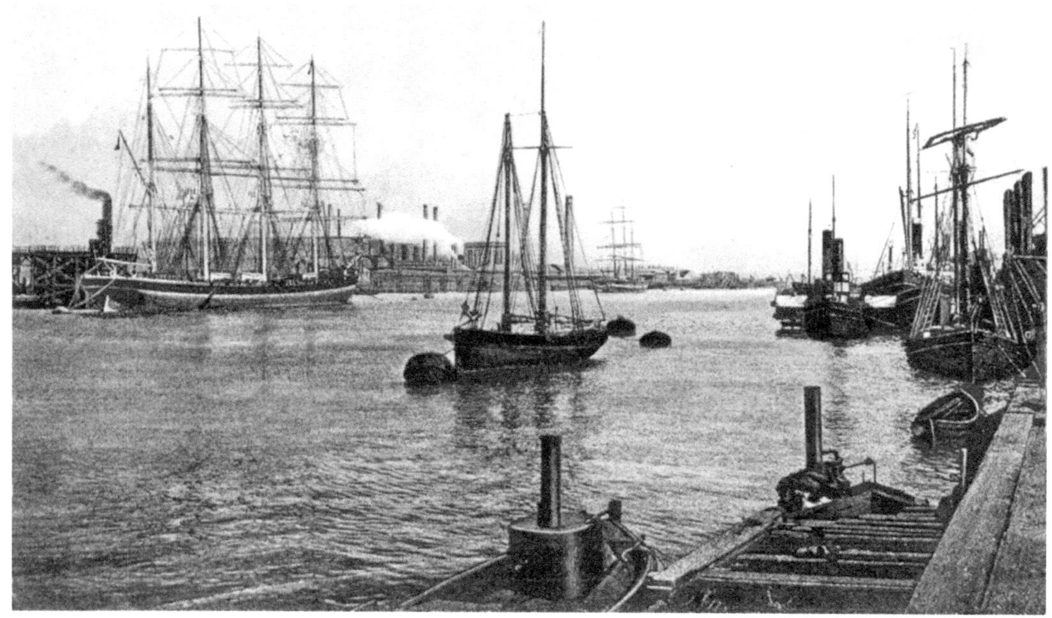

A view across to Port Clarence, showing the river banks lined with industry as far as the eye can see, *c.* 1907. Several ships are visible, including the four-masted vessel berthed at the staithes at Port Clarence. The distant chimneys are the Bell Brothers Ironworks. This picture was taken close to the point where the Transporter Bridge would later be built.

This view is quite unusual in that not only does it give a view across the river from the southern quay of the docks but it also shows one of the partially constructed towers of the Transporter Bridge at Port Clarence. Construction is obviously at an early stage, dating this image to around 1910.

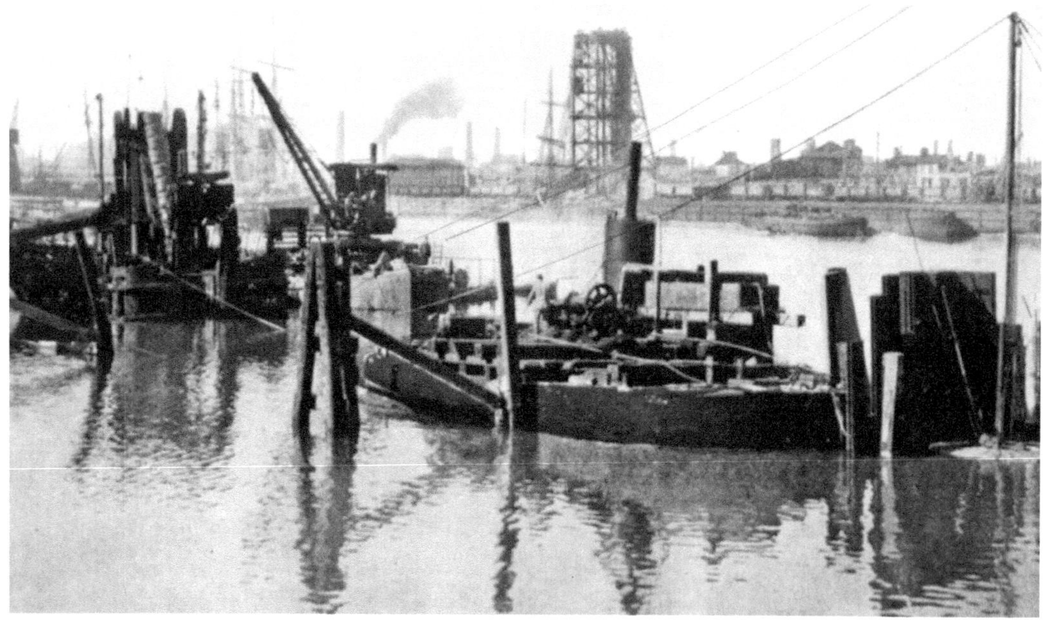

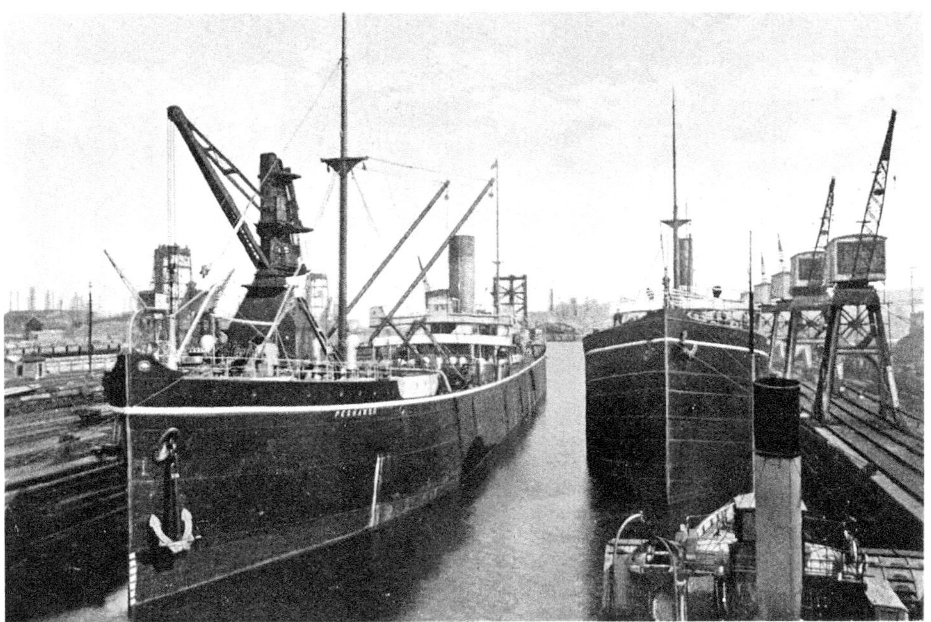

Two ships are berthed here in 1912 at one of the new quays. Behind them is the swing bridge across the dock entrance and alongside the ships further evidence of refurbishment can be seen, including the installation of more cranes to increase the capacity for loading and unloading a variety of cargoes.

This view, also from one of the docking points in the early twentieth century, shows how ships had increased in size. Competition with the Tyne and Wear as well as the Hartlepools ensured that the Tees Conservancy Commissioners, the body charged with responsibility for the port, had to be efficient in their maintenance. The new Clock Tower, which was built in 1870, can be seen in the distance.

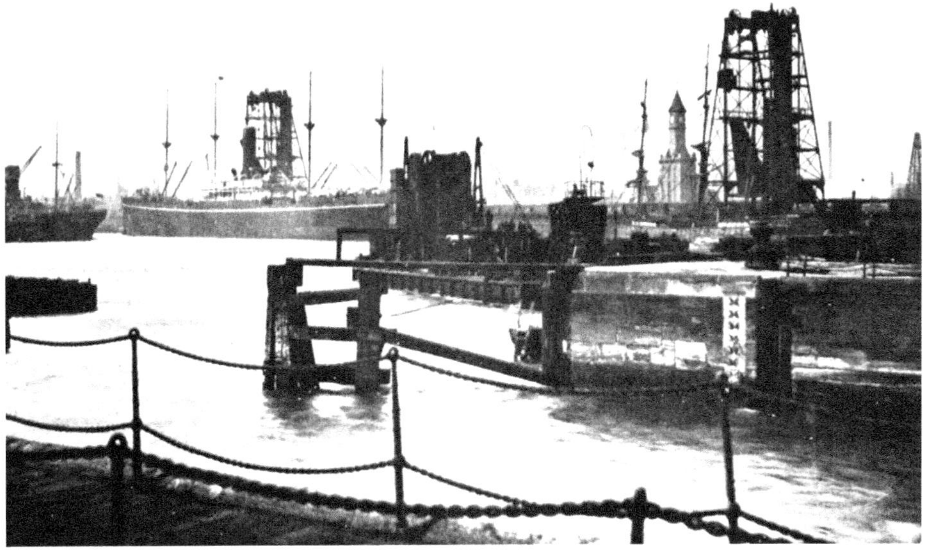

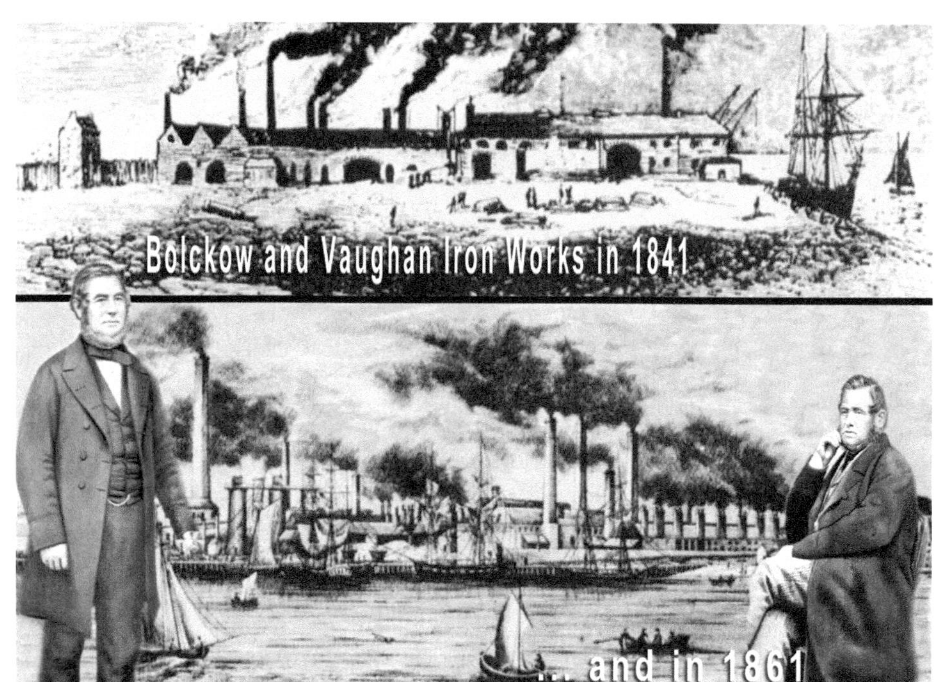

The role of Joseph Pease was again crucial when the partnership of John Vaughan (right), with his experience of the iron industry, and wealthy businessman Henry Bolckow (left) were looking to set up an iron works on Teesside. Unable to find a suitable site in Stockton, they were invited by Pease to purchase six acres of land close to Commercial Street in Middlesbrough – a move which would prove to be vital to the future of Middlesbrough. The iron works began the manufacture of iron on 1 May 1841 and these two images demonstrate the expansion of the works by 1861.

Other factories followed Bolckow & Vaughan to Middlesbrough including the Darlington and Middlesbrough Sailcloth, Shoe Thread and Patent Rope Co. in 1842 and Gilkes Wilson & Co. Tees Engine Works in 1844. On 9 October 1862 the Chancellor of the Exchequer and future Prime Minister, the Right Honourable W.E. Gladstone, visited local factories, including the Bolckow & Vaughan Ironworks, in Middlesbrough. At a banquet which followed his official welcome at Middlesbrough Town Hall, Gladstone famously referred to Middlesbrough as an 'infant Hercules'. William Taylor's painting shows the flotilla of ships – including Gladstone on board the steamship *Confidence* – sailing to Middlesbrough after visiting Eston Ironworks.

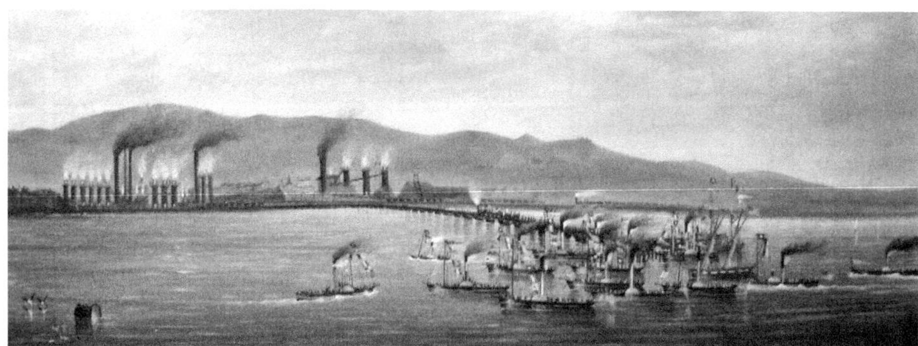

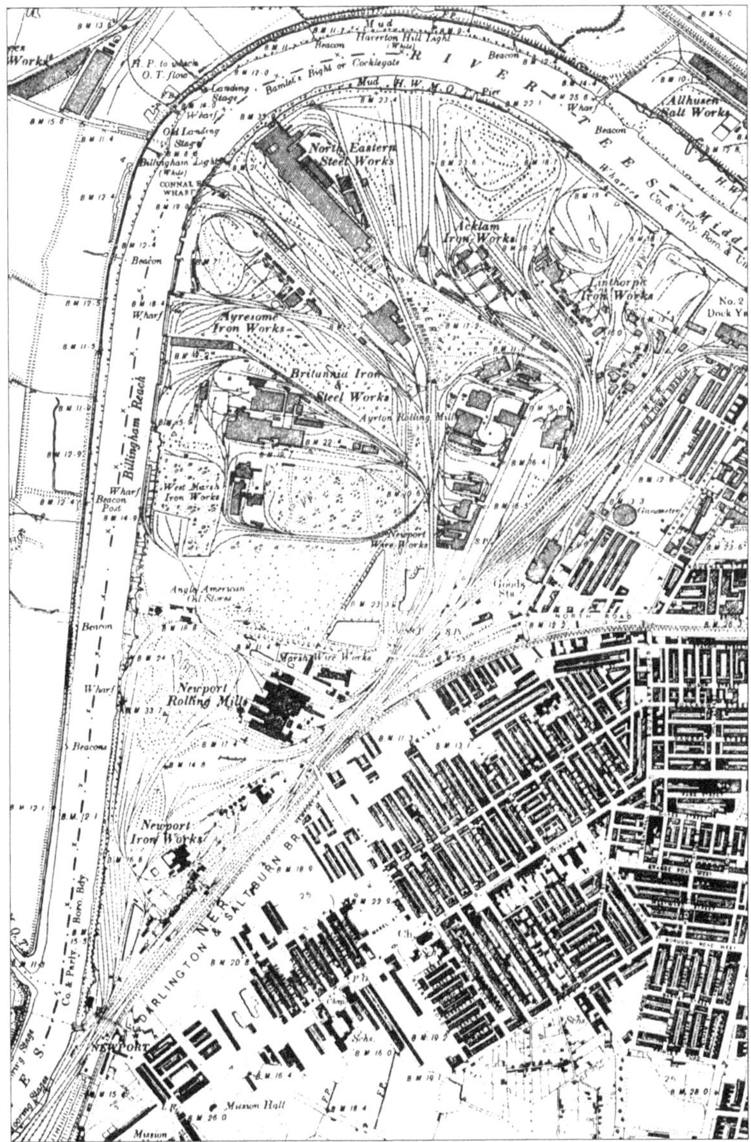

The financial support of Joseph Pease proved invaluable in helping Bolckow & Vaughan deal with problems of resources, particularly during their first decade. The turning point was the discovery of substantial deposits of local iron ore in June 1850, a catalyst for the rapid expansion of the iron industry on Teesside as a whole, led by Bolckow & Vaughan opening their blast furnace in 1851. Fuelled by the continued demand for iron from Victorian industry, an increasing number of other furnaces opened locally. Many were built on reclaimed marshland between Newport and the old town, the area being aptly named the 'Ironmasters' District'. Both the industry and the town grew rapidly; by 1901 Middlesbrough had a population of 90,000 and Teesside accounted for a third of the country's iron output. Despite depressions in the industry, local innovation helped to maintain momentum, exemplified in the 1870s by the opening of the Bessemer Steel Plant in Middlesbrough to meet the growing demand for steel. (Reproduced from 1897 Ordnance Survey map, 6 inch series, with the kind permission of the Ordnance Survey)

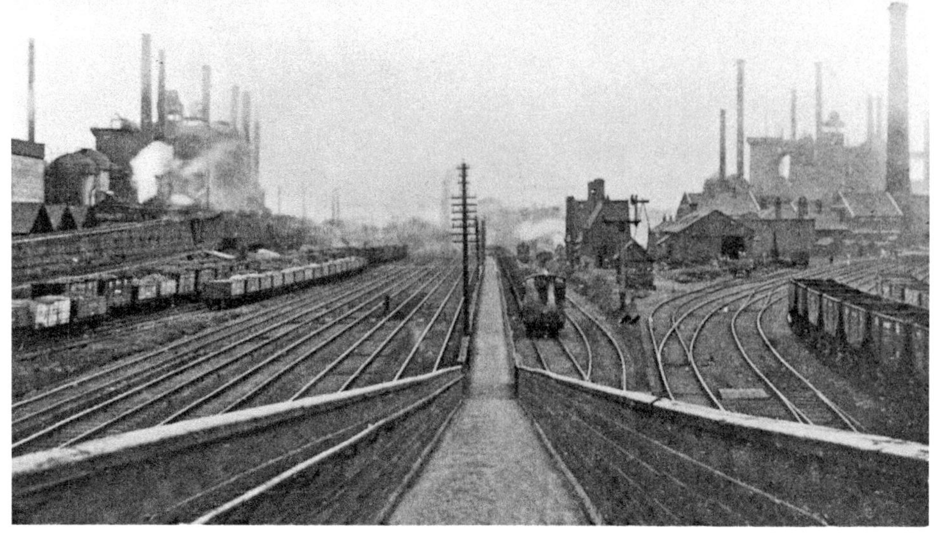

Bolckow & Vaughan had several iron foundries along the riverside, part of the rapid expansion in the number of works in the area. This works close to Middlesbrough is certainly an impressive scene with smoke pouring out from numerous chimneys, trains pulling wagons laden with coal and other trucks waiting to disgorge of their loads. When the steel industry began to dominate towards the end of the nineteenth century, new factories were located on unused land further down river as the deeper water there made it easier when importing the large amounts of haematite ore needed for the making of acid steel.

Newport Ironworks, *c.* 1912. It was founded in 1864 when Bernard Samuelson began calcining ironstone. This development was part of the rapid expansion of the industry which followed the finding of local iron ore. In 1871 there were already seven blast furnaces operating at the works, the resultant smoke and grime pouring out over the adjacent area of housing. Newport ironworks, like many others, was finally taken over by Dorman Long in 1917 and eventually closed in 1930.

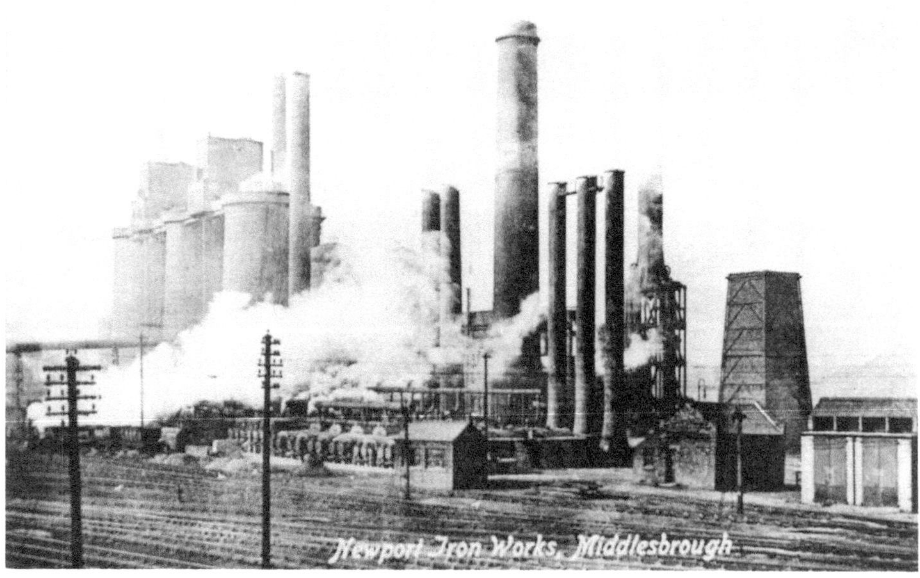

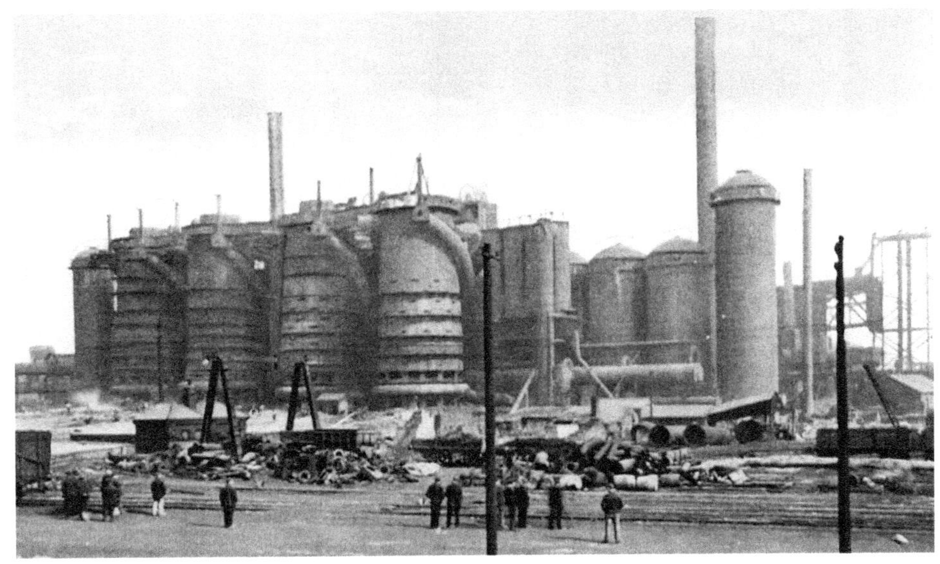

Acklam Ironworks, owned by Stevenson, Jacques & Co., was situated in the northern area of the Ironmasters' District, next to the Linthorpe Works. These two works were close to the old town of Middlesbrough and across the river from the Bell Brothers Ironworks at Port Clarence. This view of the blast furnaces, taken around 1912, shows how large they were compared with the workers who are standing in the foreground.

This view is taken from Dock Point looking towards the blast furnaces on the southern bank of the river. Many of the small companies formed during the rapid expansion of the iron industry in the latter half of the nineteenth century had, by 1914, been absorbed by three major businesses – Bolckow & Vaughan & Co., Dorman Long and South Durham Steel & Iron Co. As larger companies they could compete better against the large companies abroad, particularly in America. Difficult trading conditions in the 1920s would see Bolckow & Vaughan & Co. merge with Dorman Long, making it the largest iron and steel company in the country at the time, employing 33,000 men – though this was truly the end of an era for the pioneering company Bolckow & Vaughan.

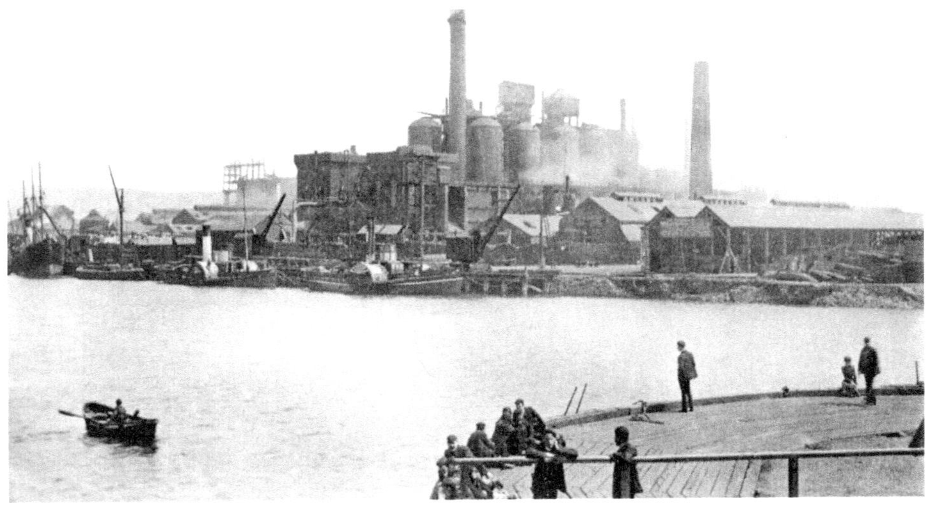

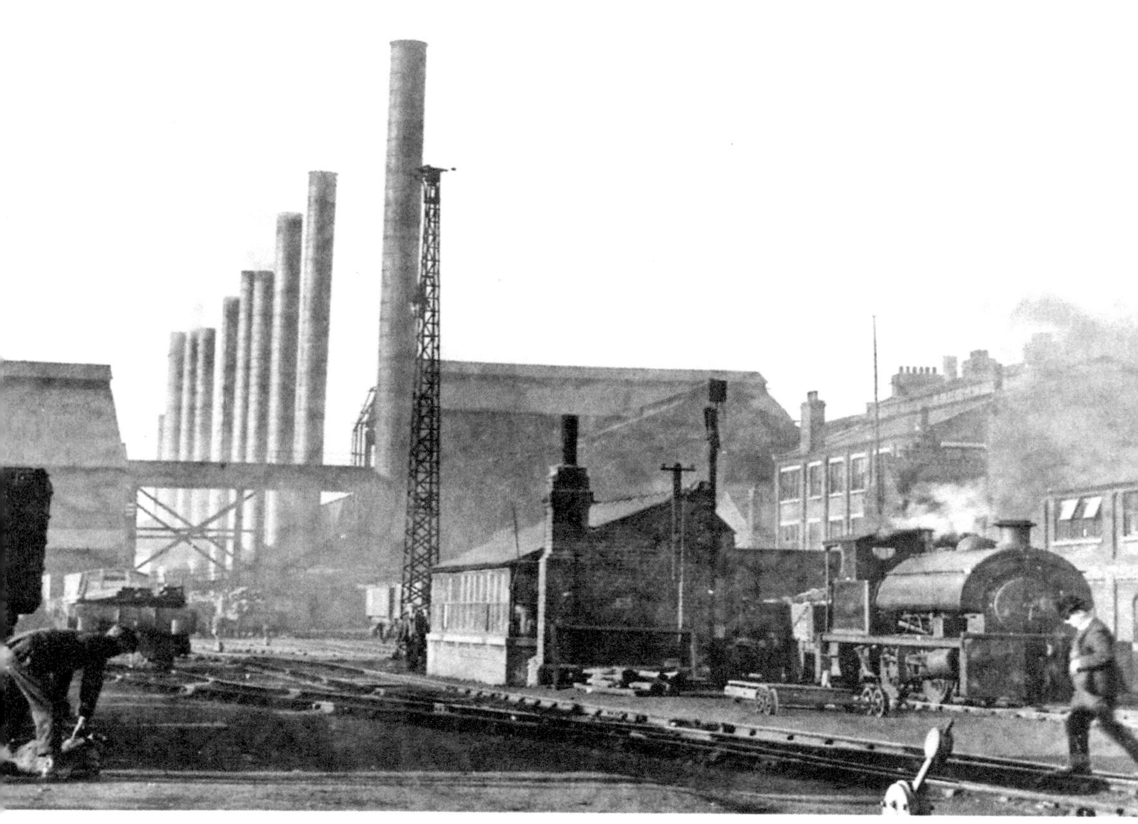

The 1920s was a decade of depression for iron and steel companies. At one point Dorman Long, the leading company in the industry on Teesside, were only operating at 30 per cent capacity. It was decided to re-organise its haphazard collection of plants, created through years of taking over smaller companies, closing the obsolete and ensuring the modern were utilised to their strengths. The Britannia Works, seen here around 1930, had originally been leased from Bernard Samuelson to increase the company's pig-iron capacity. Now it became part of Dorman Long's long-term reorganisation process – a move which would prove very successful.

4

'LITTLE BROWN STREETS'

Life in the town in the early twentieth century was tough for many inhabitants. Author Lady Florence Bell described Middlesbrough as 'rows and rows of little brown streets' overhung by 'pillars of cloud by day ... pillars of fire by night'.

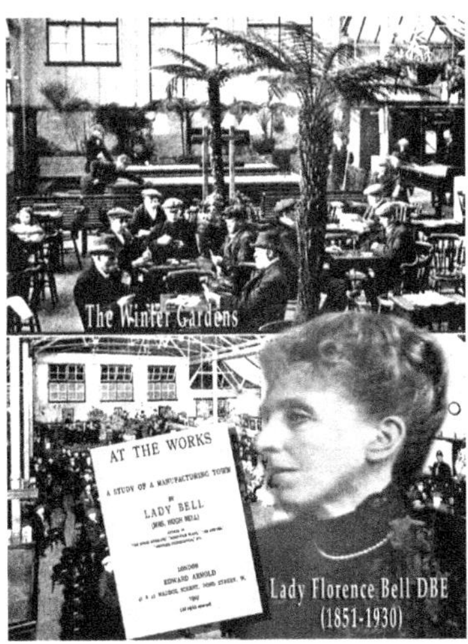

Lady Florence Bell DBE, wife of ironmaster Sir Hugh Bell and mother of famous explorer Gertrude Bell, is remembered for *At The Works*, a book she wrote about Middlesbrough in 1907. This study of the lives of workers highlighted the importance of women in managing the household. Although no individual inhabitants were identified in the book, it paints a pastiche of life for the masses at that time. The book was well received, with the *North-Eastern Evening Gazette* saying it deserved 'to be read by all [who are] interested in the welfare of the ... working classes'. Another legacy from Lady Bell was the ever popular Winter Gardens, shown here. Opened in October 1907, this was a club for the elderly built on the site of eight cottages in Dundas Street and Dundas Mews. Admission was one penny; tea and biscuits were also available as were cards, games and a billiard table.

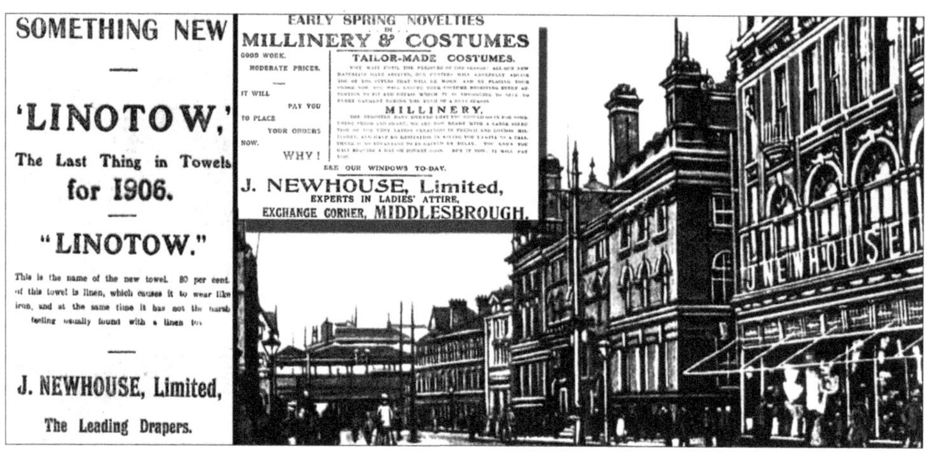

One of the best known shops in Middlesbrough was Newhouse's Department Store. John Newhouse set up as a draper when he arrived in Middlesbrough in 1865 and was successful enough to warrant a move to the larger premises (shown here around 1905) on the corner of Albert Road and Wilson Street. In 1912 the business moved to the site of the King's Head Hotel, on the corner of Corporation Road and Linthorpe Road, where it remained a popular store for more than fifty years until being replaced by Debenhams. The advertisements are from February 1906.

Having terminated at the Albert Road Railway Bridge, the No. 51 tram travels back down Albert Road, passing the Newhouse draper store where the white awnings provide shade for the front of the shop, c. 1907. The trams were a popular mode of transport at this time, providing links to the town centre from newer housing areas like Linthorpe. This tram is travelling on one of the main routes, from Linthorpe village to the terminus at Ferry Road in the old town. Note it is single decker to enable it to pass under the Albert Bridge.

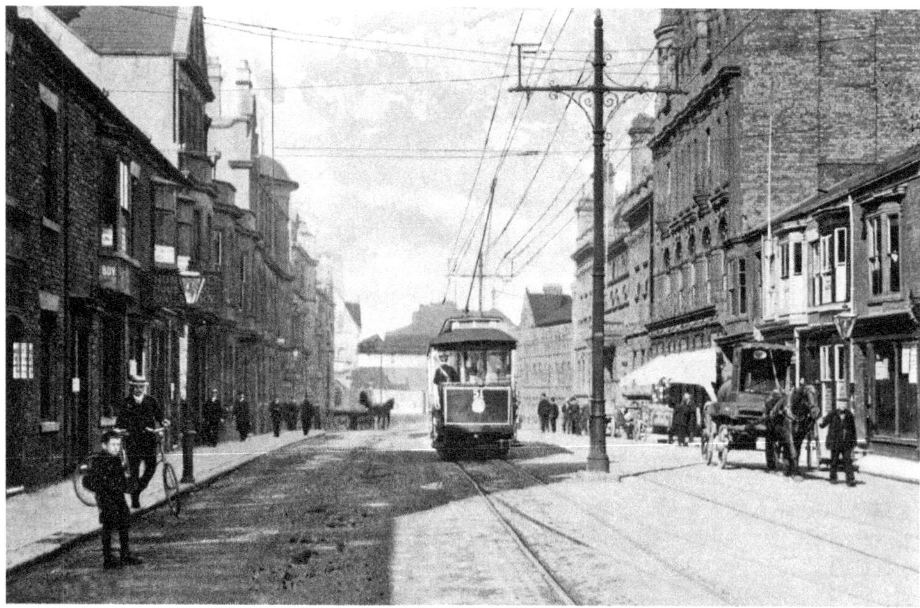

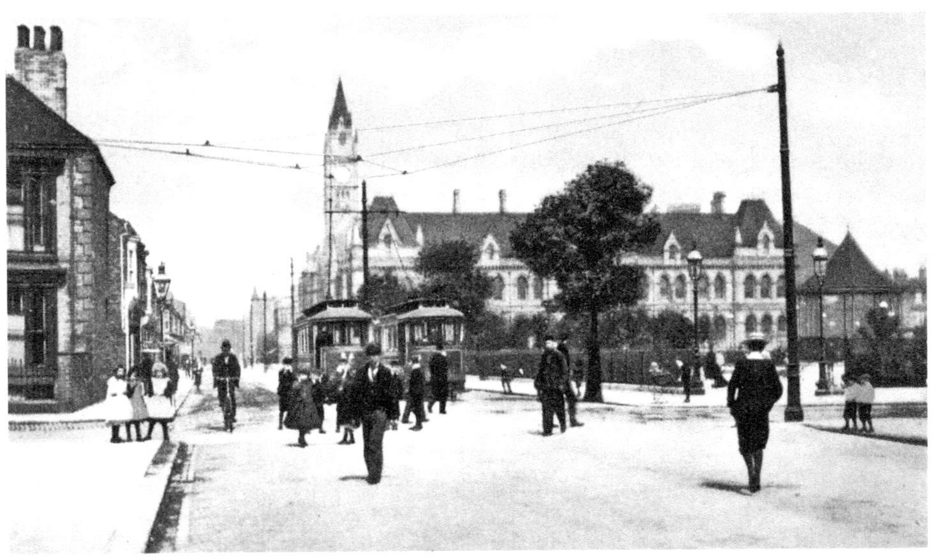

This view is taken further south in Albert Road, at the junction with Grange Road, *c*. 1910. The Town Hall, which had been opened in 1889, dominates the horizon while in front of it is Victoria Square – a popular facility for people in the town after its opening in 1901. The houses seen on the left have today been replaced by the Cleveland Centre, while the Square has survived as a public leisure area.

This view looks down a quiet Corporation Road towards the Town Hall, *c*. 1912. The provisions shop on the corner of Gurney Street on the right, belonged to merchant Robert Denis. On the left, next to the Empire Theatre, is Martin's Garage advertising Singer cycles for sale while beyond is the Corporation Hotel. The crowds are just visible in the busier area around Linthorpe Road.

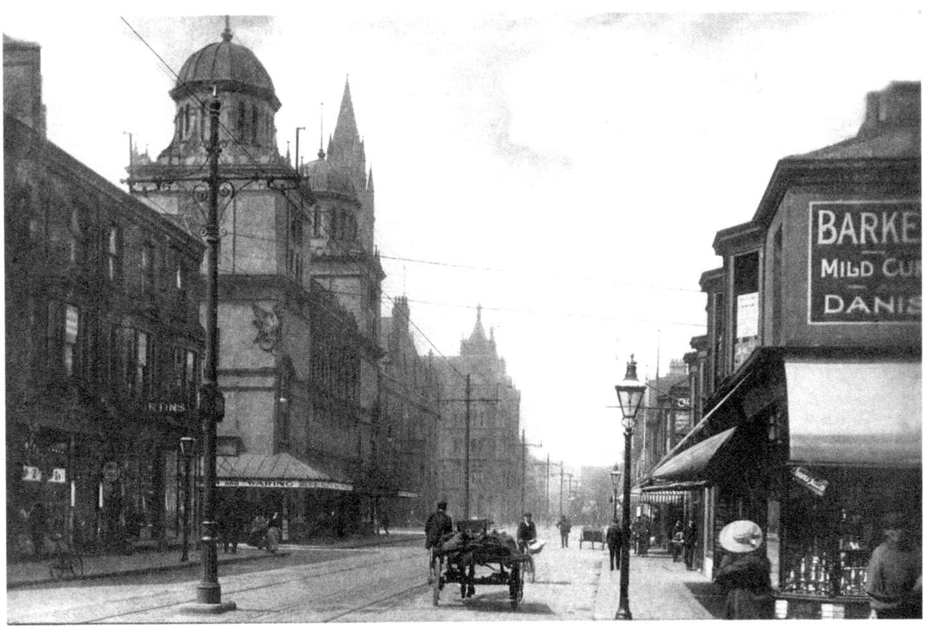

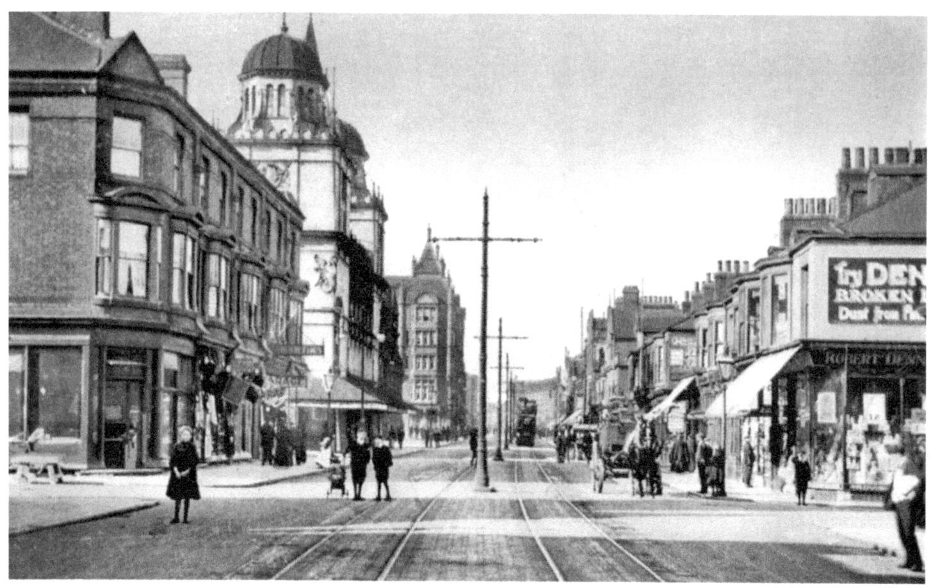

Taken from a point slightly further east, this similar view shows Peacock Street on the left and a clearer view of Denis's shop on the right. As always, the presence of the photographer attracts one or two children – note the two boys in the middle of the road along with a pram and occupant. They could not know their place in posterity would be secure, a moment in time preserved forever.

This busy scene is taken from the corner of Corporation Road and Linthorpe Road. A No. 36 tram passes the Wesleyan Chapel with the Corporation Hotel, Town Hall and Empire Theatre all visible. The shop on the left is Collingwood's the jewellers, another long-established name. Mathew Collingwood had first opened a jeweller's shop in the old Market Place in 1855, after which he moved to South Street and then to Cleveland Terrace before moving to the site shown here.

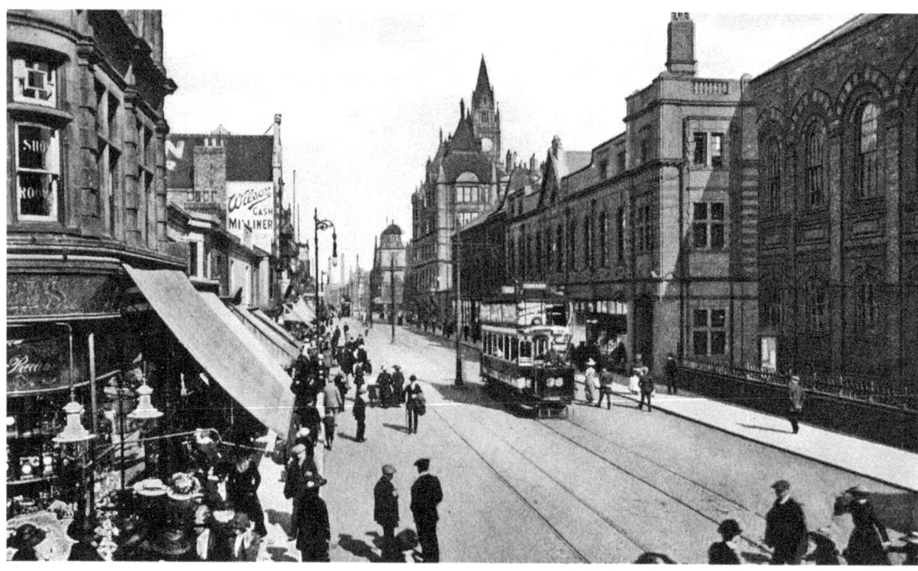

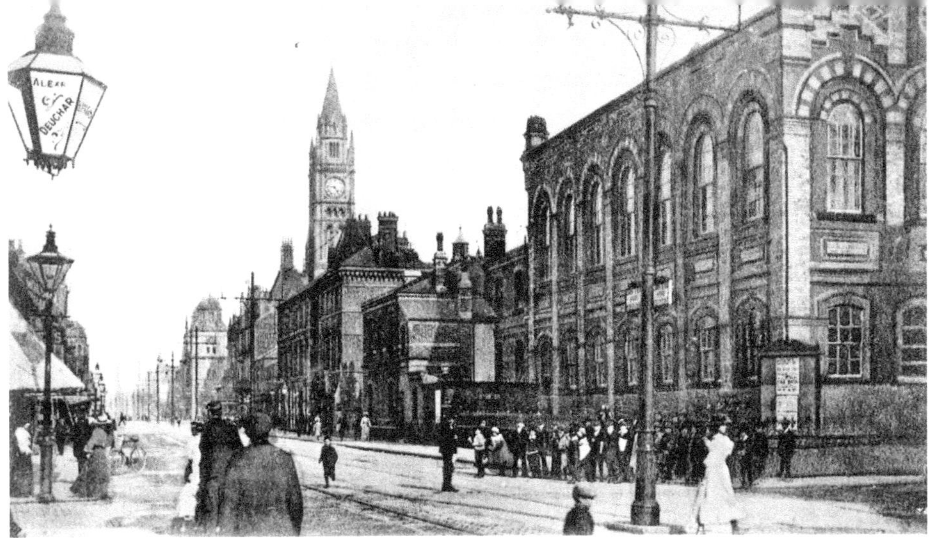

An early morning view, with the clock at the Town Hall showing 9.25 a.m., looking along from the corner of Corporation Road and Linthorpe Road. Close to Big Wesley (as the Wesleyan Chapel was affectionately known) a group of schoolchildren are patiently waiting to cross the busy road. Nearby a small boy has decided to take his chance and dash across. Beyond the chapel is the Athenaeum Building and then the Corporation Hotel.

This scene looks down Linthorpe Road from the busy intersection with Newport Road. On the immediate right is Manfield's Boot Store, which stood on the site occupied today by Binns. Opposite is the Wesleyan Chapel, which cost £6,000 to build and could seat 840 worshippers. When the chapel opened on 20 September 1863, this site was on the southern edge of the town. A school was housed here until 1908, when it was replaced by a large hall which became very popular for lectures and concerts.

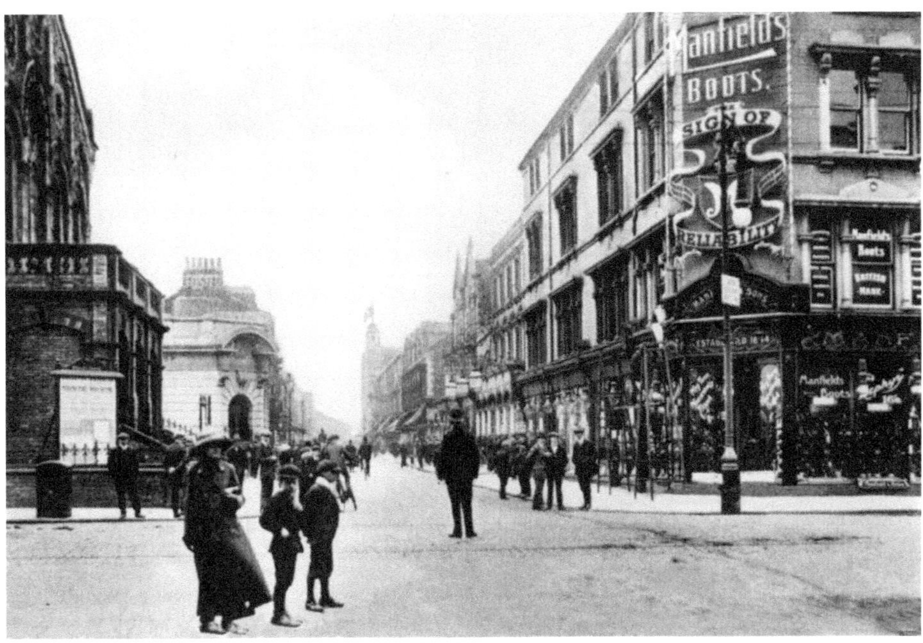

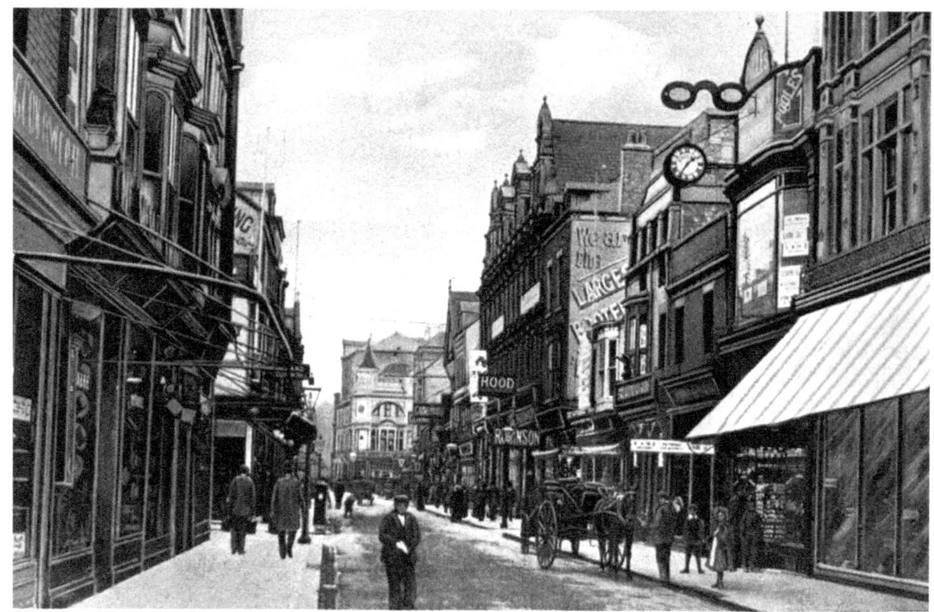

By 1900 Linthorpe Road was well established as the main shopping area in the town. This view is taken from a point which today is close to the Next clothing outlet. There is a degree of familiarity about the scene but a closer look shows little has remained the same. One hundred years ago many shops were still owned by local retailers, in an era before the national high street names became established. At 14 Linthorpe Road, in the distance on the right, is the Leeds Hotel, a popular venue until it was bombed during the Second World War.

This view, showing the northern part of Linthorpe Road, is remarkable for its clarity. As well as the Leeds Hotel, visible in the distance, the Masham Hotel can also be seen on the left at 49 Linthorpe Road, a public house which only closed in recent years. In the foreground to the left is the Cleveland Book Store, which was on the junction with Johnson Street. In the distance lies the old town just visible across the railway.

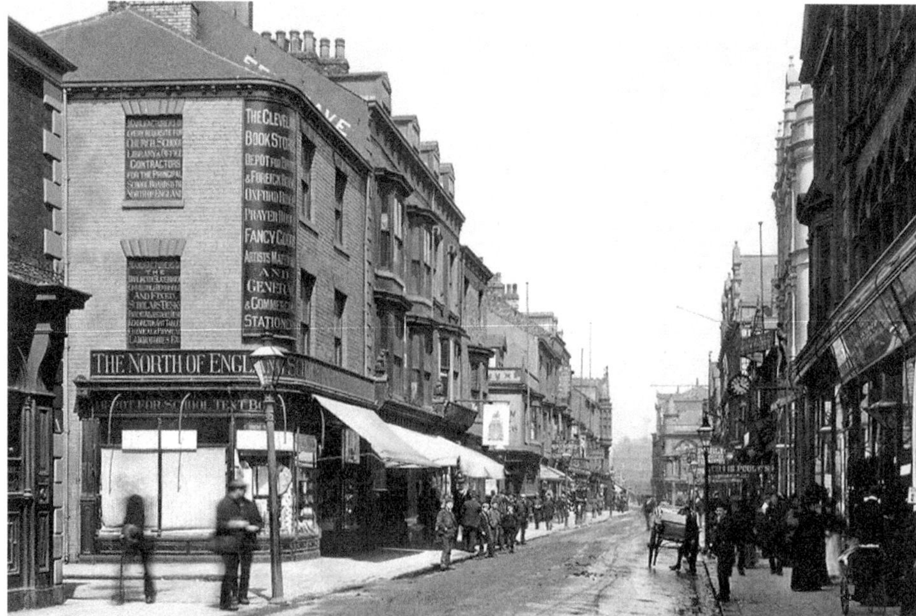

Right: These two images show the King's Head Hotel, which stood at No. 1 Newport Road on the corner of Linthorpe Road, *c.* 1908. The King's Head opened in 1862 as part of the building of the first section of Newport Road. It was a popular venue for local inhabitants, only closing when John Newhouse bought the site for his new store in 1912. Even a century ago this area was popular for shopping, as shown by the crowds of people spilling across from the pavements. This section of Linthorpe Road was never part of a tram route; the only traffic here is a pair of cyclists.

Below: Moving further south down Linthorpe Road this is a more distant view of the King's Head and the premises of Manfield's Boot Store. Three large ornate lanterns hang down over the frontage of the Imperial Hotel on the left while opposite is the corner of Wesley Street which was adjacent to the chapel.

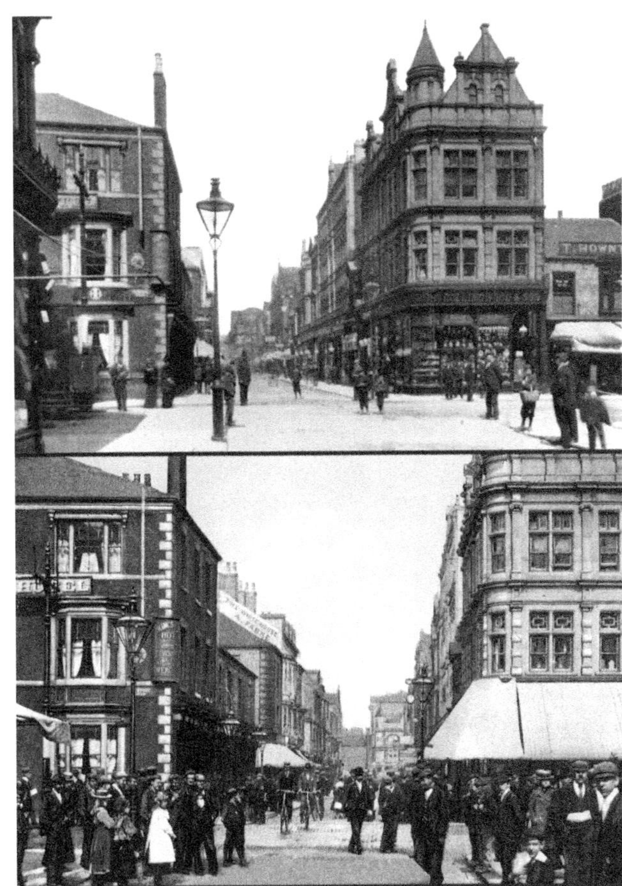

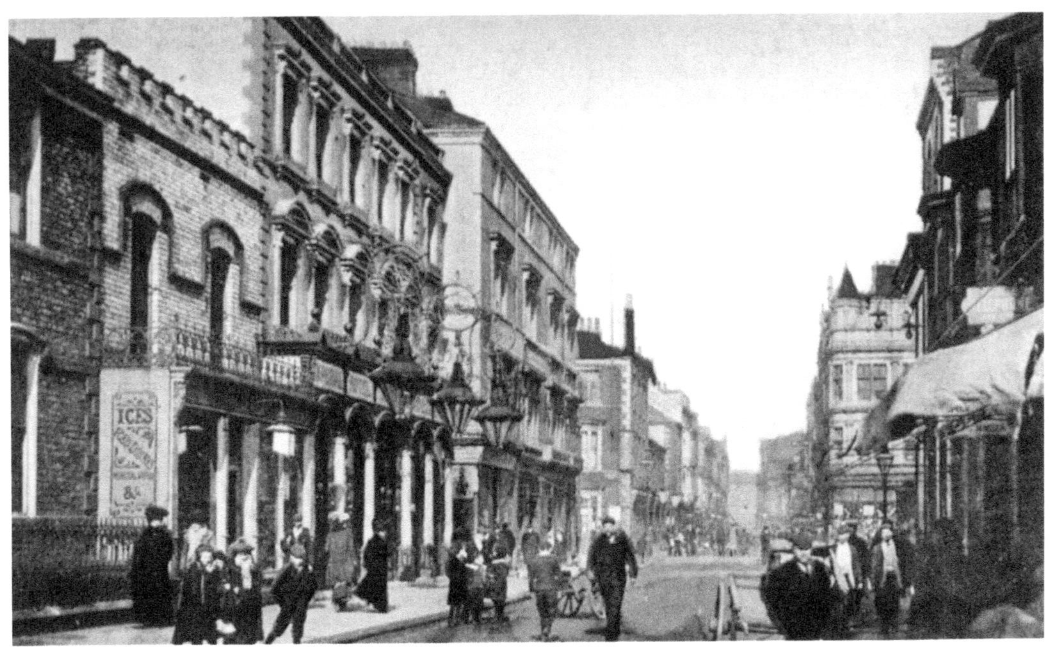

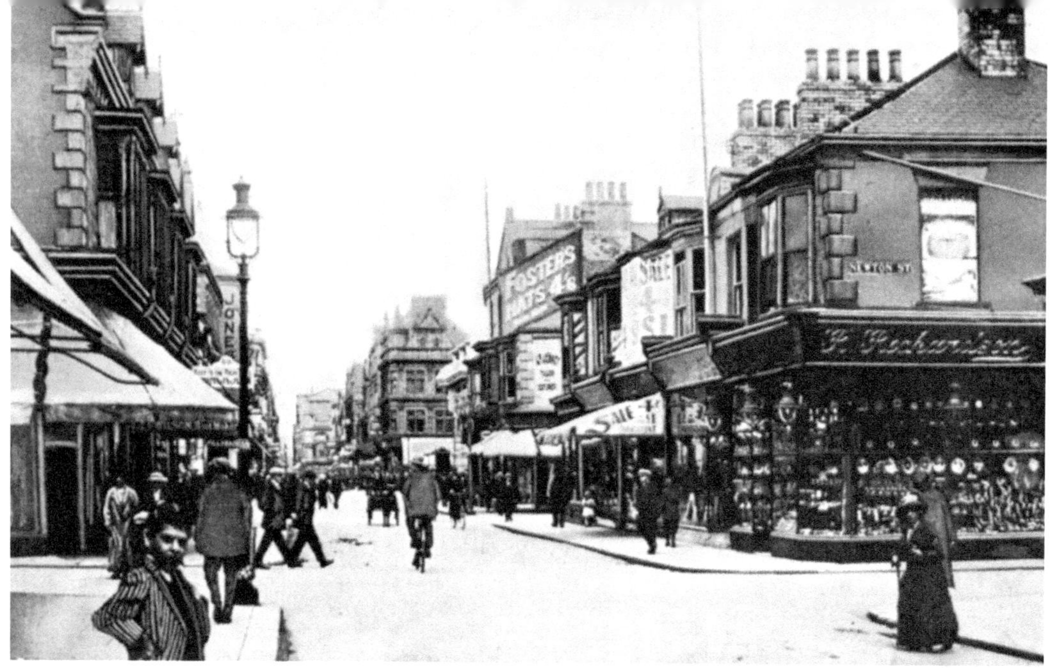

As it went southwards Linthorpe Road was joined by several other roads which no longer exist, such as Newton Street, seen here in around 1910 behind the lady crossing the road. Richardson's the jewellers are on the corner of Newton Street while Foster's hats – available at 4s 6d – are advertised on the end of the building in Fallow Street. The boy in the foreground stands close to the corner of Gilkes Street and the premises of Francis Wilson the bootmaker. Today this is the premises of Curry's electrical stores.

Linthorpe Road, probably one of the town's best known roads, was once a country lane to old Linthorpe. It quickly developed as a major route when Middlesbrough expanded south of the railway. This view was taken around 1910, close to the junction with Grange Road. On the left is an early Woolworth's store, on the corner of Davison Street with Red Cross House (a chemist) opposite. Further down is the Café Royal, a popular meeting place for many people in the era before the First World War. To the right is Norton Street.

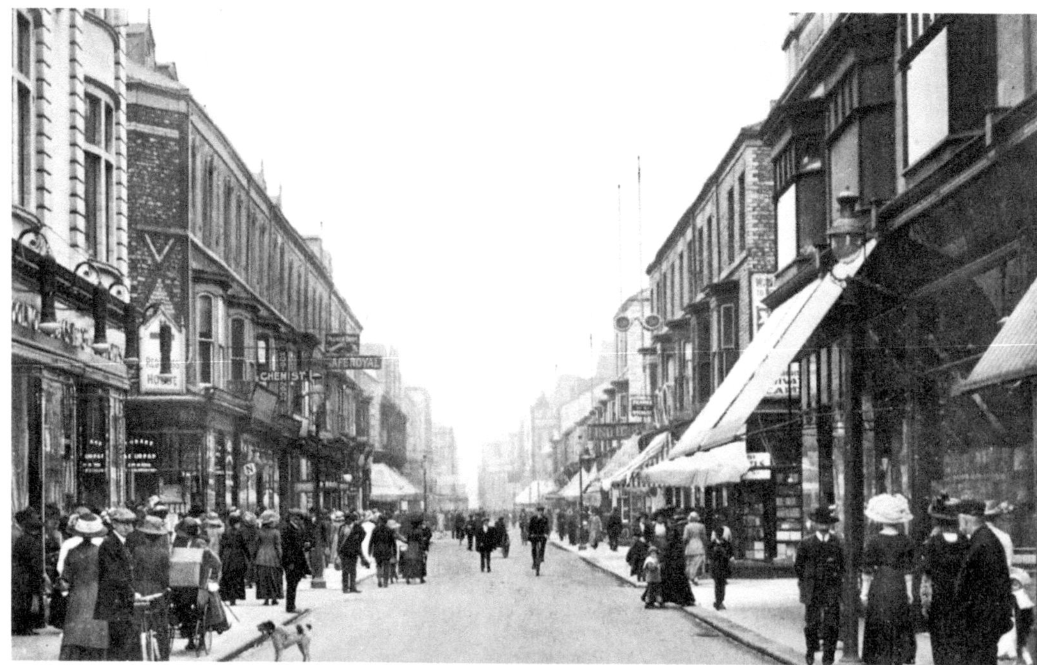

'Wright's Tower House' was a familiar building in Middlesbrough before being demolished in 1986 and replaced by a McDonald's restaurant. Lawrence Wright originally came to Middlesbrough in 1865 when he established with Richard Archibald 'Wright and Archibald' in premises at 2-8 Sussex Street. By the time the flagship store (seen here) opened on the corner of Grange Road West in 1910 it was known as Wright & Co. Previously four large terraced houses, this was another example in central Middlesbrough of private houses becoming commercial properties. It's interesting to note that the trams turned right here down Grange Road East, thus avoiding the northerly section of Linthorpe Road.

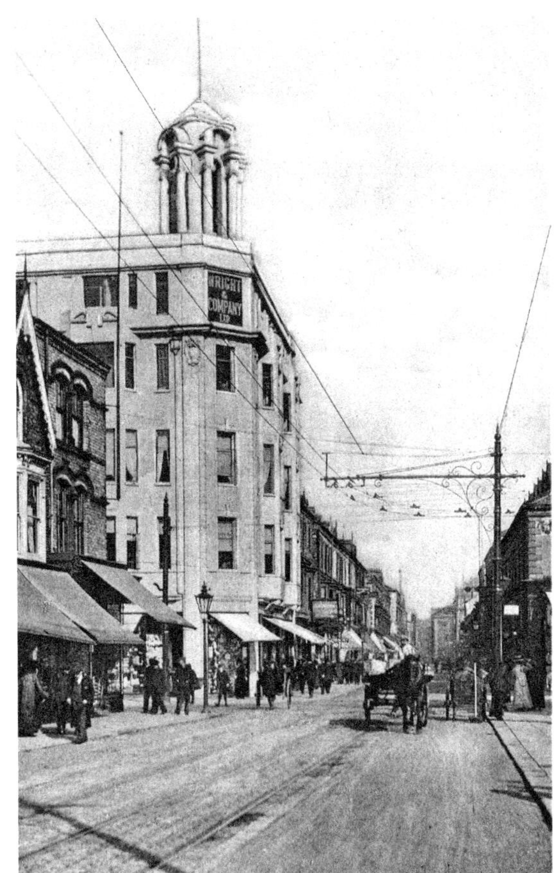

By the early 1870s horse-drawn trams were seen regularly in Middlesbrough. William Oliver was the first person to run an organised service, with several routes linking the town with Grove Hill and North Ormesby. From 1876 the Imperial Tramways Company were also running services – these images feature two of the early horse-drawn trams. Routes within the town went from the Exchange to the Ferry Landing at Newport and from 1876 a service went every fifteen minutes from the Cleveland Hotel in Linthorpe village to the corner of Ferry Road and Vulcan Street in the old town. The single-decker trams carried fourteen passengers while double-deckers carried sixteen passengers on each deck.

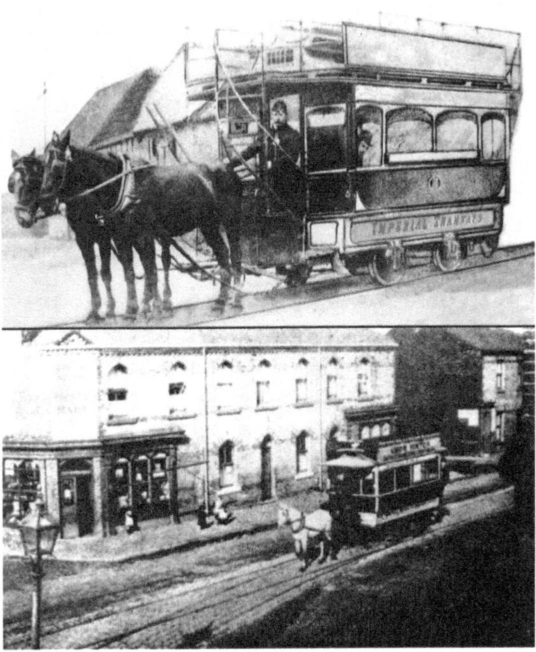

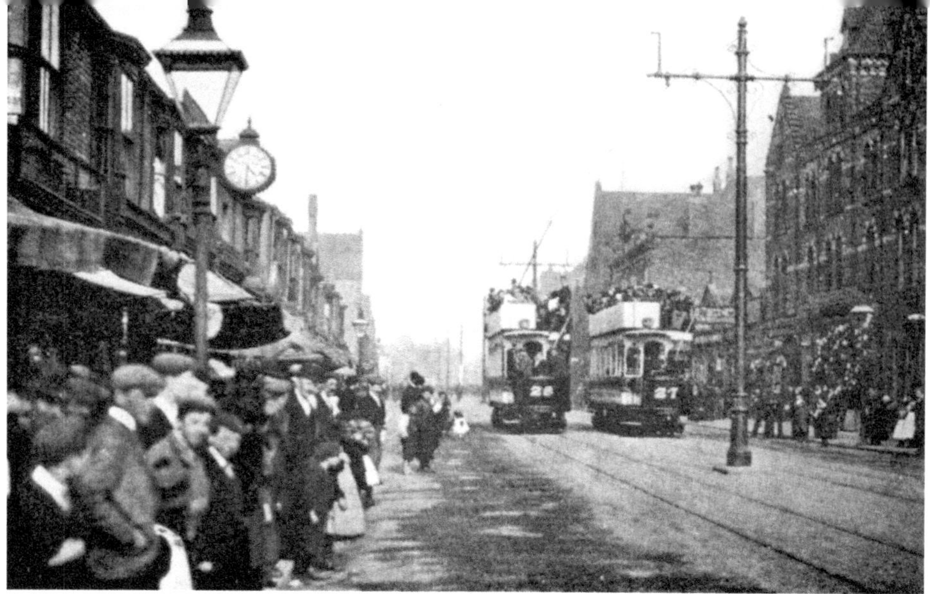

In 1897 a Parliamentary Bill sanctioned the building of an electrified tram system from North Ormesby to Norton Green. As new tracks were laid the end was looming for the horse-drawn services and the last horse-tram from the Exchange to Newport ran on 13 December 1897 and on the route to Linthorpe a week later. The new service began operations on 16 July 1898, bringing one of the most up-to-date systems of the time to the town. This image shows some of the crowds who turned out on the first day, here watching No. 27 and No. 28 tram as they travel along Newport Road close to the Cleveland Hall, today the site of the town's bus station.

Another image of the new electrified tram service shows crowds around a vehicle at the intersection of Albert Road and Corporation Road. The destination board shows the new route. Despite only having wooden seats and giving a fairly bumpy ride, the electrified tram service was very successful and enabled many ordinary people to travel much further than before.

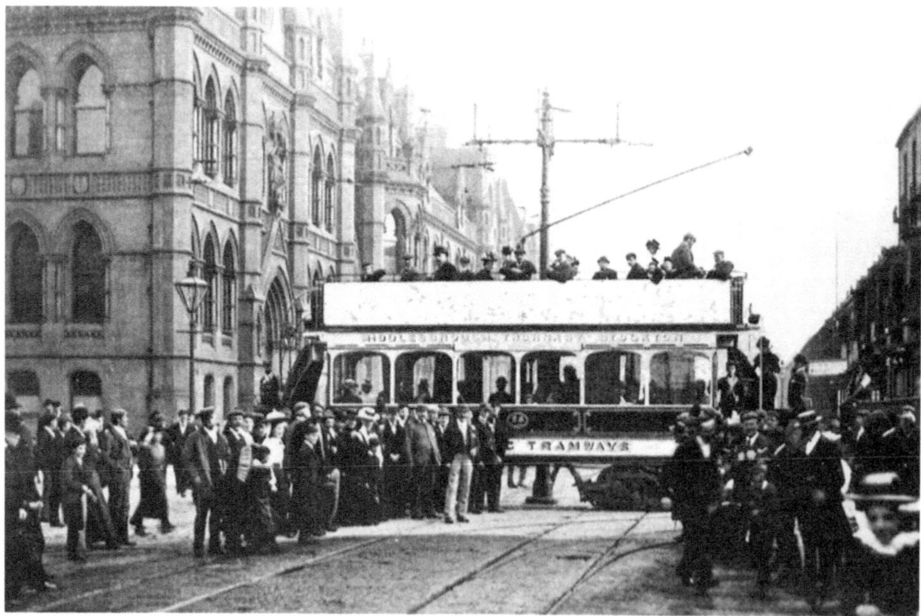

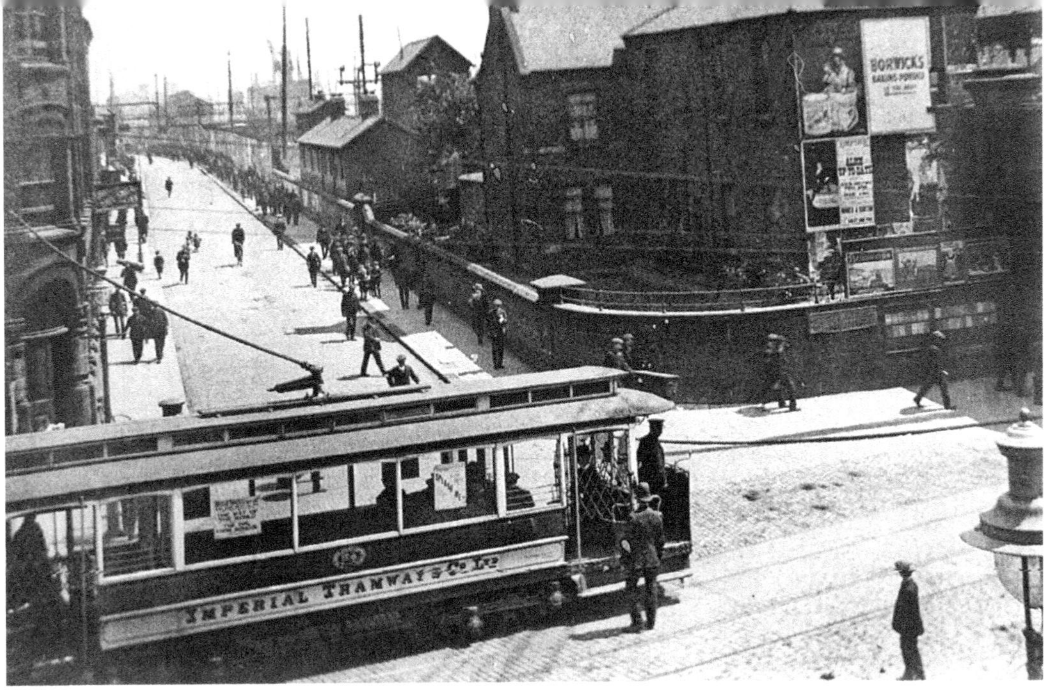

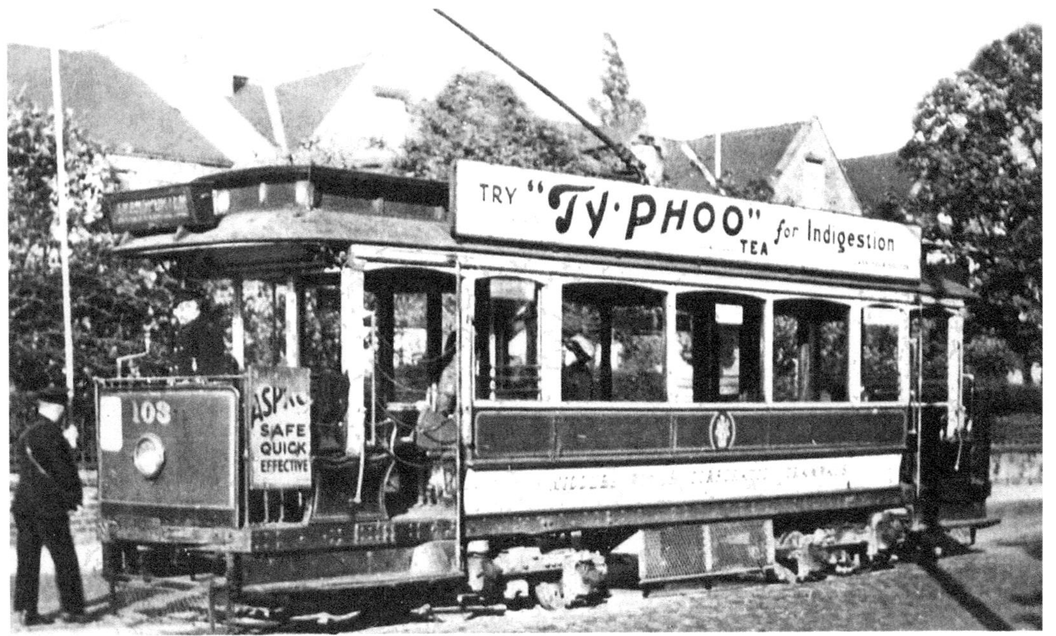

This single-decker Imperial Tramways service travelling from Ferry Road towards Linthorpe village is passing the entrance to Bridge Street East and approaching Albert Bridge. A number of workers are walking home from the docks, which can be seen in the distance.

On 2 April 1921, Middlesbrough Corporation used their option of purchasing the successful tram operation. Consequently, their logo appears on the side of this tram. However, some of the rolling stock was in severe need of maintenance, as can be seen by the flaking livery of this tram in Linthorpe village.

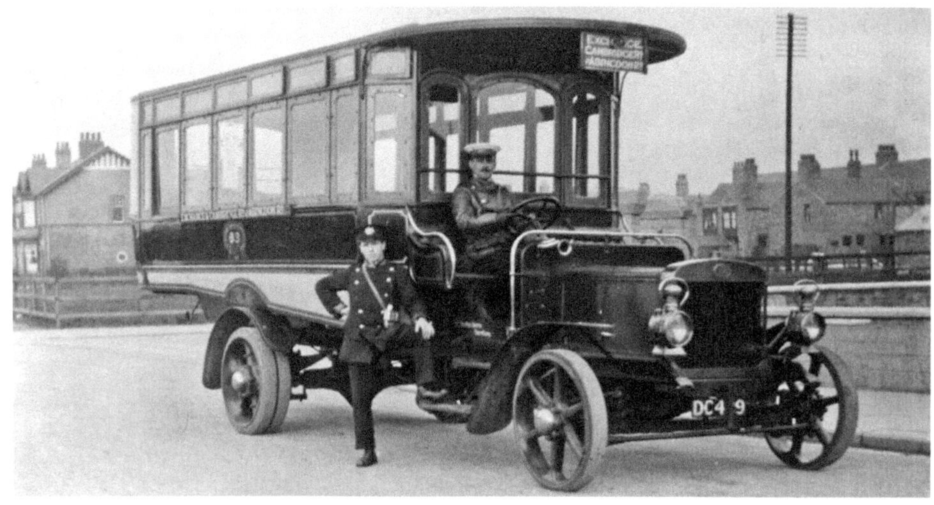

The first motor omnibuses, which were all single-deckers, first appeared in Middlesbrough on 29 January 1914. They were operated by Imperial Tramways along two routes – from the Exchange to Grove Hill Toll Bar and from the Exchange to Park Road South. As can be seen here, the service was later extended to Cambridge Road, where a crew stand outside their vehicle in about 1921.

As well as using the transport provided by the railway and the various tram services, people in Middlesbrough also had the use of ferry services. Rival services operated by Mr C.C. Duncan and a Mr Dixon sailed from Newport Landing to Stockton, with an additional service being operated later by Imperial Tramways. The unreliability of the services as well as the coming of the electrified tram service eventually reduced passenger numbers and the ferry service was discontinued in 1898. Passengers for the ferry are shown here at Newport Landing.

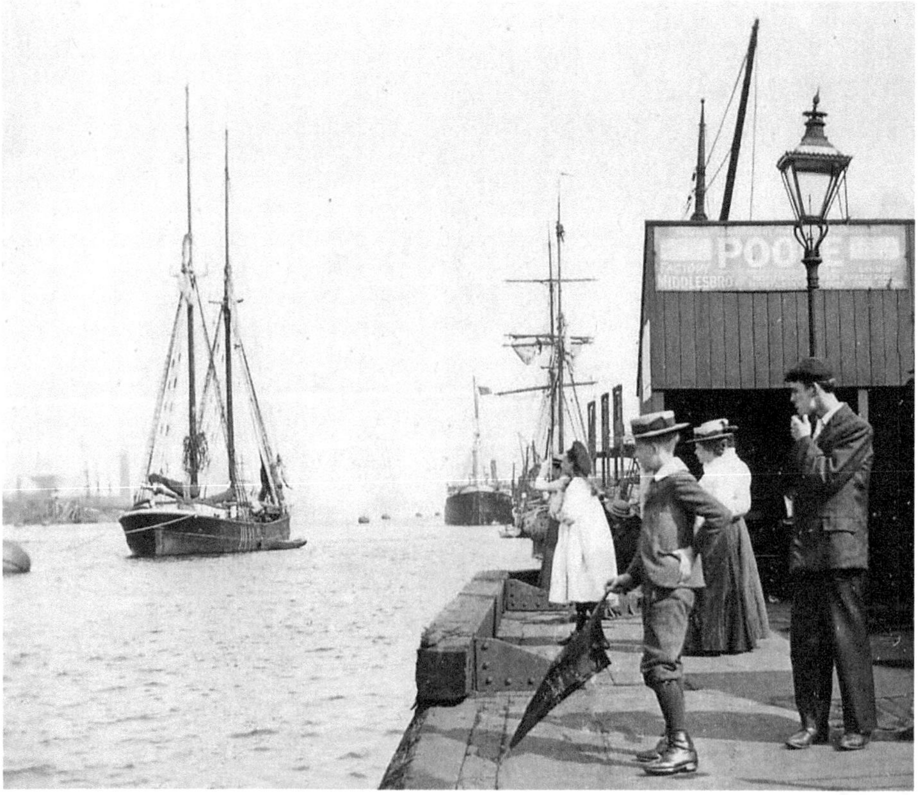

The other main ferry service operated across the river from the quay at Ferry Road, in the old town, to Port Clarence. This was heavily used by workmen as seen in these images of two of the boats, the *Hugh Bell* launched in 1884 and the *Erimus*, launched on 15 September 1888. The *Erimus* was licensed to carry 927 passengers. Both boats operated until the Transporter Bridge opened in 1911, when they were sold to Messrs Pollock, Brown of Southampton – the *Erimus* incidentally being sold for £725!

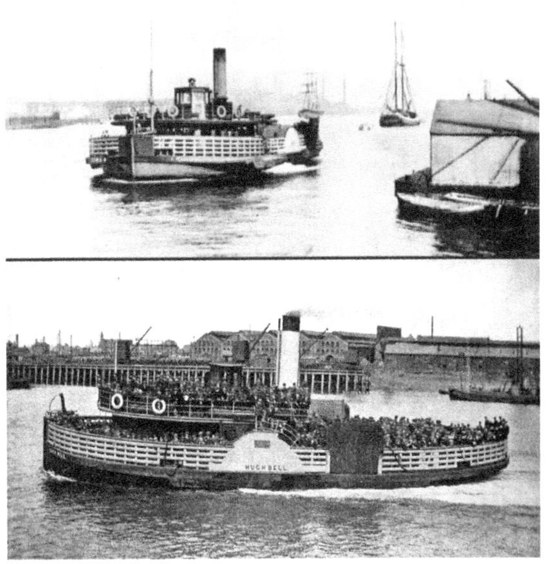

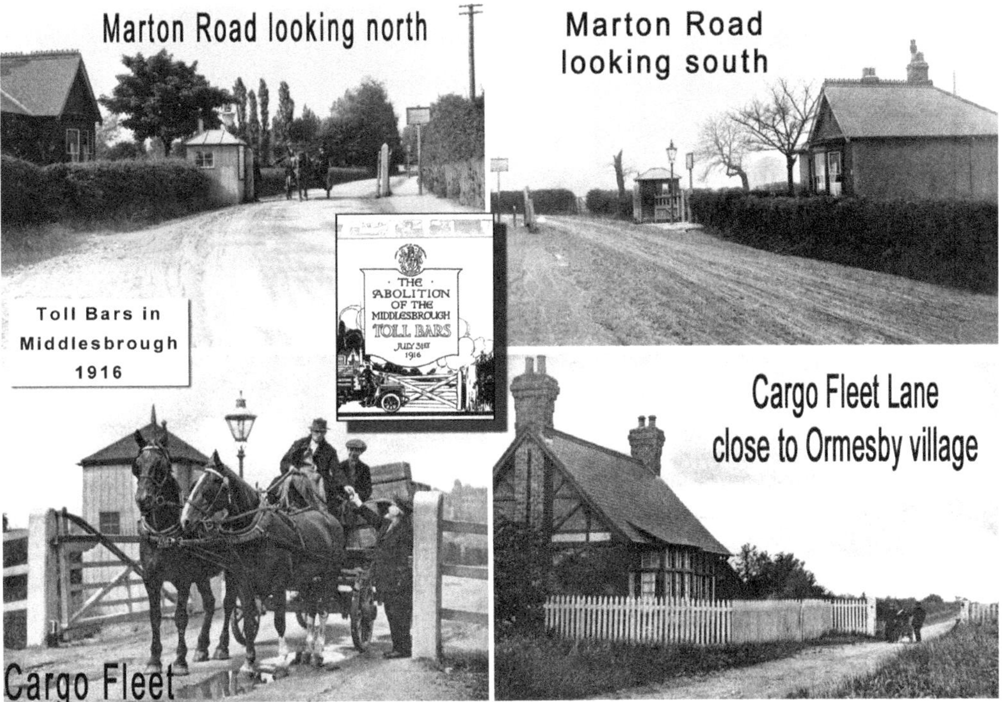

Toll Bars had been erected in the nineteenth century on all privately owned roads into the town. Although some had been abolished before 1914, an Act was passed abolishing the five which remained in the Middlesbrough area from 31 July 1916. A commemorative programme accompanied the formal ceremony bringing an end to the toll bars. Three of the toll bars abolished on that day are shown here. The toll bar cottage on Marton Road still stands nearly a century later but is no longer on the perimeter of the town.

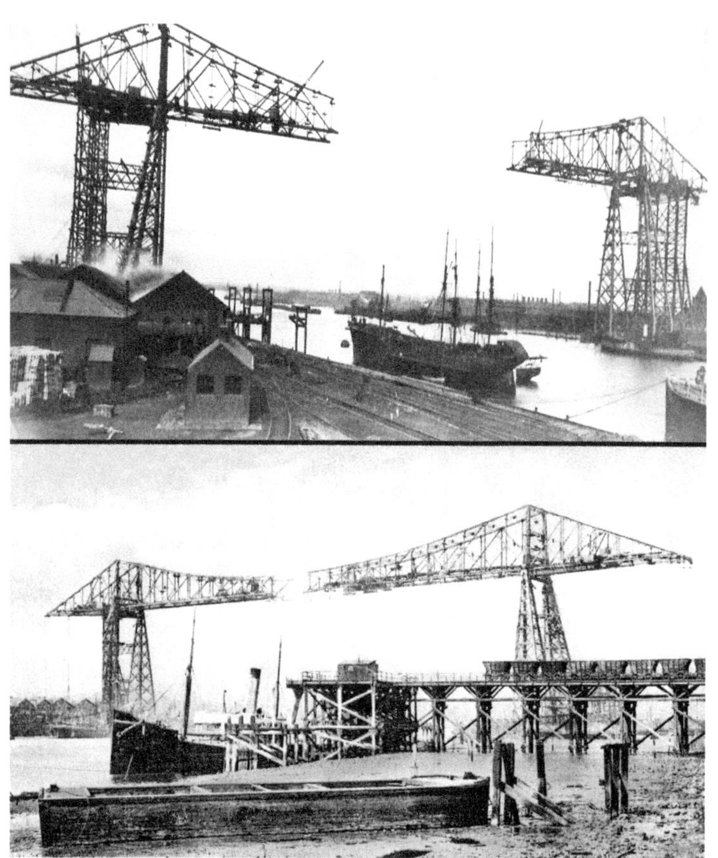

The Transporter Bridge has become a well-known landmark for many inhabitants of Middlesbrough. The Bill for building the bridge received Royal Assent on 4 July 1907 and on 3 August 1910 two foundation stones were laid by the Mayor Lt-Col. T. Gibson-Poole and Alderman Joseph MacLauchlan, who had first instigated the scheme. The bridge, which cost just over £87,000 to build, can be seen here in the latter days of construction from Middlesbrough (upper image) and from Port Clarence (lower image), where the coal staithes are also visible.

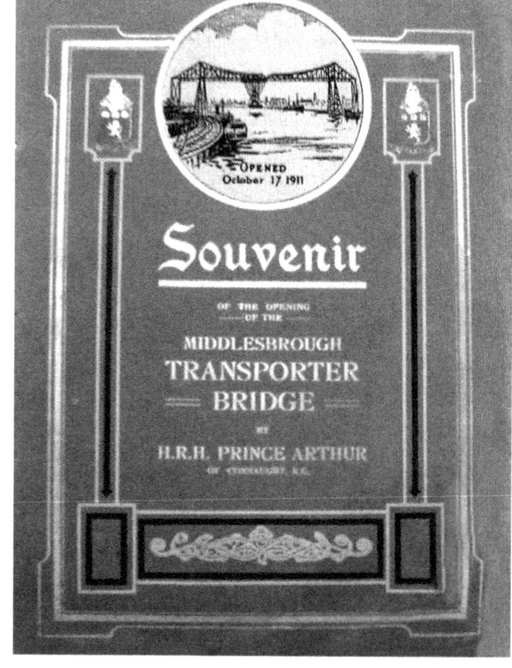

The official opening of the bridge by HRH Prince Arthur of Connaught KG was commemorated by the printing of an official programme; the front cover of which was royal blue with gold lettering, as seen here.

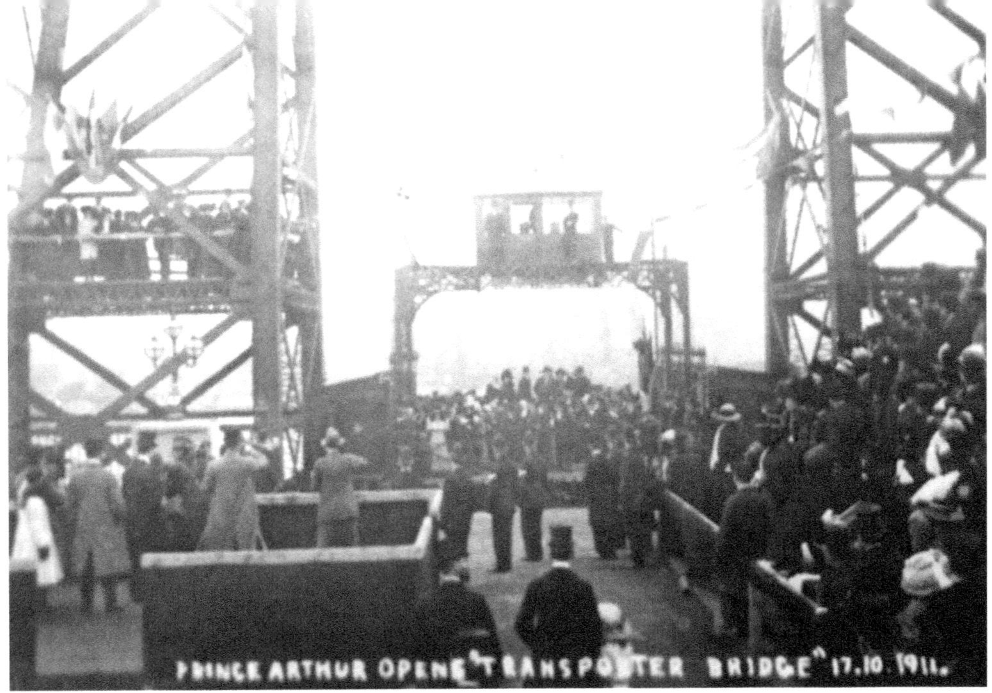

The Prince was the guest of the mayor, Sir Hugh Bell, and stayed at his country home, Rounton Grange. On the day he was driven to Middlesbrough he passed through the same Grove Hill toll bar as his father had done in 1868. From there he was escorted to the Transporter Bridge by a troop from the Yorkshire Hussars. This image is a scene from the official opening showing the Prince about to press a button which would set the car in motion.

Having set the cable car in motion, the Prince is given a demonstration trip. The cable car is seen here with a page from the commemorative programme giving details about the ceremony. The Prince then boarded a steam boat and inspected the river before being taken to the offices of the Tees Conservancy Commissioners in Queens Square for luncheon.

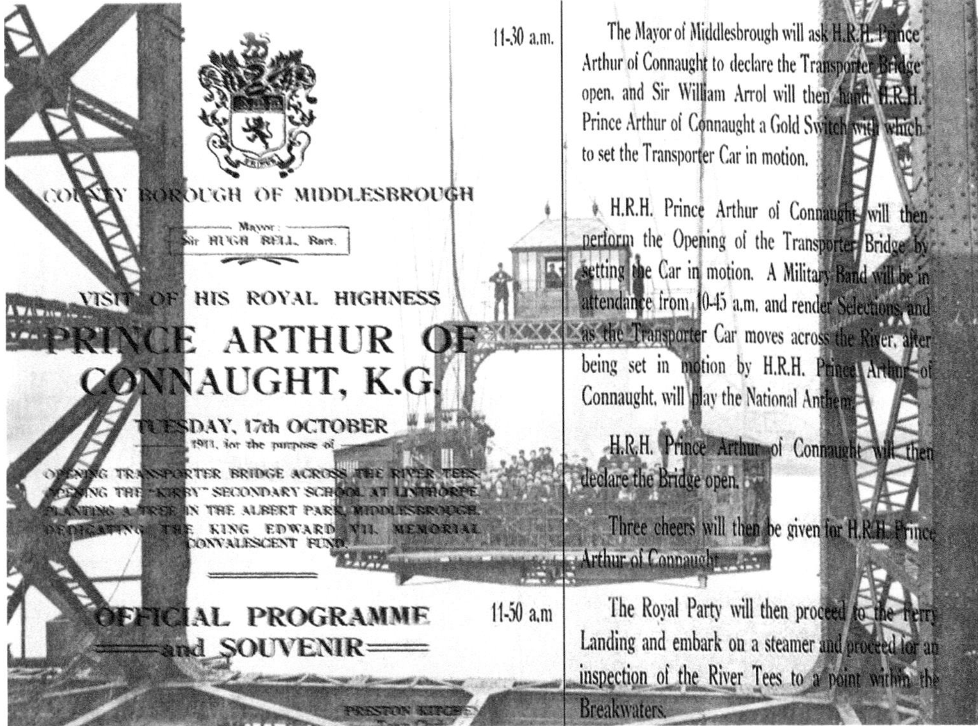

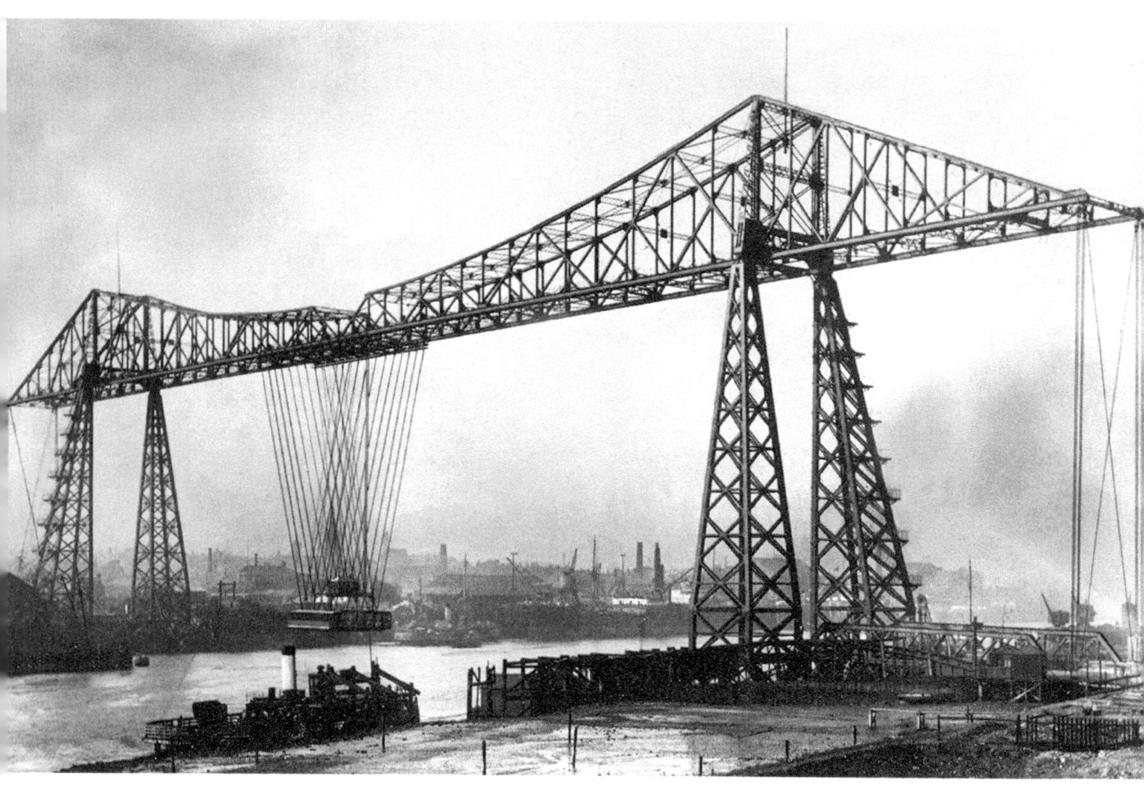

This image gives a view of the Transporter Bridge in operation looking from Port Clarence across to the old town of Middlesbrough, *c*. 1921. The bridge was an immediate success with 6,290 people using it on the first day, many paying an extra three pence to walk across the top. In the first year the bridge carried over 2,657,206 people.

5

OH, WHAT A LIFE!

Some varying aspects of daily living in Middlesbrough around a hundred years ago ...

AT THE ALBERT PARK.

3-40 p.m. — A Guard of Honour from the North Riding Fortress Royal Engineers (under the command of Capt. Hy. Winterschladen) will be mounted at the Entrance to the Albert Park.

3-45 p.m. — On arrival at the Enclosure in the Albert Park, situated on the second turning to the right, on entering from Linthorpe Road, H.R.H. Prince Arthur of Connaught will plant a Tree in close proximity to the one planted in the year 1868 by his father, the Duke of Connaught.

4-0 p.m. — The Procession will then be re-formed in the same order as on entering the Park, and will proceed by way of Linthorpe Road, the Avenue, and Orchard Road to the " Kirby " Secondary School, at Linthorpe.

In the afternoon large crowds watched along Albert Road and then Linthorpe Road as HRH Prince Arthur of Connaught KG travelled to Albert Park, where he planted a commemorative tree close to the one planted by his father in 1868. In this image we see crowds waiting in the park to see the Prince along with a page from the commemorative programme giving details of the proceedings.

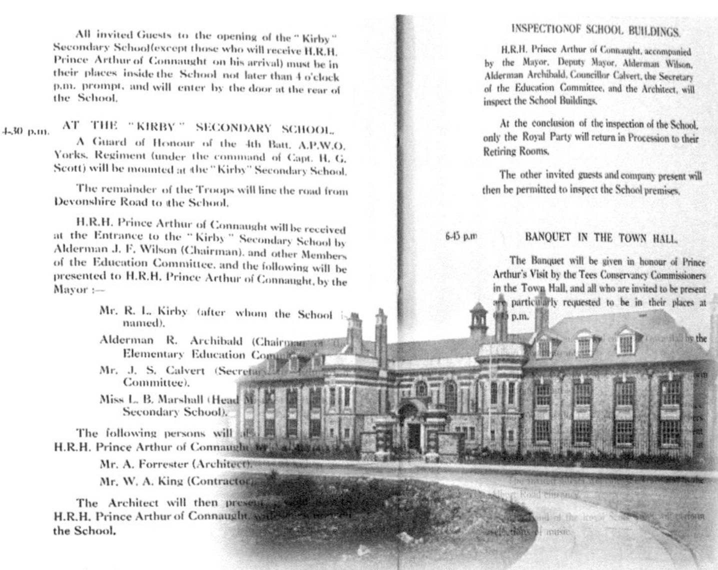

All invited Guests to the opening of the "Kirby" Secondary School(except those who will receive H.R.H. Prince Arthur of Connaught on his arrival) must be in their places inside the School not later than 4 o'clock p.m. prompt, and will enter by the door at the rear of the School.

4.30 p.m.   AT THE "KIRBY" SECONDARY SCHOOL.
A Guard of Honour of the 4th Batt. A.P.W.O. Yorks. Regiment (under the command of Capt. H. G. Scott) will be mounted at the "Kirby" Secondary School.

The remainder of the Troops will line the road from Devonshire Road to the School.

H.R.H. Prince Arthur of Connaught will be received at the Entrance to the "Kirby" Secondary School by Alderman J. F. Wilson (Chairman), and other Members of the Education Committee, and the following will be presented to H.R.H. Prince Arthur of Connaught, by the Mayor :—

Mr. R. L. Kirby (after whom the School is named).
Alderman R. Archibald (Chairman of the Elementary Education Committee).
Mr. J. S. Calvert (Secretary Committee).
Miss L. B. Marshall (Head Mistress Secondary School).

The following persons will be presented to H.R.H. Prince Arthur of Connaught by
Mr. A. Forrester (Architect).
Mr. W. A. King (Contractor).

The Architect will then present to H.R.H. Prince Arthur of Connaught the School.

INSPECTION OF SCHOOL BUILDINGS.

H.R.H. Prince Arthur of Connaught, accompanied by the Mayor, Deputy Mayor, Alderman Wilson, Alderman Archibald, Councillor Calvert, the Secretary of the Education Committee, and the Architect, will inspect the School Buildings.

At the conclusion of the inspection of the School, only the Royal Party will return in Procession to their Retiring Rooms.

The other invited guests and company present will then be permitted to inspect the School premises.

6.45 p.m   BANQUET IN THE TOWN HALL.

The Banquet will be given in honour of Prince Arthur's Visit by the Tees Conservancy Commissioners in the Town Hall, and all who are invited to be present are particularly requested to be in their places at p.m.

The final formal ceremony of the day was the opening of Kirby School, named after R.L. Kirby, Chairman of the Education Committee. Troops lined the route along Devonshire Road and a guard of honour greeted the Prince's arrival at the school. The formal presentations and opening having taken place, the Prince was then given a tour of the building before leaving for a banquet at the Town Hall in the evening, where the band of the Royal Scots Grays provided the musical entertainment. One hundred years later, Kirby School is being converted into residential buildings.

Many thousands of visitors went to Albert Park each year and these images show the park as it was in Edwardian Middlesbrough. One of the well-known landmarks in the park was an ancient tree trunk of a prehistoric oak dredged from the Tees and presented to the park in 1872 for display. At the end of the Promenade walk can be seen examples of the large detached residences which were built close to the park. The main entrance gates on the west side of the park facing Linthorpe Road were made by Walker's of York and purchased for donation by Henry Bolckow.

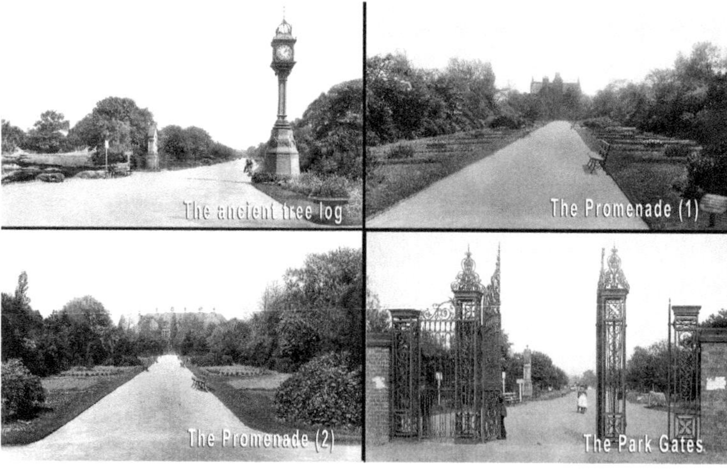

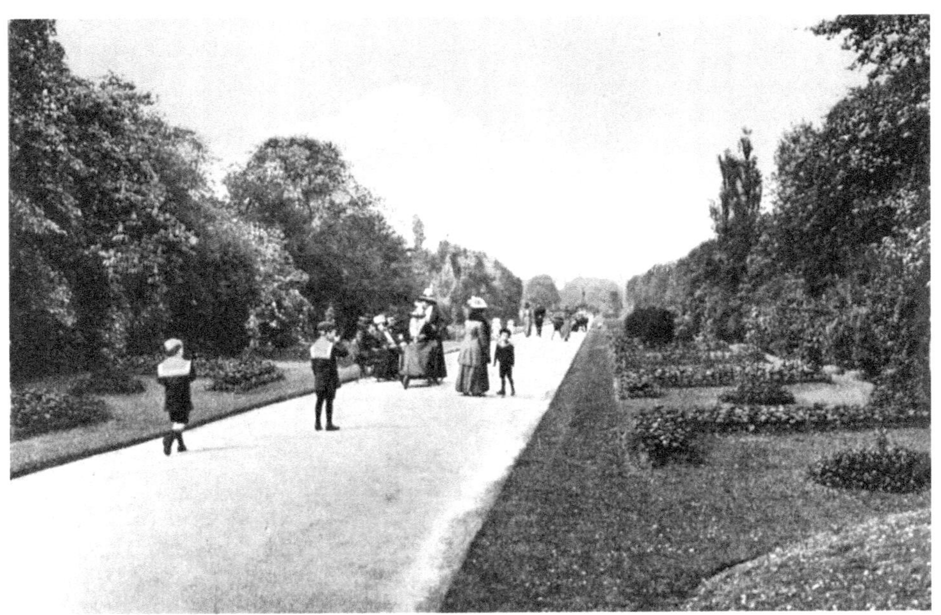

Like these strollers in 1907, many generations of people from Middlesbrough have enjoyed a walk in Albert Park. The park, which has recently undergone major restoration work, still continues to be popular today, 142 years after it first opened.

As a result of a group of industrialists meeting in June 1870, Middlesbrough High School first opened for boys on a site at No.1 Grange Road on 15 October 1870. Fees were charged and twenty-five pupils were enrolled. By 1874 this number had increased to ninety-three and a school for girls had also opened at 37 Grange Road on 11 August, aided by a grant from local ironmaster Bernard Samuelsson. This too proved to be a success, with a preparatory school added in 1876. This image shows the school in Albert Road in 1896 – originally the site had been allotments.

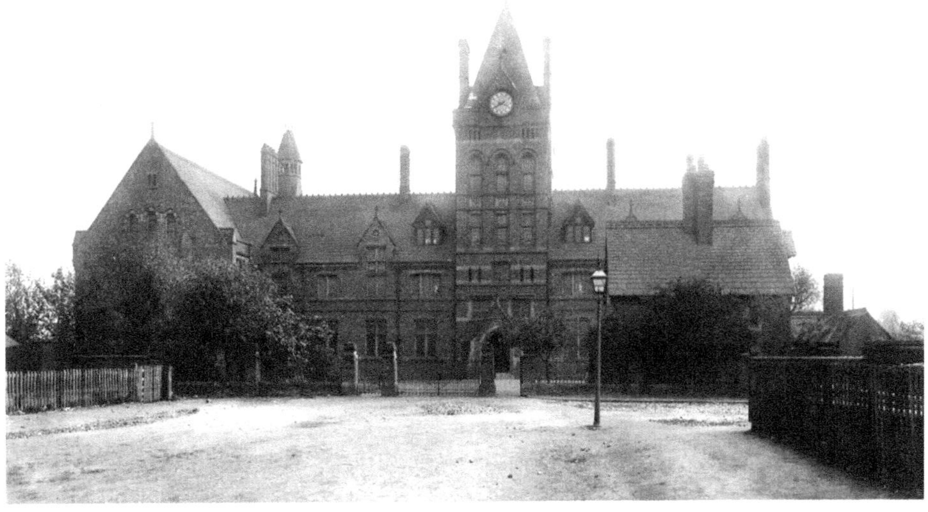

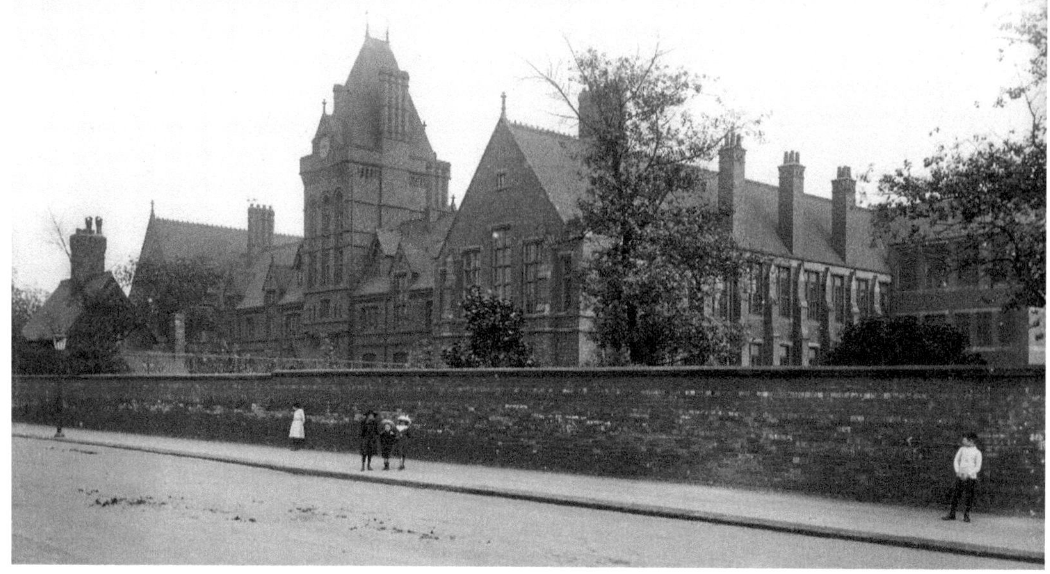

When increasing numbers of pupils meant that a new site was needed, J.W. Pease offered a piece of land at the southern end of Albert Road. Middlesbrough High School opened on this site on 15 January 1877 for the use of both boys and girls. In 1879 there were 179 pupils but by 1882 this had increased to 267. The school closed in 1959 and today the site has become part of Teesside University – with the clock tower building still standing.

The Hugh Bell Schools were on a site which faced onto Victoria Square. The original site was purchased on 11 September 1889 for £3,375 from the OME and was opened as the Grange Road Schools on 2 May 1892 by Alderman T. Hugh Bell. They were renamed the Hugh Bell Schools on 6 December 1898, marking the roll of Hugh Bell (seen here) as Chairman of the Middlesbrough School Board.

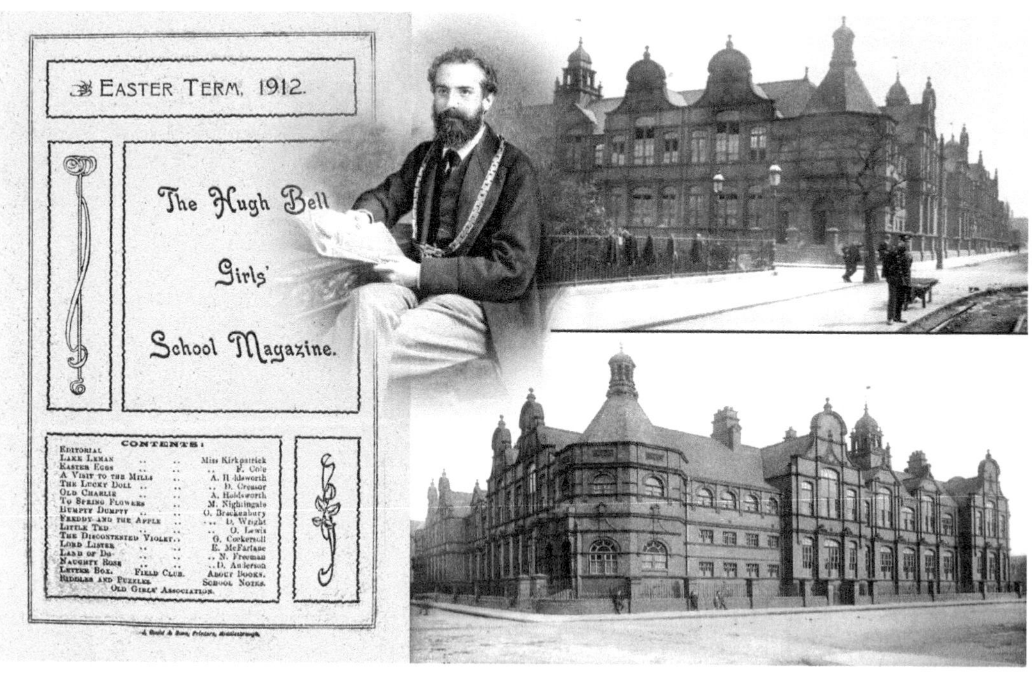

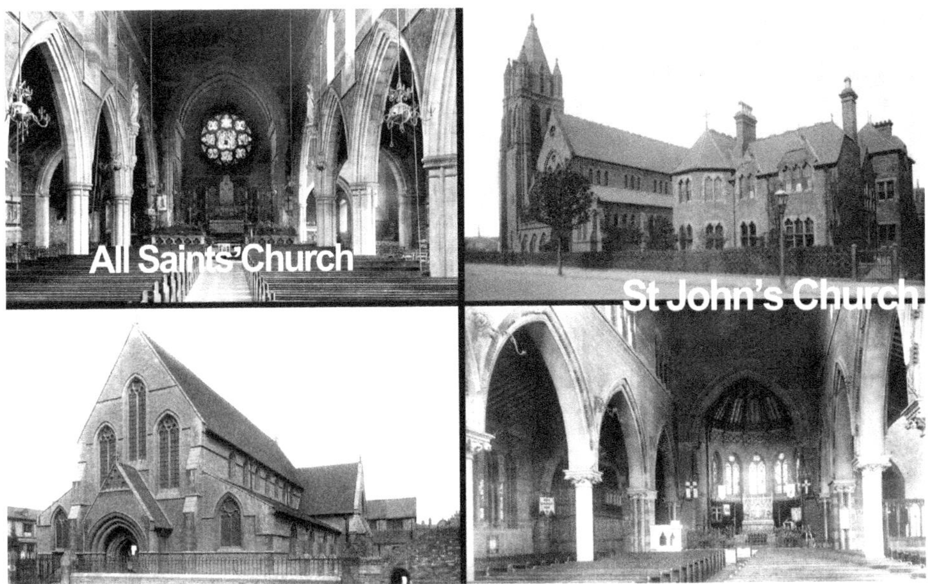

A number of new churches were built when the town expanded south of the railway, two of which still survive today. All Saints' Church, located on a site at the corner of Grange Road and Linthorpe Road, was consecrated on 20 July 1878 and became known as the 'Ironmaster's Church' because funding came from W. Hopkins and John Gjers, both ironmasters. The interior of the church is also shown here with its fine east window of painted glass paid for by ironmaster John Gjers in 1890. St John's Church on Marton Road was consecrated on 30 November 1865, costing £5,500 to build. The view on the right shows the interior of the church, looking towards the original high altar.

The Wesleyan Chapel, shown here in exceptional clarity, stood on a site occupied today by British Home Stores. Opening on 20 September 1863, 'Big Wesley', as it became fondly known, is still remembered by many local people. Beyond the Wesleyan Chapel is the Athenaeum Building, which was where the Cleveland Literary and Philosophical Society was based. For many people it was a sad day when the last service was held at the chapel in March 1954, with the building being demolished soon afterwards.

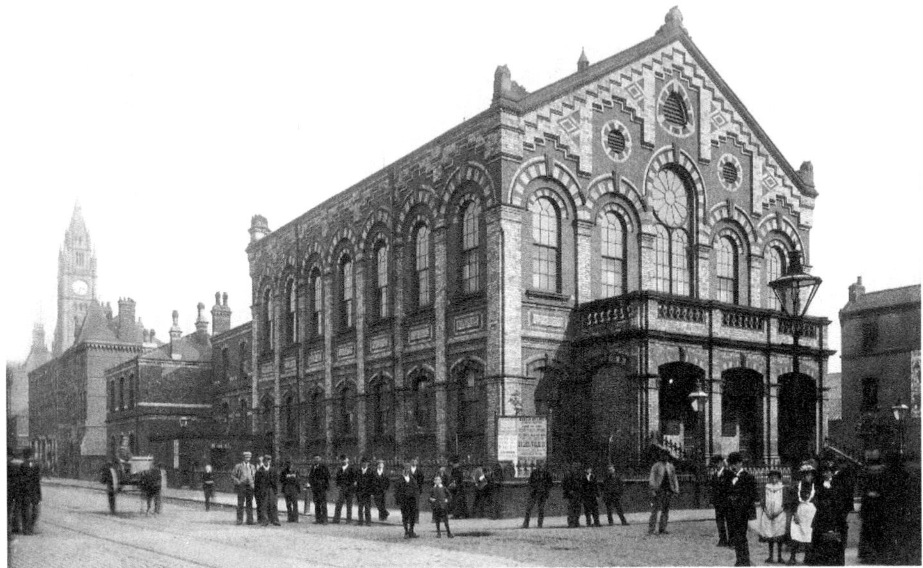

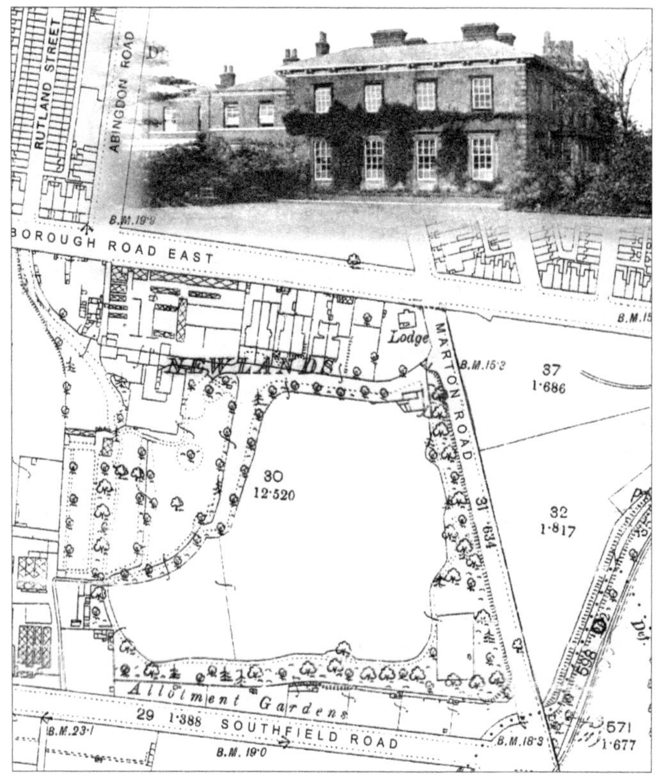

This map shows details of the grounds of Newlands, home of Sir Hugh Gilzean Reid, founder of the *North Eastern Daily Gazette* in 1869. Having arrived in 1858, Reid became a prominent citizen of Middlesbrough, even editing a book to mark the town's fifty-year jubilee in 1881. In the early 1880s Newlands was rented by the Nuns of the Faithful Companions of Jesus to be used as larger premises for the school they had recently opened. They finally purchased the building in 1896 and it became known as St Mary's Newlands Convent. The building, seen here around 1907, was demolished in 1965. (Reproduced from 1893 Ordnance Survey map, 25 inch series, with the kind permission of the Ordnance Survey)

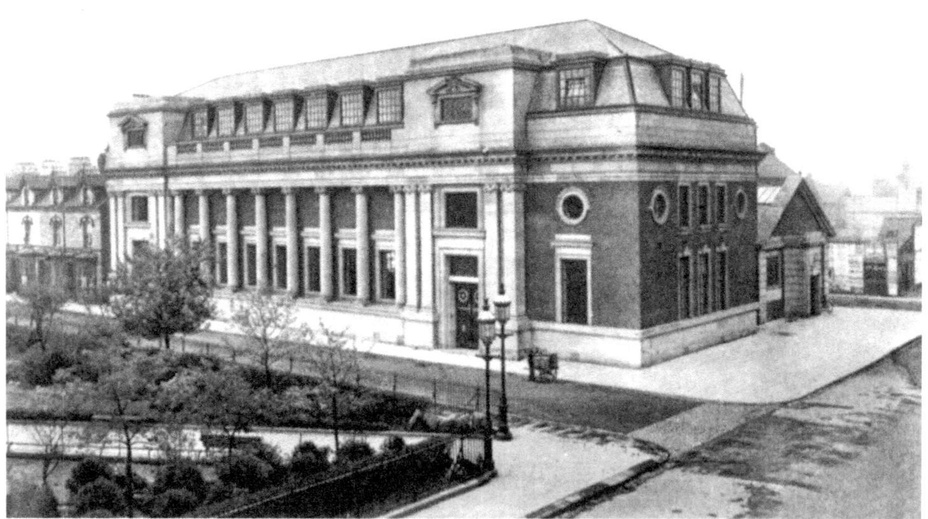

The Carnegie Library, as it was originally known, is shown here from the south-west shortly after its opening by Alderman Amos Hinton on 8 May 1912. It was a replacement for the Free Library housed in rooms at the Town Hall on the corner of Russell Street and Albert Road. A generous donation of £15,000 from Andrew Carnegie in January 1908 enabled the new library to be built on land donated by Sir Hugh Bell on Grange Road and by Amos Hinton on Dunning Street.

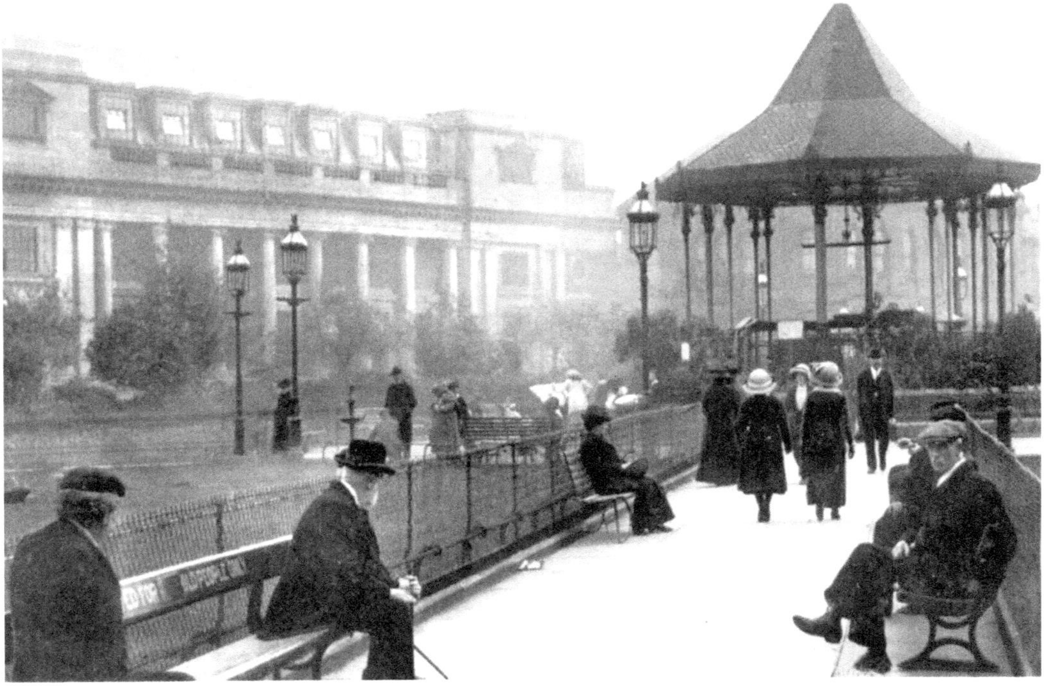

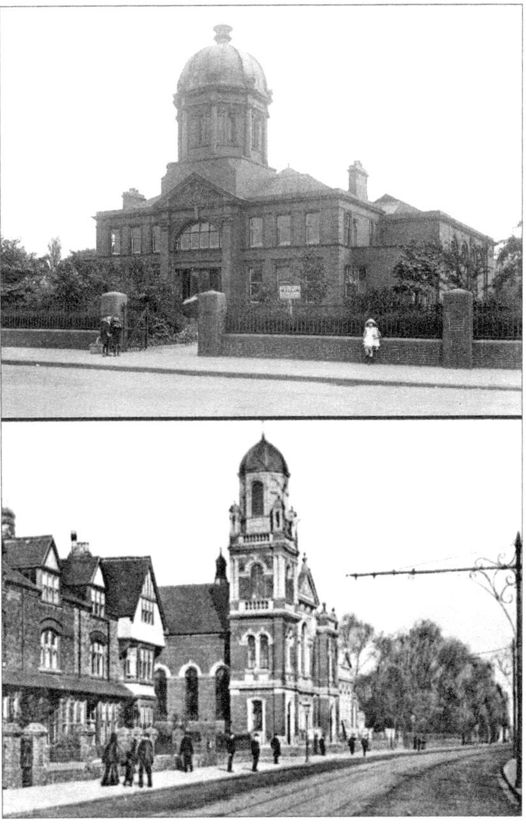

Above: The land immediately south of the Town Hall was used as a cattle market, a circus, a cycle track and as a skating-rink in winter before it was opened as Victoria Square, complete with ornamental garden and bandstand, by Colonel S.A. Sadler on 12 July 1901. Music was provided by the Coldstream Guards. By 1912, as this image shows, seats had been provided for the 'sole use of old people'. The statue of John Vaughan was moved here from Exchange Place on 23 October 1914, joining the statue of Sir Samuel Sadler which had been placed here on 21 June 1913.

Right: The Dorman Museum was opened on 1 July 1904, on land donated by Sir Arthur Dorman, founder of Dorman Long & Co. Ltd, as a memorial to his son George Dorman who had died in the Boer War. The building costs of £15,000 were also donated by Sir Arthur Dorman. The museum has become well known to several generations of Middlesbrough inhabitants, especially the collection of stuffed animals and birds which were donated by Sir Alfred Edward Pease. The lower view looks across from the Dorman Museum to Park Wesleyan Chapel and the row of houses that today are Fellini's restaurant.

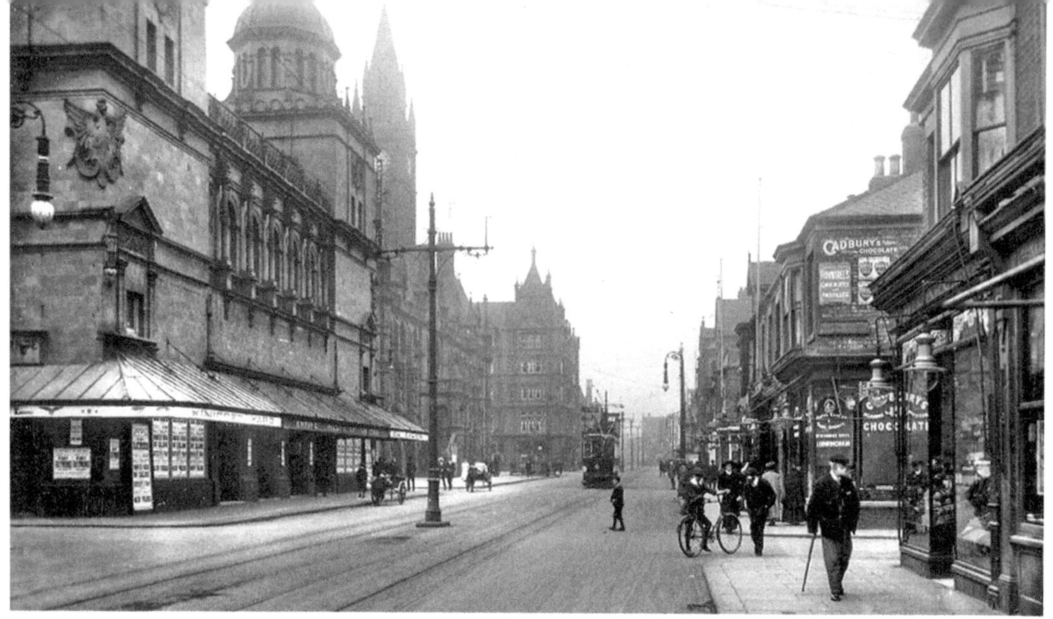

The Empire Palace of Varieties, shown here on the left, has a distinctive history stretching back to the days of the music hall. Built on a site previously used for circus shows, the Empire had six private boxes and other seating for more than a thousand people. Here a tram passes the Town Hall as it approaches the Empire, with the Corporation Hotel in the background.

Many famous entertainers have appeared at the Empire since it opened on 13 March 1899, including Charlie Chaplin, Stan Laurel, Gracie Fields, George Formby, Will Hay, W.C. Fields and Marie Lloyd. In 1937 Sir Harry Lauder, returning to the Empire after an absence of thirty-three years, paid tribute to the 'spirited nature' of the audiences there.

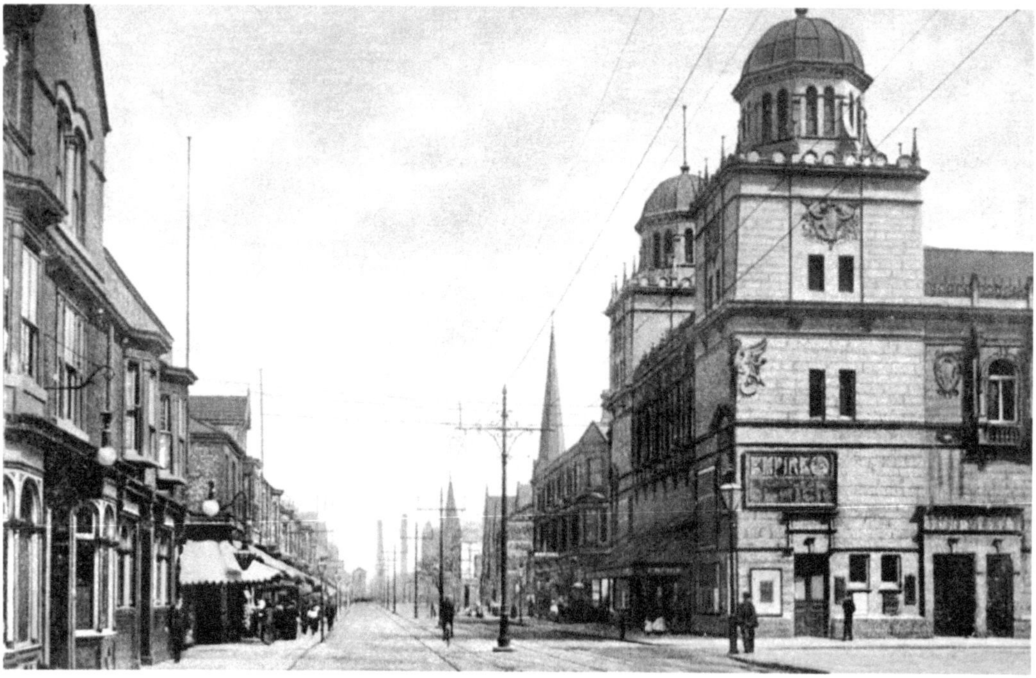

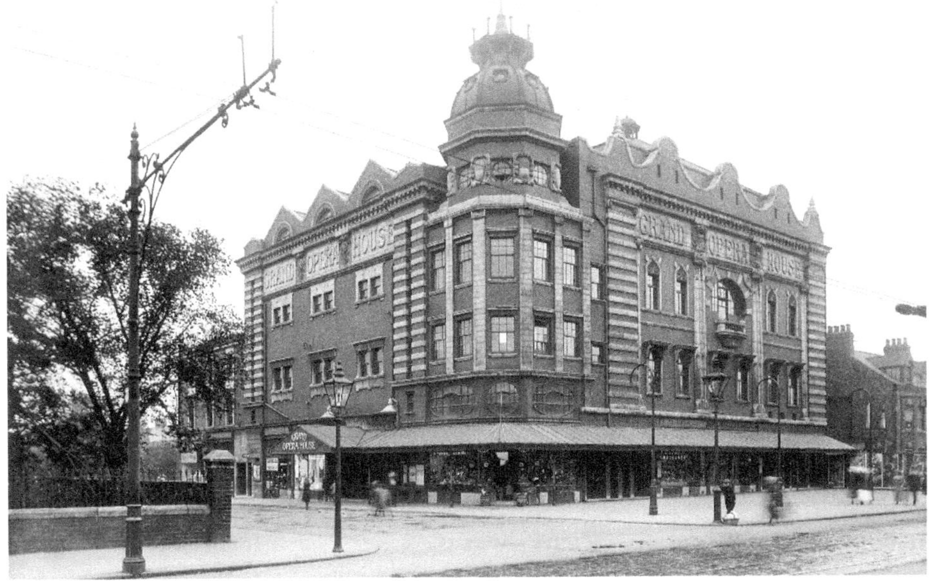

Another great venue which carried on the tradition of entertainment established in the old town during the nineteenth century was the Grand Opera House. Built at a cost of £38,000 on the site of Swathers Carr, the Opera House opened on 7 December 1903. Many famous artists came here including Charlie Chaplin along with Fred Karno in 1912, Gracie Fields and Jack Buchanan. It closed on 21 June 1930 and reopened on 31 March as the Gaumont Cinema.

The Hippodrome Theatre of Varieties, which opened in Wilson Street on 17 August 1906, was built on the site of a Quaker burial ground, necessitating a night-time exhumation of the bodies. Florrie Ford topped the bill on the opening night but thereafter the Hippodrome had a chequered history. In 1908 fierce competition forced it to close, only to reopen again shortly afterwards as a venue showing films in addition to variety acts – as shown in this advertisement from 1912. The first full length 'talkie' seen in Middlesbrough, *The Singing Fool* with Al Jolson, was shown here in August 1929.

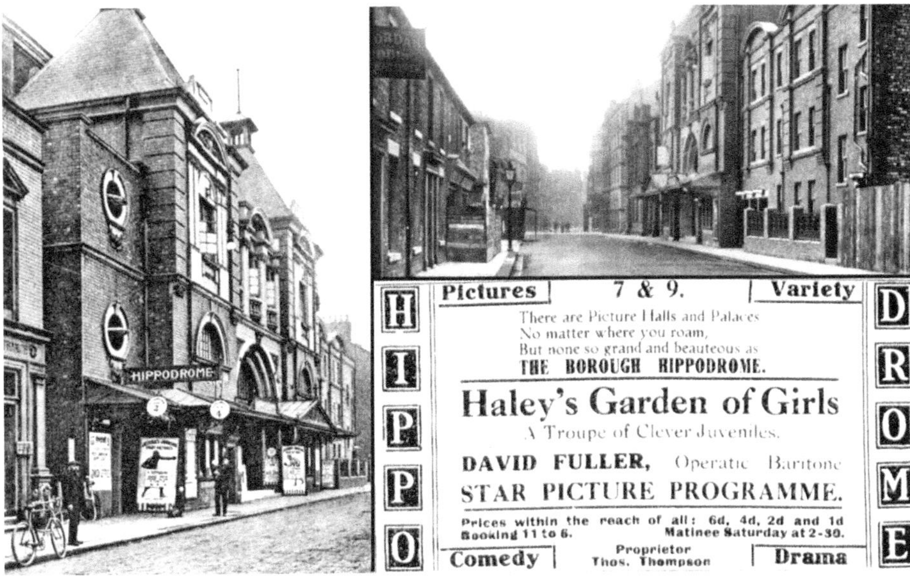

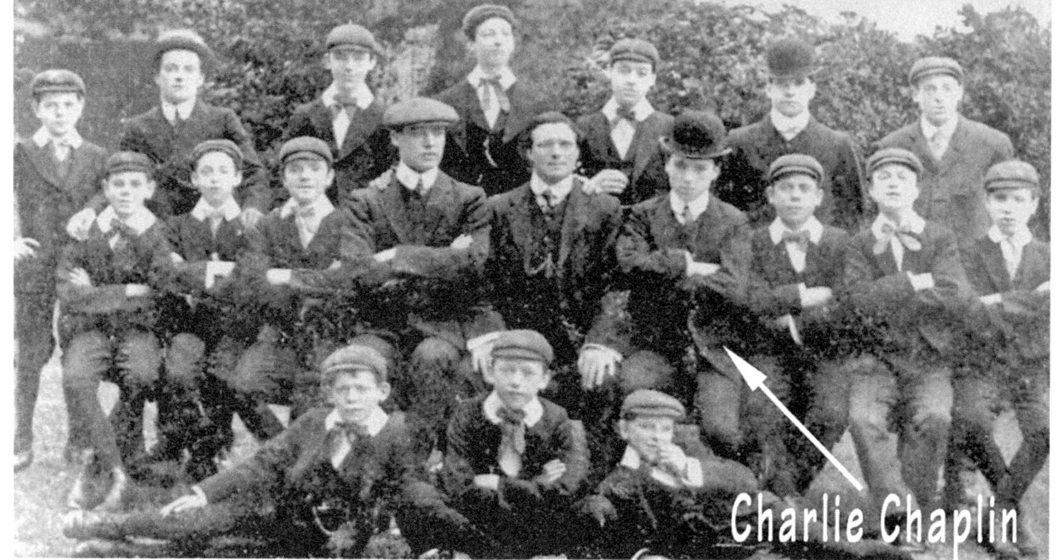

Charlie Chaplin appeared more than once in Middlesbrough but this advertisement marks his appearance on 21 February 1906 with Casey's Circus at the Empire. Stan Laurel is second from the left in the middle row.

Middlesbrough Football Club, formed in 1876, had by February 1880 moved to a ground in Linthorpe Road, where they remained for twenty-three years before moving to Ayresome Park. The ground, designed by the doyen of football ground designers, Archibald Leitch, was built on land belonging to Old Gate Farm. The map shows the farm as well as the nearby Ironopolis Football Ground, where rivals Middlesbrough Ironopolis were based during their brief spell in the Football League in the 1890s. (Reproduced from 1893 Ordnance Survey map, 25 inch series, with the kind permission of the Ordnance Survey)

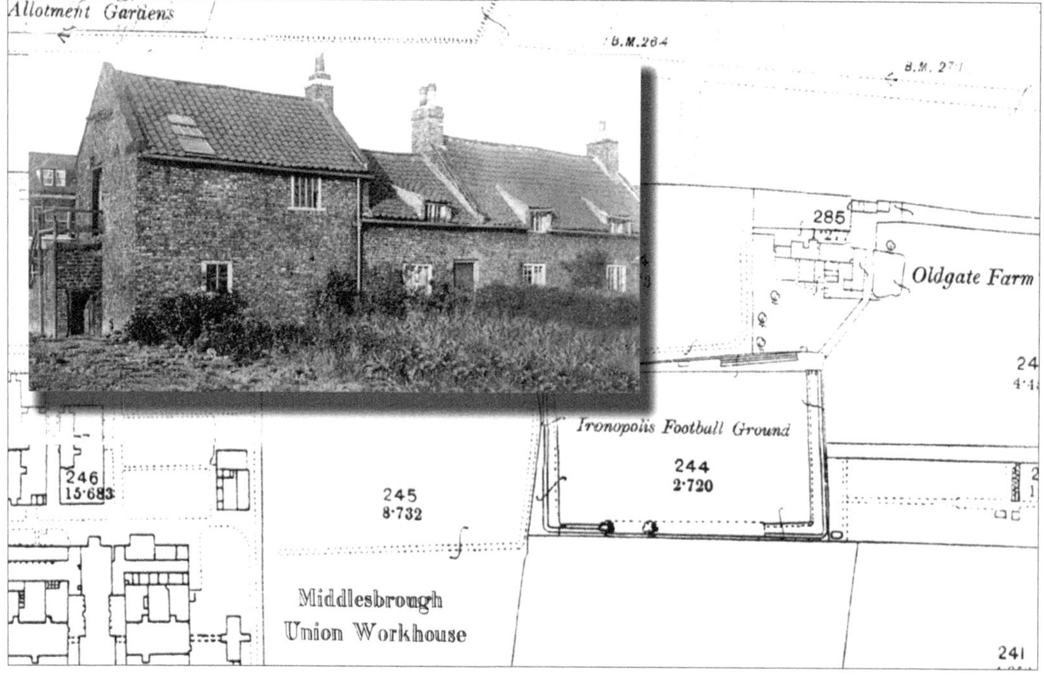

The official opening of Ayresome Park took place on 12 September 1903, when a crowd of 30,000 people saw Sunderland defeat Middlesbrough 3-2. The move to Ayresome Park followed the admission of the club into the Football League in 1899 and subsequent promotion to the First Division in 1902. The top view looks across to the North Stand while the lower image shows the team from that first game at the ground.

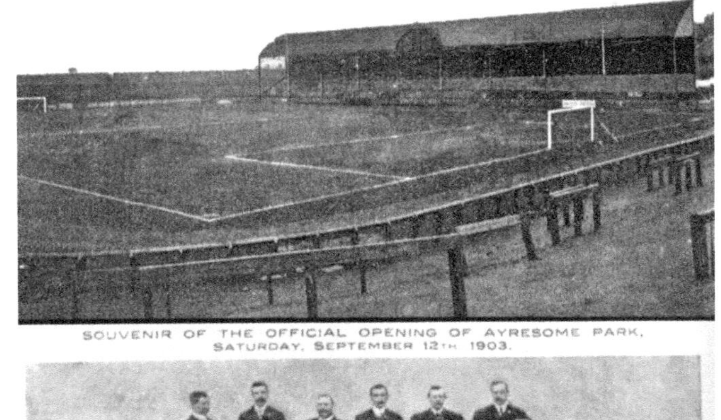

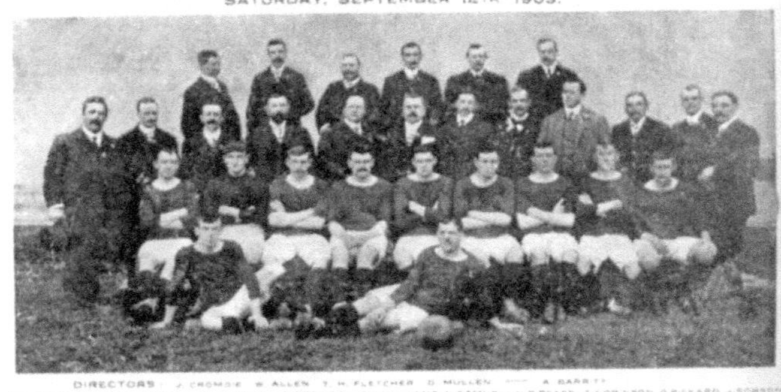

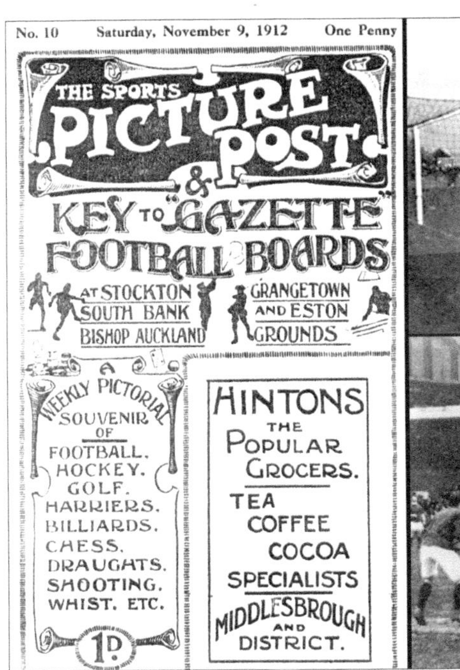

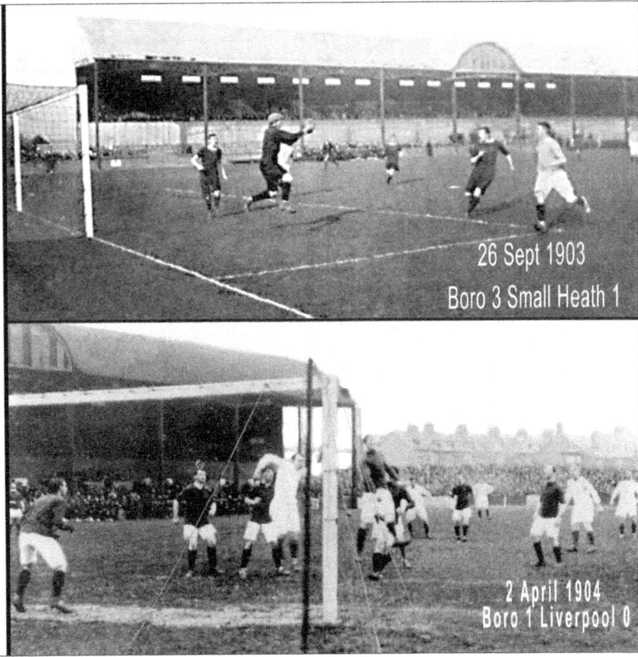

These images show action from two games played in those early years. This was to be one of the best periods in the history of the club as they had a team which by 1914 was able to mount a serious challenge for the League Title. The front page of a programme from the game against Liverpool in 1912 is also shown. The win over Small Heath, was only the second ever game at Ayresome Park. The goalkeeper is the legendary Reginald Garnett (Tim) Williamson from North Ormesby, who made 602 appearances for the club between 1901 and 1923. He was also an England international player.

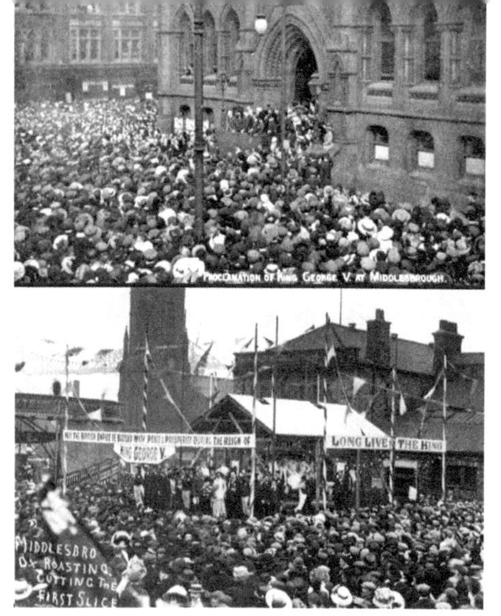

These images show the celebrations at the accession to the throne of King George V in 1910. A large crowd gathered at the Town Hall to hear the proclamation of the Accession being read out on 22 March 1911. Coronation Day was 22 June 1911, with a public holiday on the following day. One of Middlesbrough's main celebrations was the roasting of an ox in the old Market Place. It cost one shilling to buy a piece of roasted ox on a special commemorative plate – the proceeds going towards a special tea for elderly people and a trip to Redcar for the children.

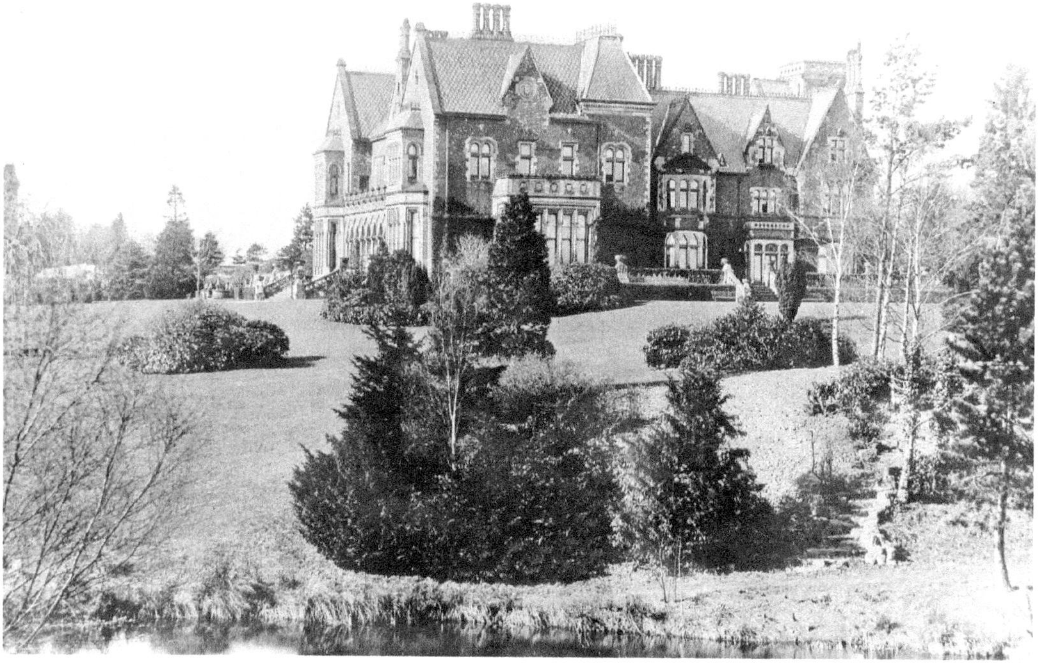

Those individuals who had played a key part in the rapid growth of industry also accumulated a great deal of wealth. This was particularly true of Henry Bolckow and John Vaughan, who both moved from homes in the old town to country mansions. Gunnergate Hall, seen here around 1870, was a magnificent brick house built in Gothic style in 1857 in parkland near Marton, for the Quaker banker Charles Leatham. Two years after his death in 1858 it was purchased by Vaughan. After his death in 1868, his son Thomas took over the house and proceeded to enlarge it considerably. When Vaughan's company crashed in 1879 all work ceased, leaving a banqueting hall and ballroom unfinished. The house and contents were sold in 1881 to Henry Bolckow's nephew, Carl. The final resident of the Hall, shipbuilder Sir Raylton Dixon, purchased it in 1888 and lived here until his death in 1901. The Hall was never occupied again other than by troops during the First World War and it was demolished in 1946.

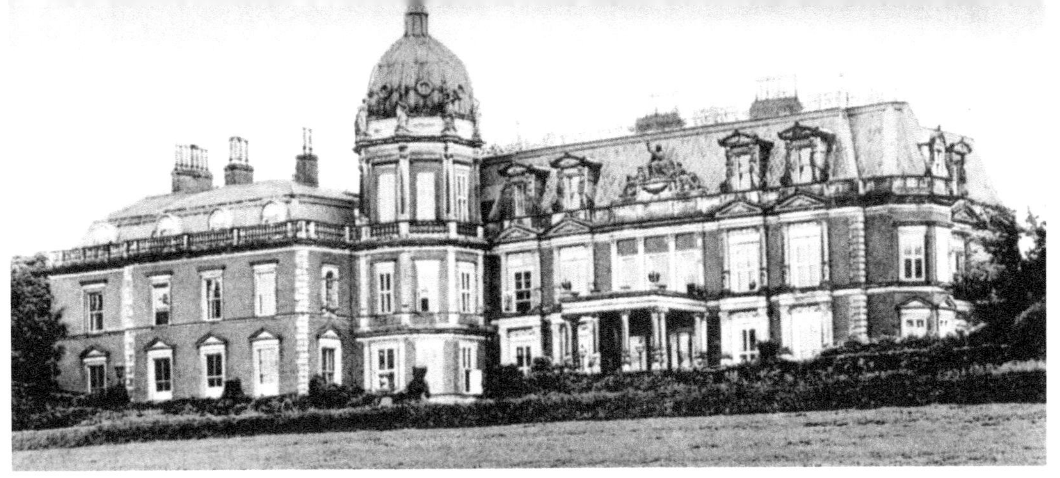

Henry Bolckow was already living in Marton Hall when Vaughan arrived at Gunnergate Hall. Bolckow, who bought the estate in 1853 as a private residence, had the Hall built before he moved there in 1856. He continued to improve the grandeur of the Hall and its grounds too, in which he planted many rare trees. He also amassed a fine art collection, which passed to his nephew Carl, but, due to the industrial recession of 1888, it was sold in London on 5 May of that year. The elegance of the Hall was exemplified by its Carrara marble columns and staircase and many other decorative features.

During the early 1900s more inhabitants of Middlesbrough took up cycling and walking and Marton Bungalow was for many years a popular venue for those enjoying the countryside around Marton village. The timber-built bungalow was situated opposite Stewarts Park on the corner of Ladgate Lane and can be seen from two different aspects in these images from around 1910 and the 1930s. Inside there were wicker chairs and tables and a veranda was also available for seating. Similarly Ormesby Bungalow situated close to where the existing garage stands today, became a popular venue. The bungalow was also well attended for dances and was very much a part of village social life.

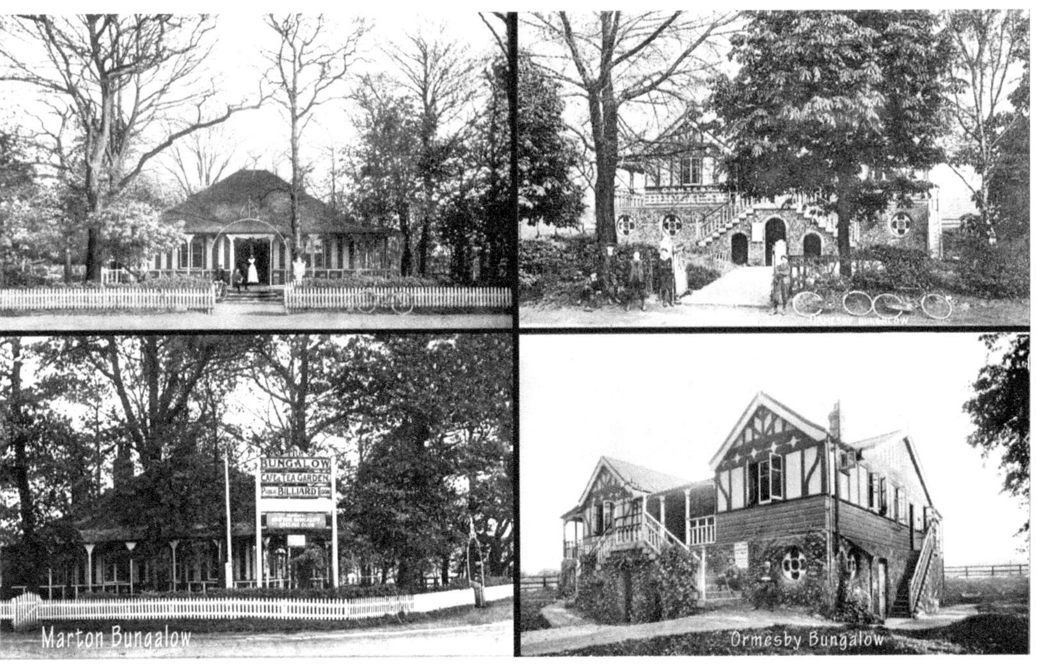

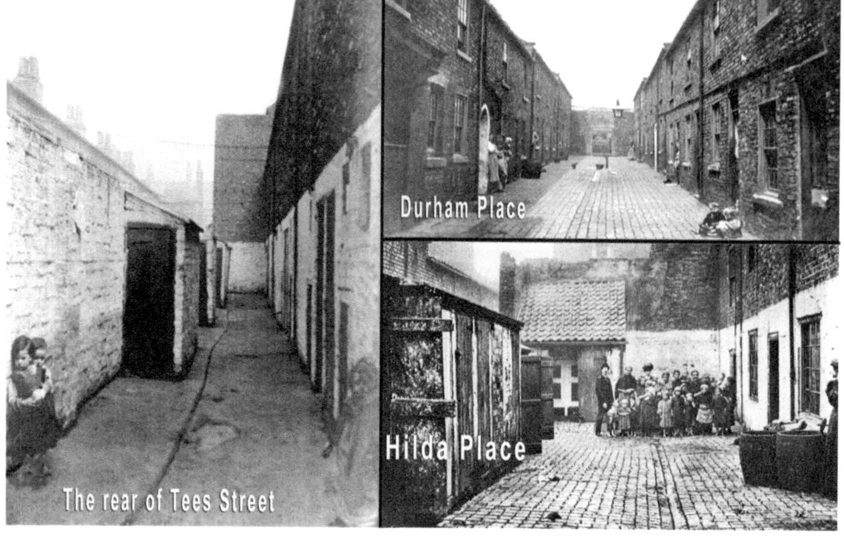

In marked contrast to an improving standard of living for many inhabitants of Middlesbrough, the conditions for some residents left a lot to be desired, as shown by these images of yards and back-to-back housing in the old town. As the population exceeded all original expectations, Otley's precise grid pattern of streets became choked by dense house building with infilling occurring on a massive scale. Dark, gloomy courtyards and small streets, houses without adequate ventilation, sewerage arrangements or even a basic water supply were built resulting in the slum housing shown here. Durham Place, for example, was one of many yards where families were served by only one communal pump.

The rear of Commercial Street illustrates the basement rooms that were common in many properties. With much of the old town built on land that was originally low-lying marshes, there were many problems in drainage, meaning that sewage was often incapable of being drained from the basement rooms in particular. Despite a series of cholera and typhoid epidemics hitting the town and several official reports by Government inspectors, including the well-known Ranger Report of 1855, there was little progress made in addressing these problems.

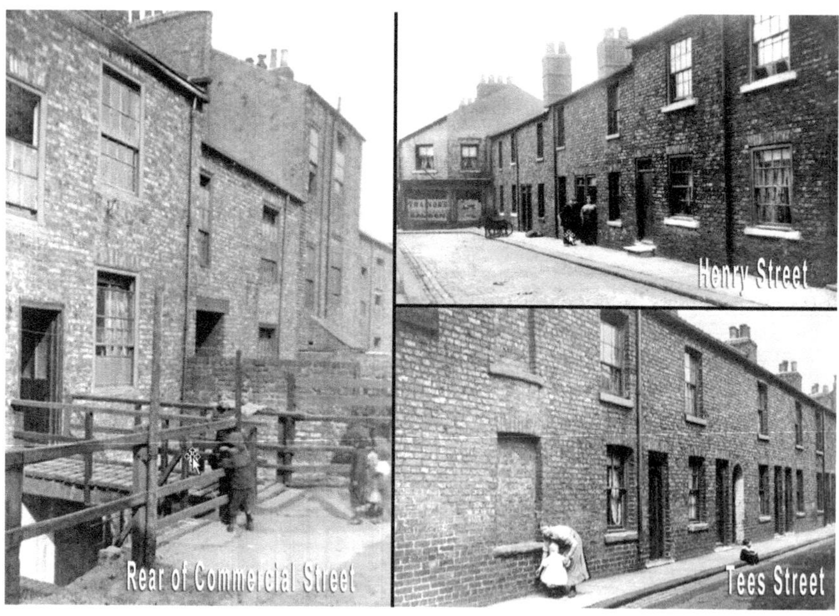

Despite the local authorities being well aware of the problems caused by slum housing, there was little willingness to acknowledge and accept responsibility, thus there was very little improvement in housing conditions. The lack of fresh water was a huge problem – the mains were laid to the area but there was a reluctance to accept responsibility for the connection to individual properties. After more virulent epidemics in the 1890s, a government inspector concluded that they were due to the 3,000 privy middens in the town in close proximity to people's homes. The removal of raw sewage from properties and the deficiencies of the sewerage system meant that raw sewage was regularly found on some streets.

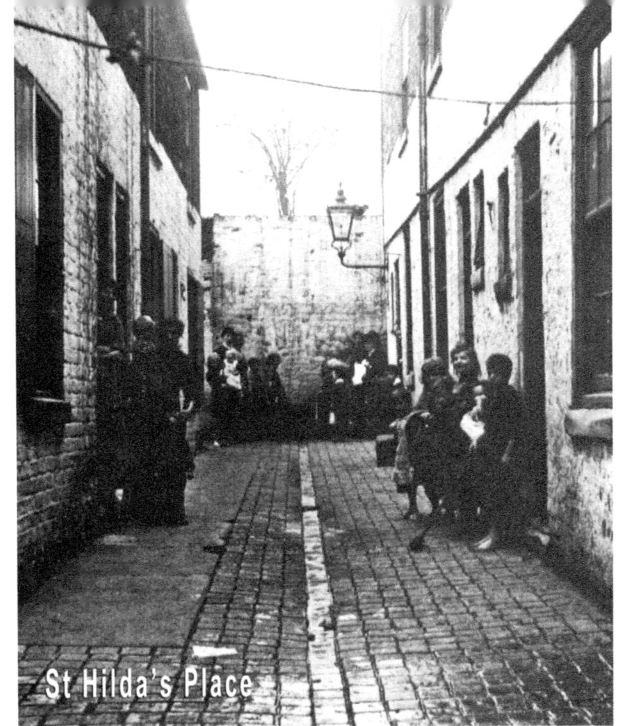

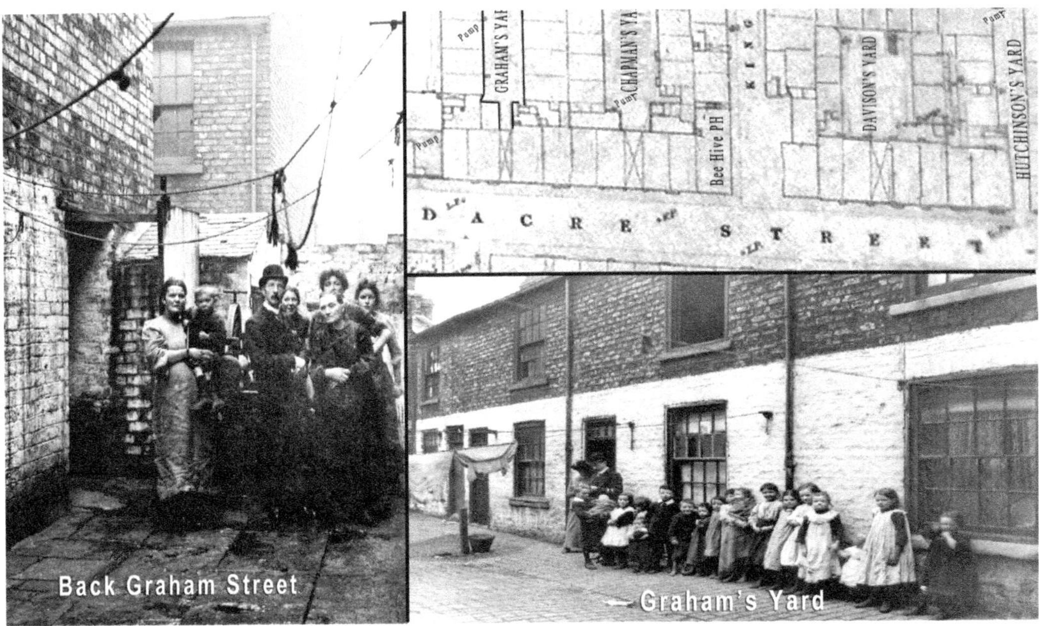

Although the Corporation voluntarily adopted legislation in 1901, which would have allowed them to address this problem by demolishing the worst slums, they were slow to act and it was not until 1914, after initial pressure from Marion Coates Hansen of the Independent Labour Party, that a report was drawn up outlining solutions to the problem. Inevitably, the onset of war delayed any further action until after the conflict was over. The map extract, from a plan of the town in 1856, shows the close proximity of the houses to each other in the yards, a key factor behind the poor housing conditions.

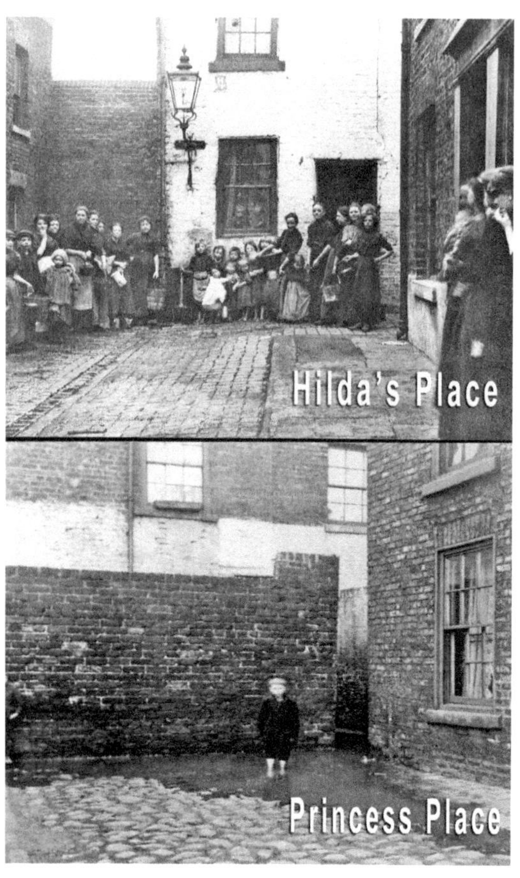

Left: Although a new, compulsory Housing and Town Planning Act required the Corporation to survey the housing needs of the town in 1919, there was a delay of a further eight years before widespread demolition of Middlesbrough's slum areas began with the Dacre Street Improvement Scheme. By November 1927 the first fifty-seven houses had been cleared. Scenes like these were to become a distant memory.

Below: The regular occurrence of epidemics resulted in the building of fever hospitals away from the town. In 1871, following another outbreak of smallpox, a new hospital was planned on land in West Lane close to the new cemetery at old Linthorpe. West Lane Hospital, or the 'Fever Hospital' as it became known, opened in 1872. Dealing with cases of smallpox, typhoid and enteric fever, the hospital was extended over a further two acres in 1890 and again in 1896. A particularly virulent epidemic of smallpox in 1897-8 meant that temporary accommodation had to be built to cope with the outbreak. (Reproduced from 1893 Ordnance Survey map, 25 inch series, with the kind permission of the Ordnance Survey)

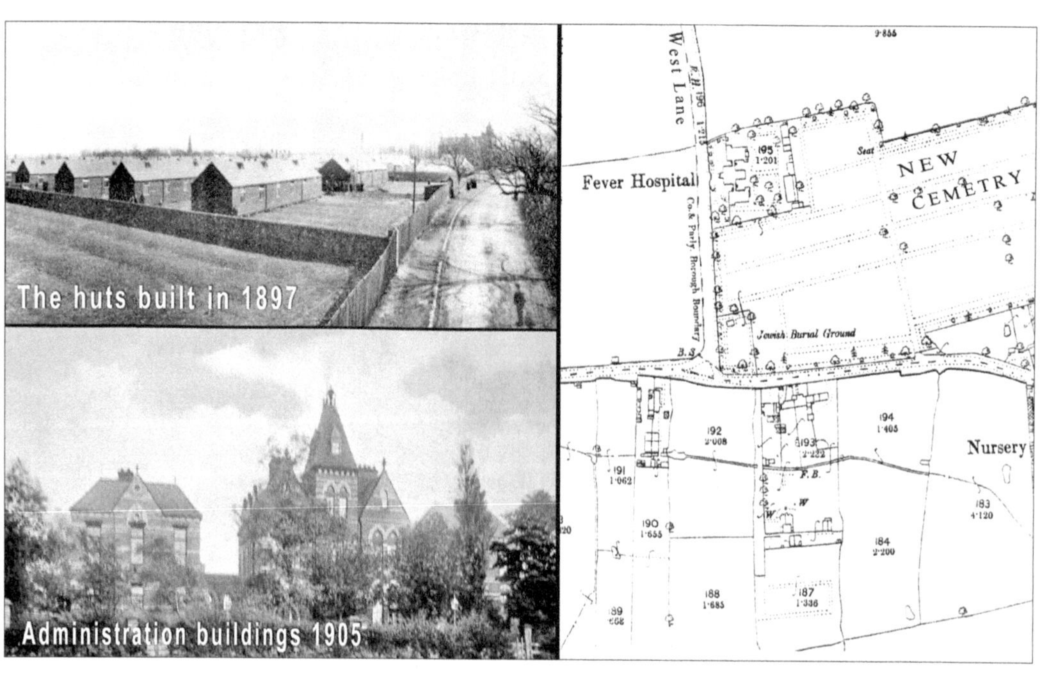

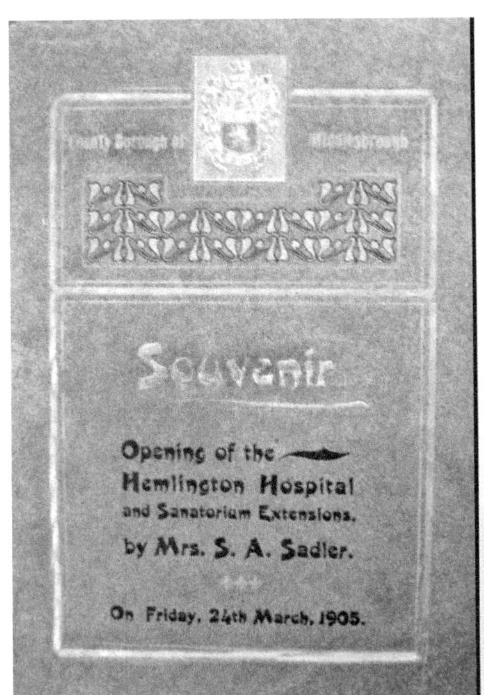

Hemlington Hospital.

The lesson learnt by the visitation of Small-Pox in 1897-1898, when temporary Hospital accommodation on an extensive scale had to be requisitioned will not readily be forgotten by the people of Middlesbrough

Immediately after the Epidemic, the Corporation wisely determined to be prepared for any emergency of a similar character which may occur in the future, and with that end in view they purchased the **Belle Vue Farm** at Hemlington, and erected thereon Hospitals and other buildings for the reception and treatment of cases of Small-Pox.

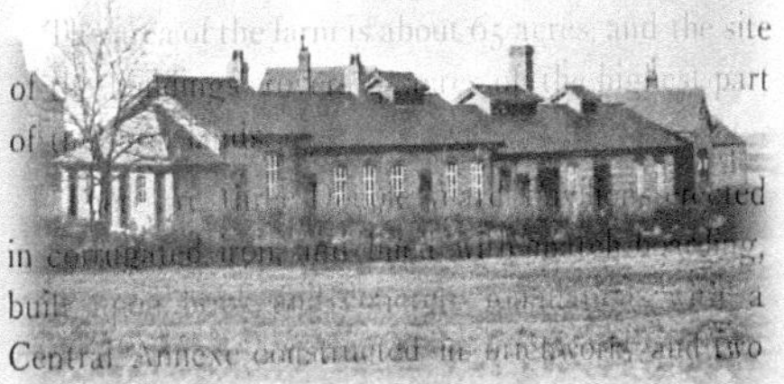

The events of 1897 highlighted the need for more facilities and it was decided in April 1900 to purchase Belle Vue Farm at Hemlington as a sanatorium for smallpox cases. This souvenir programme marks the official opening of the hospital and sanatorium extensions at West Lane on 24 March 1905 by Mrs S.A. Sadler, wife of Colonel S.A. Sadler, Chairman of the Sanitary Committee.

The sixty-five acre farm at Belle Vue was four miles south of Middlesbrough and was therefore able to offer an isolation site for dealing with cases of smallpox and, as it turned out, the increasing number of cases of tuberculosis. The buildings covered four acres of the highest part of the farm.

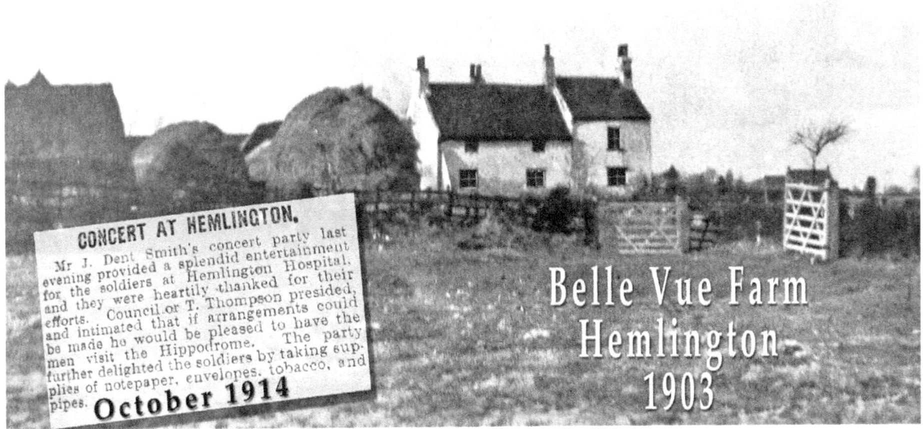

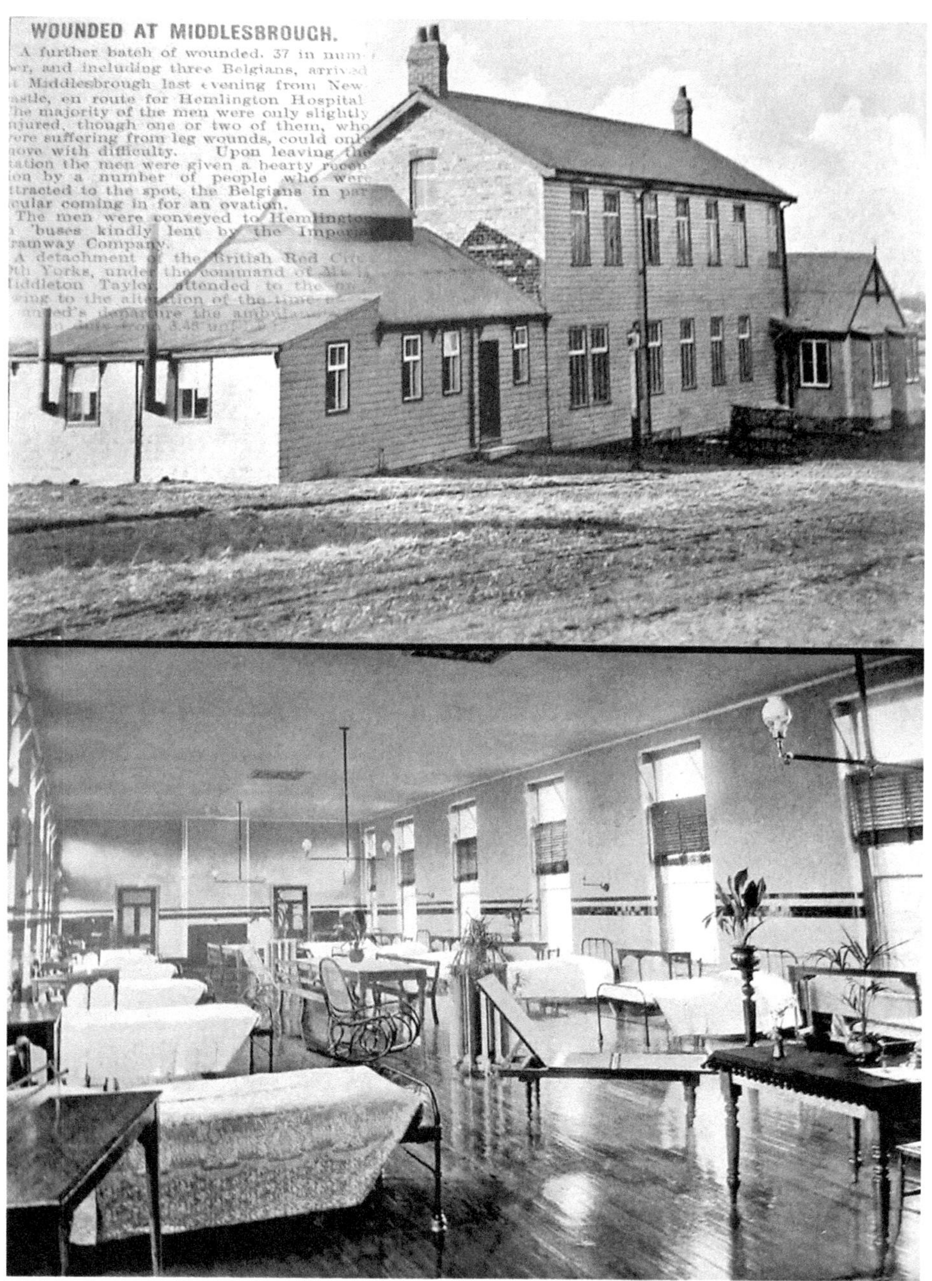

The total cost of Hemlington was £8,600 and these images show the farmhouse converted into administrative buildings. Also shown is one of the three new, double-ward pavilions erected in corrugated iron, lined with match boarding and built upon brick and concrete foundations. There was also a central annexe and accommodation for staff. During the First World War both Hemlington and West Lane took in casualties from the fighting; the inset, taken from the *North Eastern Evening Gazette* of December 1914, describes the arrival of wounded patients at the hospital.

6

MOVIN' OUT

The town spread its wings southwards ...

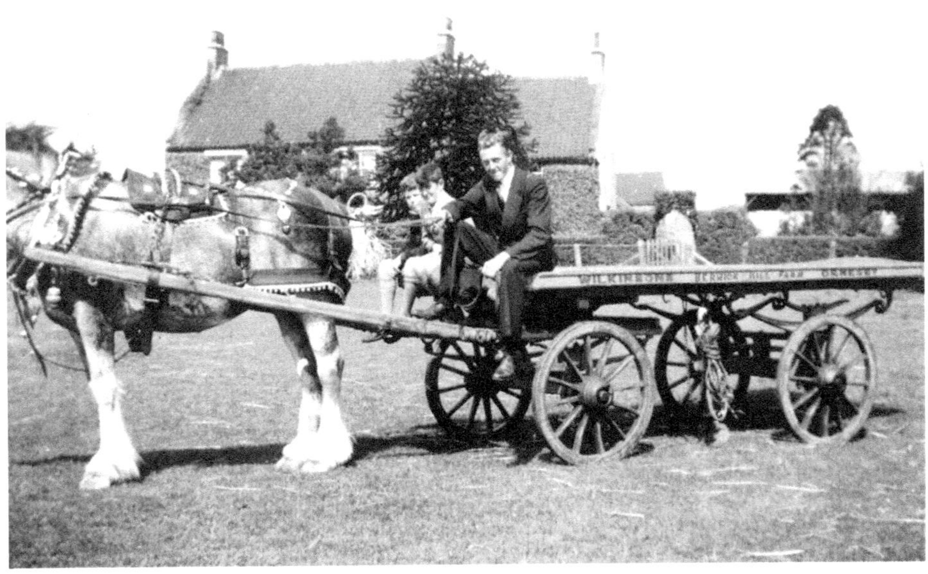

A major expansion in Middlesbrough Corporation's housing programme after 1945 meant that the land farmed by the Wilkinson family at Berwick Hills Farm was subject to compulsory purchase. This image, taken in front of the farm around 1950, shows a time before the rural area south of Middlesbrough gave way to housing estates.

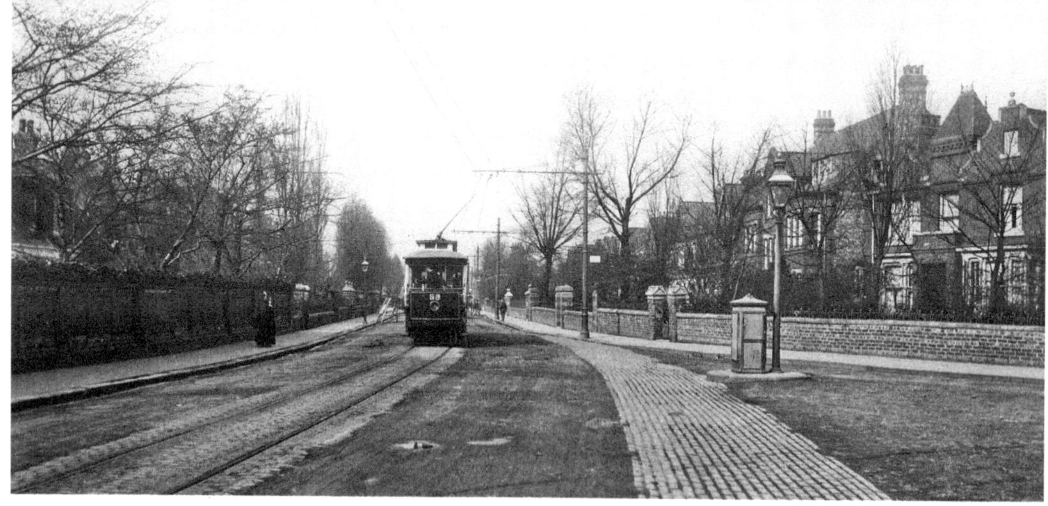

In the 1850s, as Middlesbrough expanded southwards, small pockets of land were gradually sold off for building desirable residences away from the hustle and bustle of the town, for those able to afford them. Southfield Villas was built in the 1850s, North Park Road and Grove Hill in the late 1860s and Linthorpe from the early 1970s as Middlesbrough's suburbs were born. One attraction of Linthorpe was the tram terminus there. Trams, like this one shown here in The Avenue around 1906, were an excellent link to the town.

The development of the new areas of housing was linked to the commercial progress of the town. The several downturns in commerce meant that the spread of the suburbs was often sporadic and it was not uncommon for several plots of land to be found next to finished residences. Thus rural areas co-existed next to the building developments well into the twentieth century, as shown here.

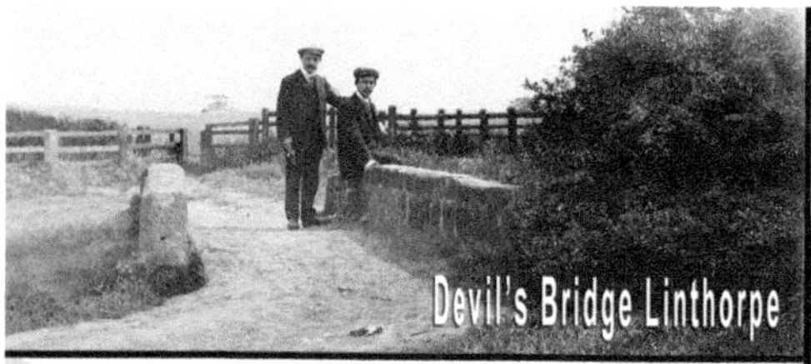

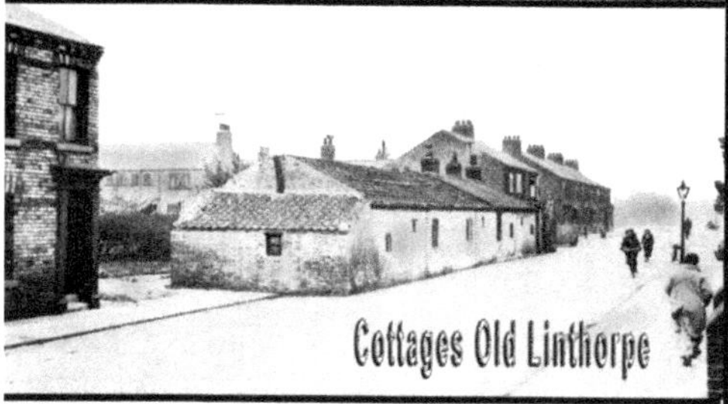

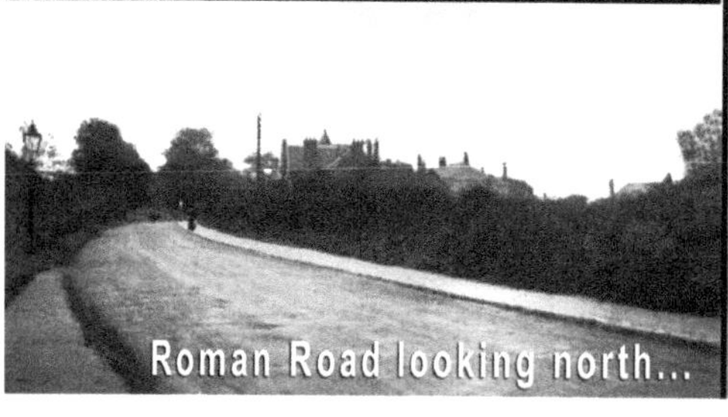

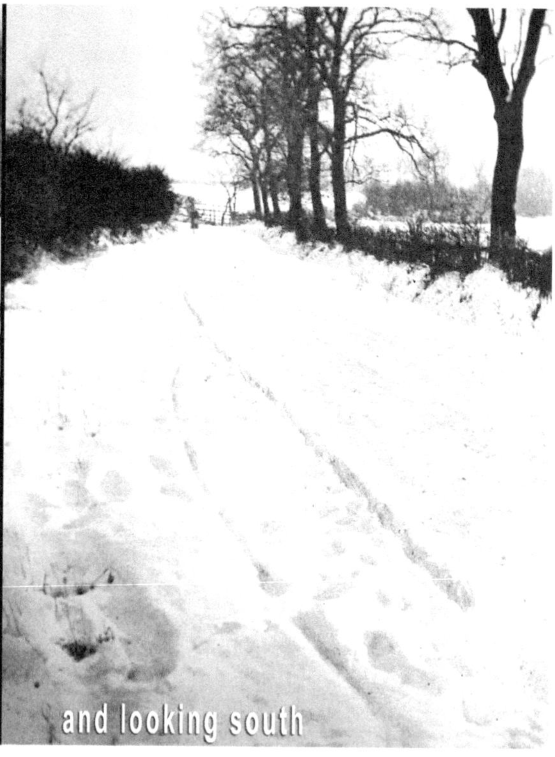

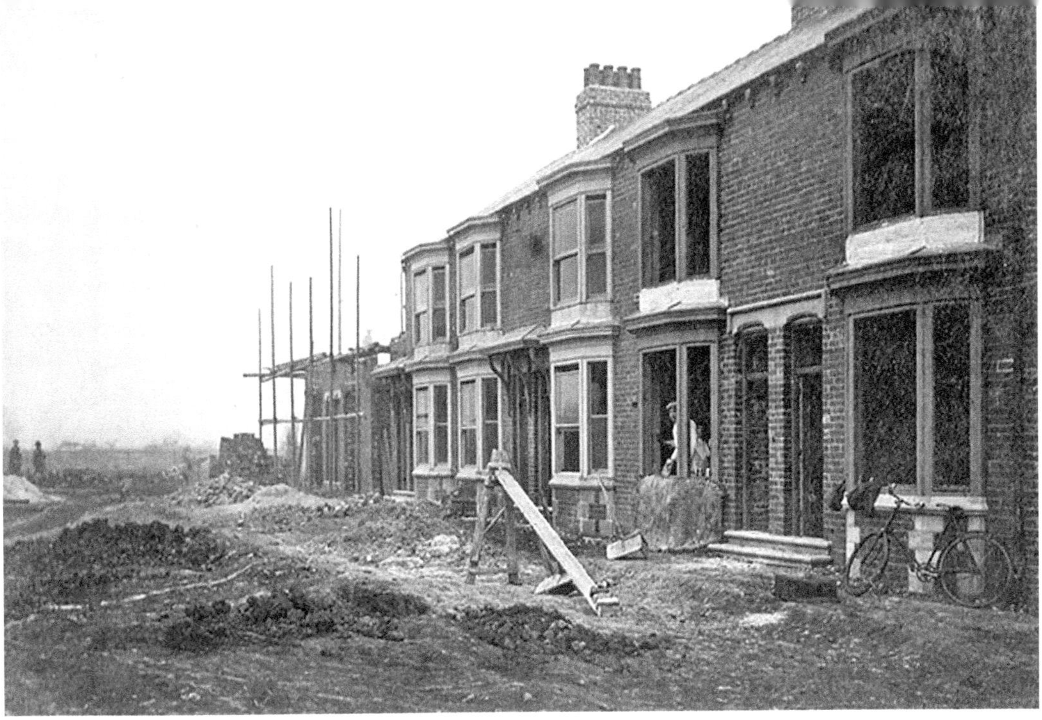

Above: Building in Clive Road, 1910. Development in this area was the culmination of residential building that had started in the 1860s as the area between Newport Road and Linthorpe Road was gradually filled in. Note the open fields in the distance towards Linthorpe.

Right: Grosvenor Terrace, Linthorpe and Woodlands Road *c.* 1905. Linthorpe Road became increasingly important during the post-1850 period, providing a link to the residential development in Linthorpe around the Avenue and the Crescent. Close by, a 'new' Linthorpe village developed, offering shopping and other community facilities to the new residents.

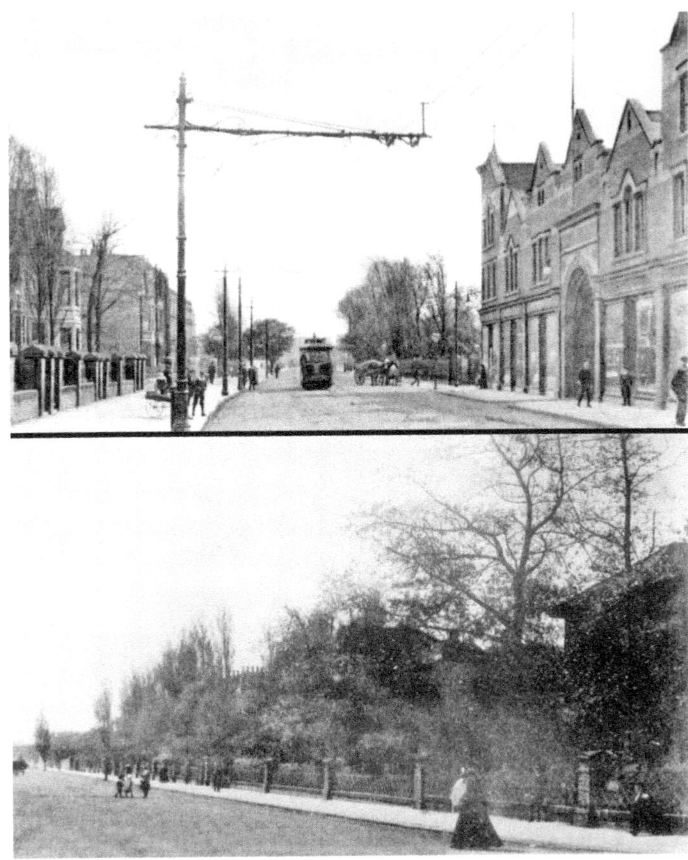

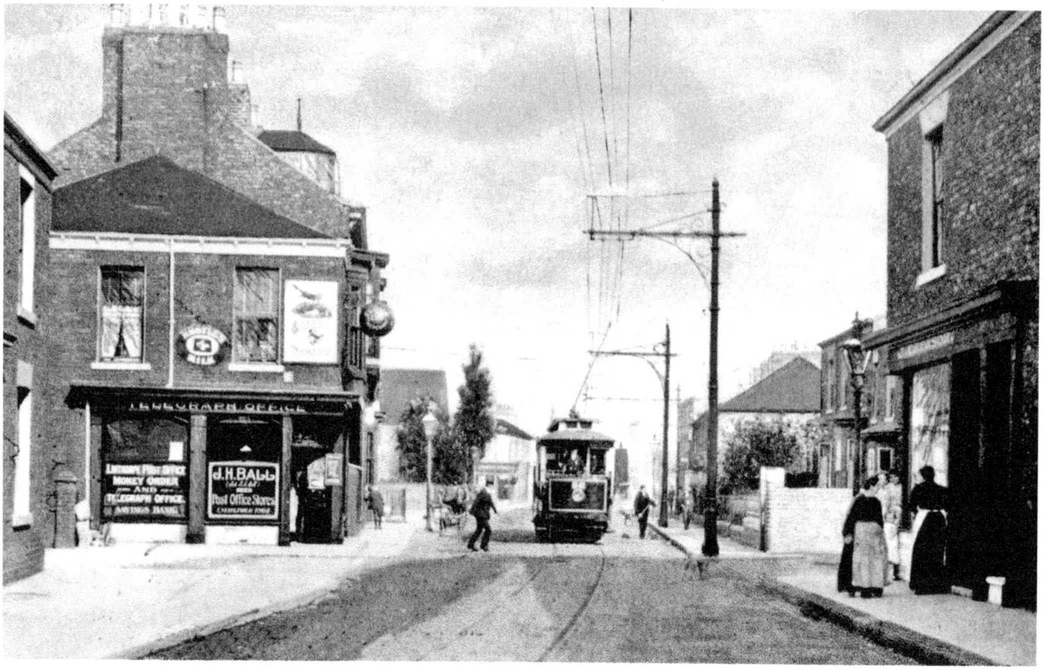

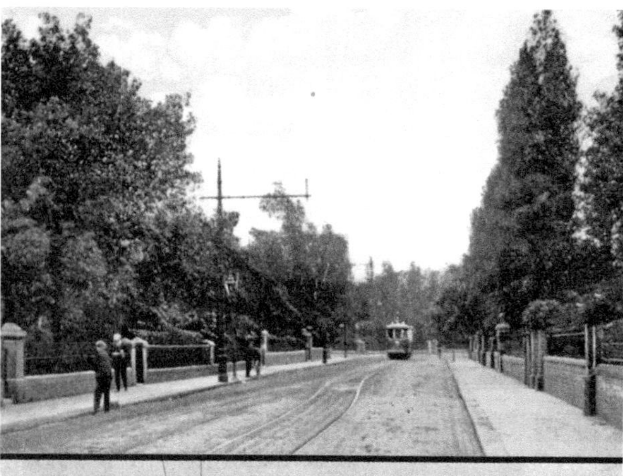

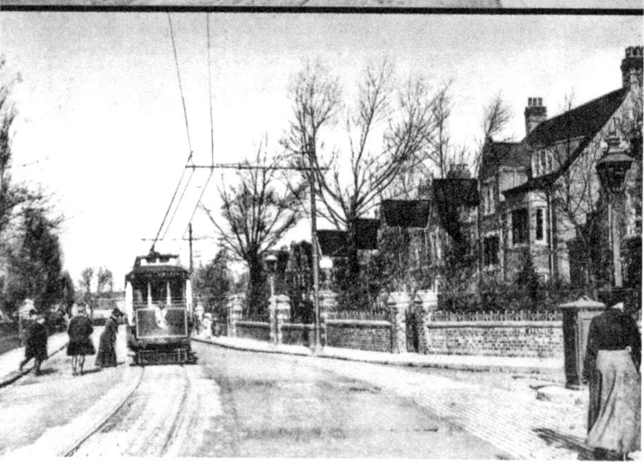

Above: Linthorpe village, *c.* 1910. James Henry Ball's post office stores can be seen on the corner of Chipchase Road. Local residents referred to this commercial area as 'the village' and it certainly offers a contrast to the housing found further north of the town. The tram heading towards us terminated at The Crescent having travelled from Ferry Road in the old town.

Left: Another two images of The Avenue, Linthorpe in the early Edwardian period. This was a desirable area to live, with properties which were pleasing to the eye. The properties in Linthorpe have retained their style today, a reflection of the quality of the design and workmanship that went into the original building. Many were architect-designed, detached and semi-detached residencies – a world away from the type of properties found closer to the town.

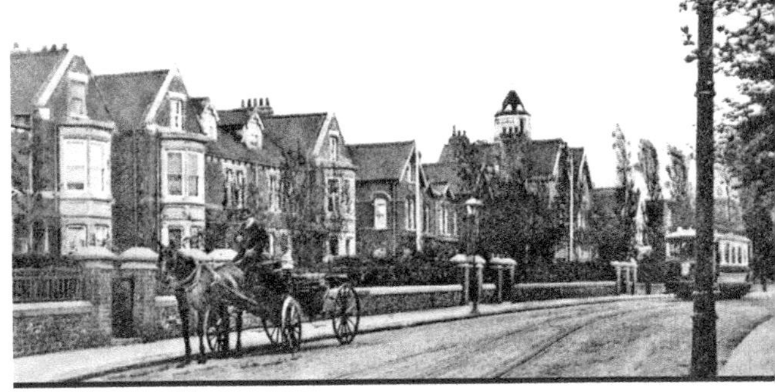

Right: These images of The Crescent (above) and Sycamore Road (below) show the existence of differing styles of property within the area; a distinct contrast to the rows of identical houses found in the terraced streets in the town. The area attracted many professional people able to afford a lifestyle which usually included employing 'staff'– servant girls who helped in running the house.

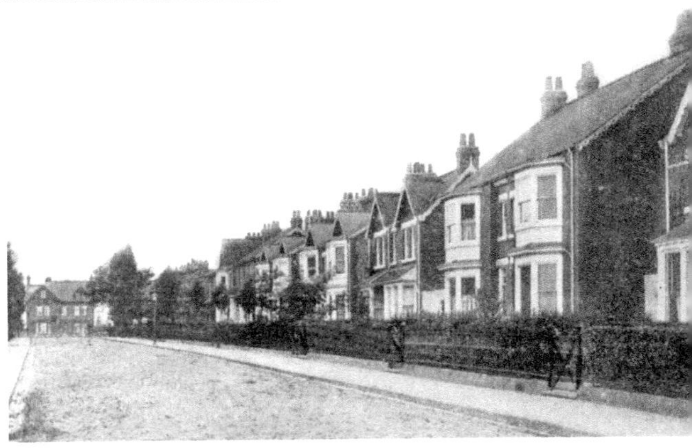

Below: Although Middlesbrough developed within a relatively short period of time, it was only after the First World War that this development began to reach areas like Acklam. This image of Acklam Road around 1903 looks south to where the modern entrances are to Church Lane and Hall Drive. The two houses featured still stand today but the changes in the area close by are quite remarkable.

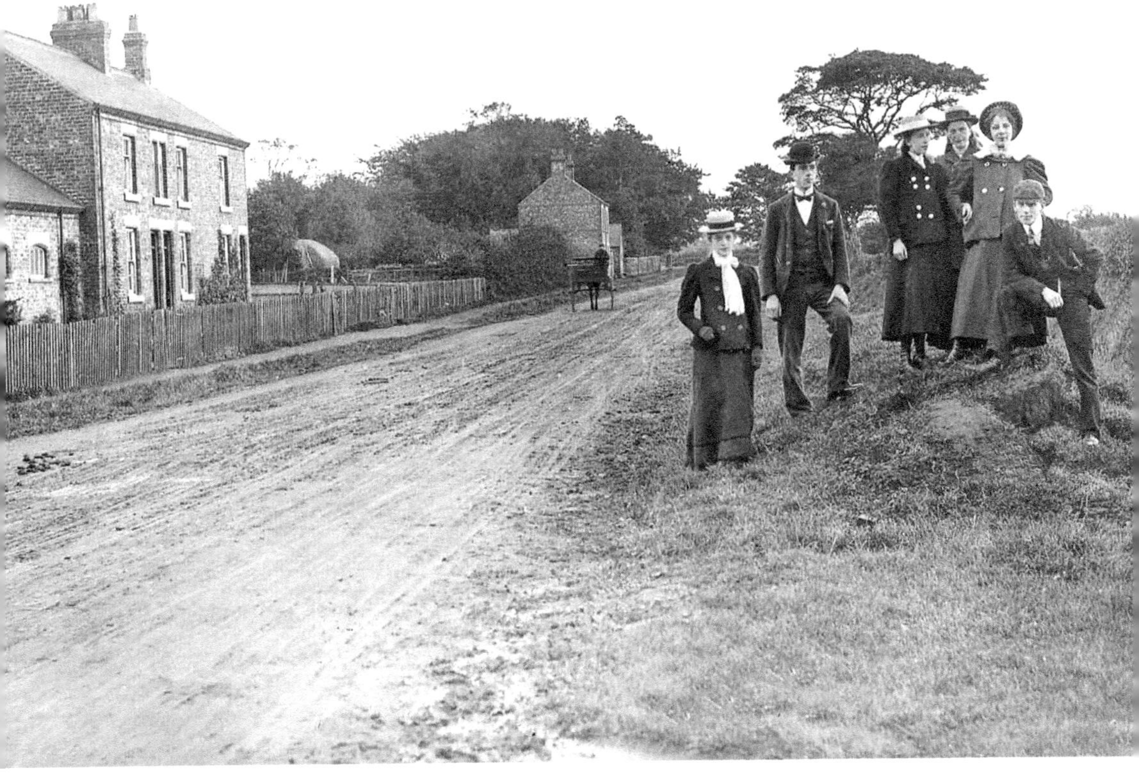

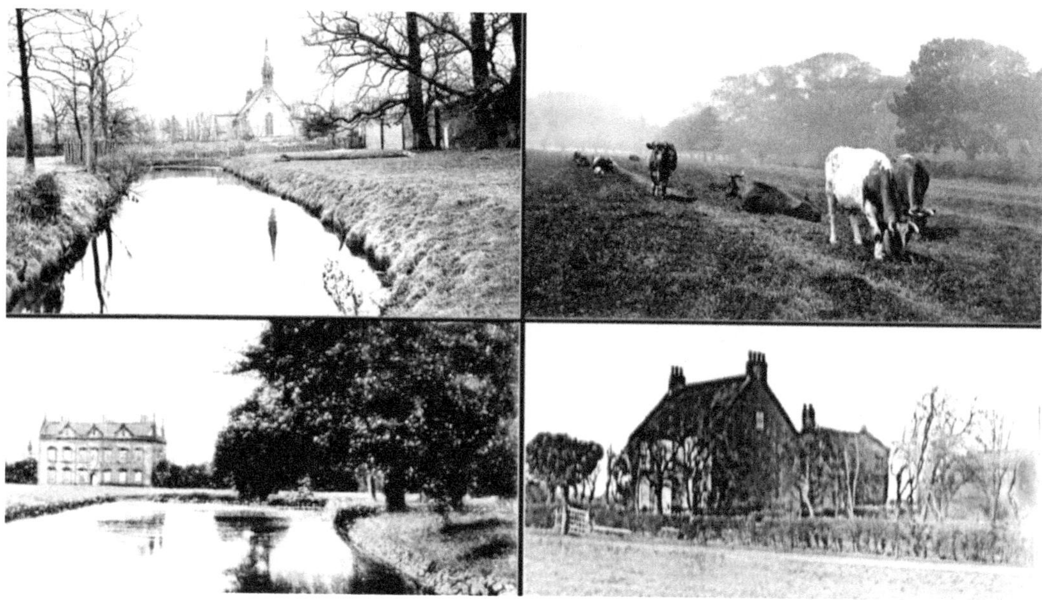

The later expansion of Middlesbrough towards Acklam meant that the rural character of the area was retained for a longer period of time than in areas like Linthorpe. These images are from around 1903 and show the rural nature of the area. The images include Acklam Hall, St Mary's Church, Acklam vicarage and part of the Acklam estate. These were to be the final years of rural tranquillity in the area.

The boundaries of Middlesbrough were extended to include Acklam just before the First World War. This remarkable image looks towards Acklam from close to the entrance from Acklam Road to Appleton Road. At this time, 1912, the road was in the process of being widened. In the distance are the buildings of Newport Lane Farm.

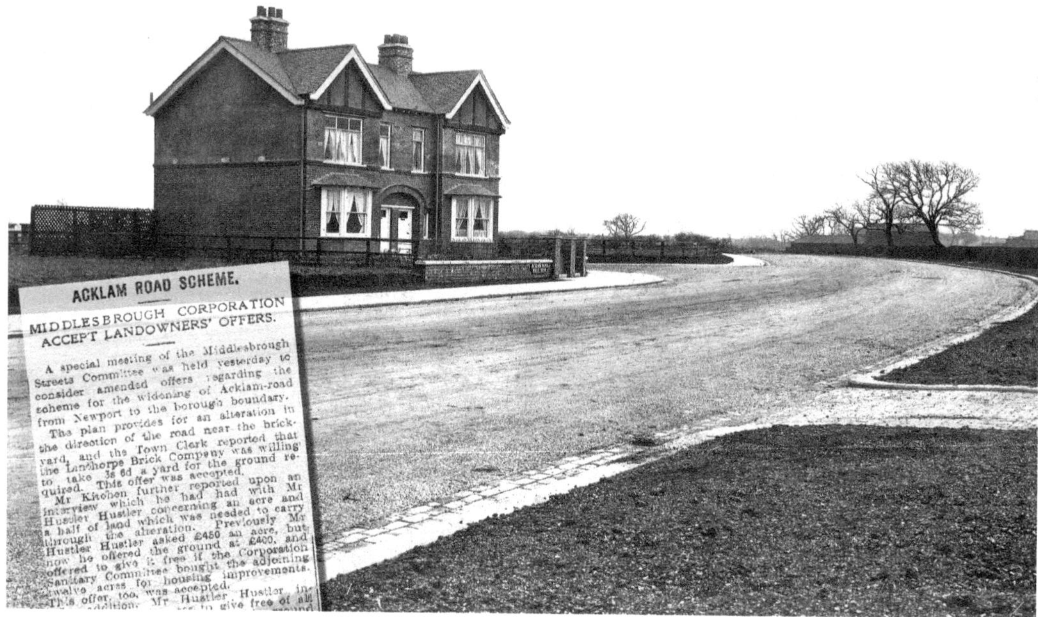

Taken at the same time as the previous image, this view provides a remarkable insight into the rural character of the area around Acklam a hundred years ago. The lane can be seen in a 'before and after state' as the process of widening the road has reached this point close to Newport Lane Farm. Within ten years this area would be covered by houses.

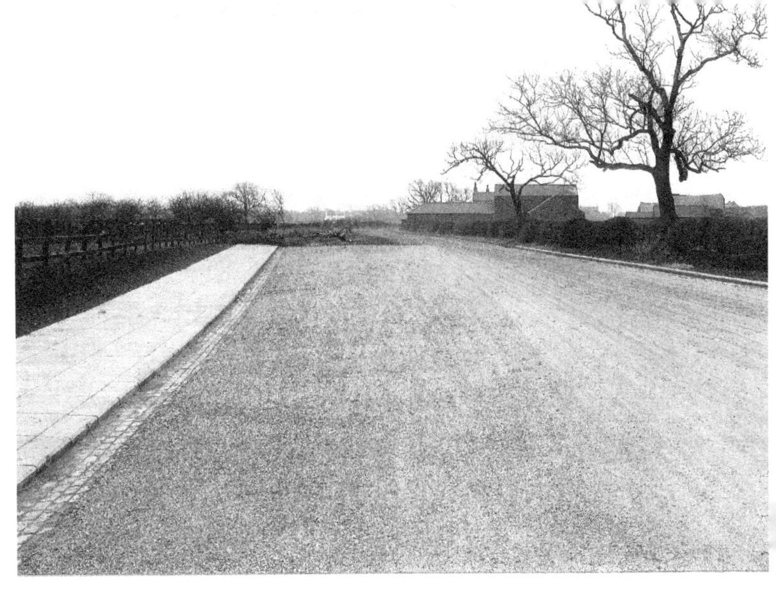

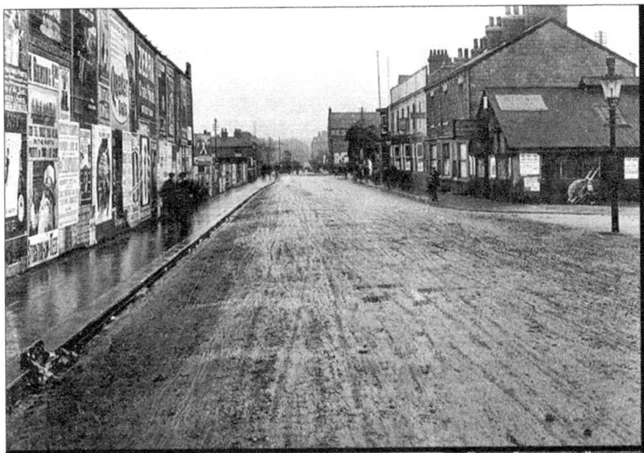

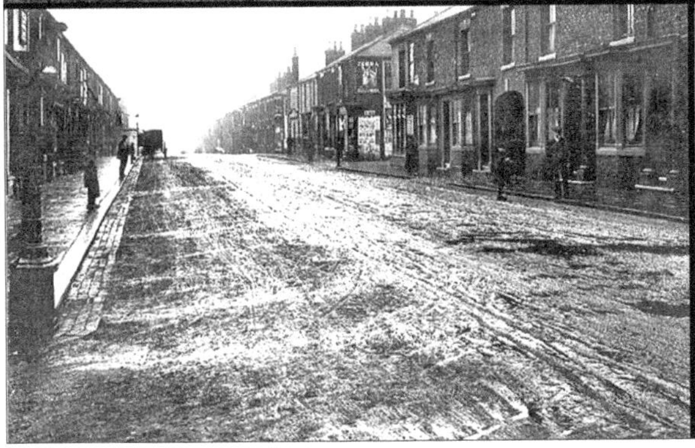

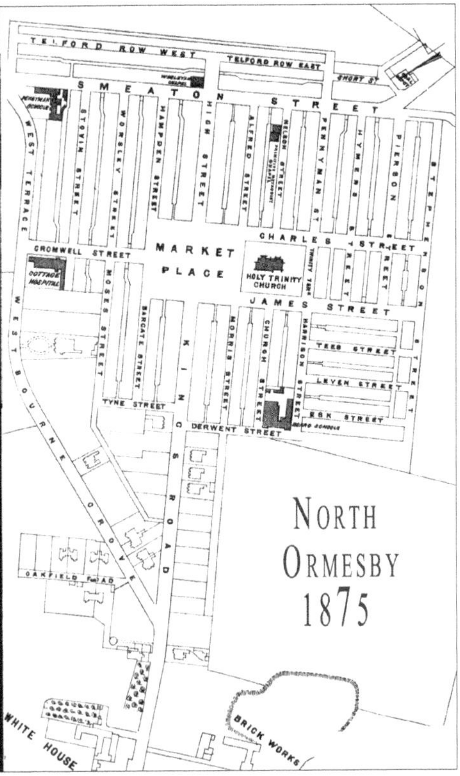

Development further east had taken place much earlier with the building of North Ormesby in the 1860s. Captain J.W. Worsley and his son, J.S. Pennyman, were responsible for the laying out of North Ormesby, selling off land for building after 1852. In association with the owners of the Middlesbrough Estate they also built a new road from Ormesby to Middlesbrough. The streets of North Ormesby were built in a grid design, centred on a market place, similar to Middlesbrough. The upper image looks to Middlesbrough from Langbaurgh Place, while below is Smeaton Street looking east from the High Street.

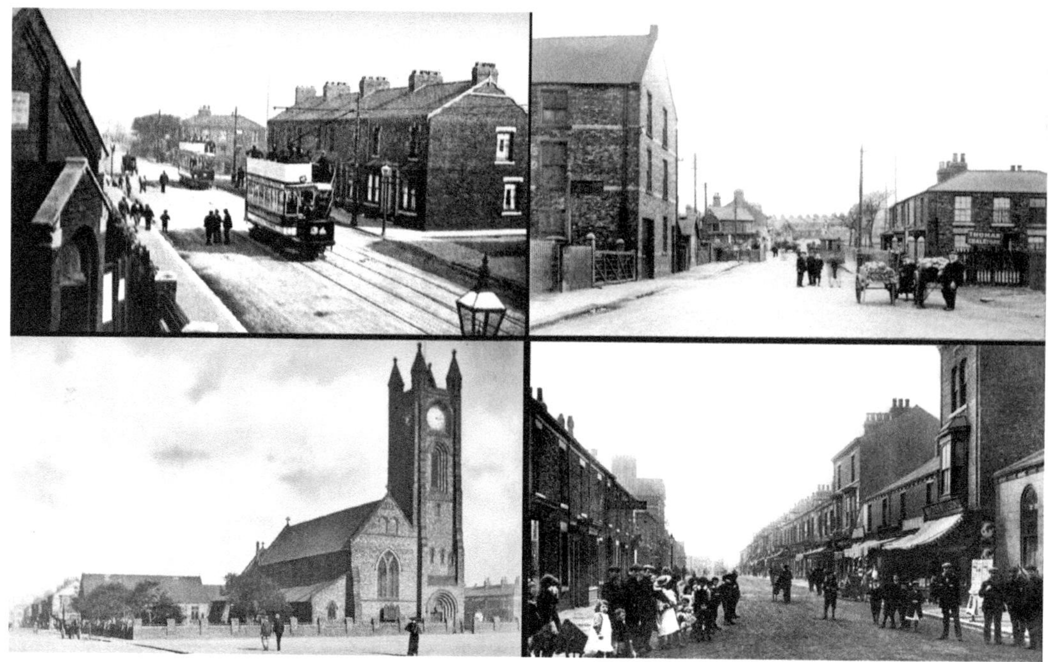

The two upper images look towards the railway crossing at North Ormesby. Holy Trinity Church (lower left) on the corner of Charles Street and the Market Place was consecrated on 26 November 1869. It has had various extensions, including the addition of the tower in 1880 and the clock in 1883. Smeaton Street (lower right) became one of North Ormesby's best known shopping areas and is still remembered today by many people.

Flooding was a regular occurrence in North Ormesby and this image, taken close to the railway crossing in 1903, shows how serious the problem was.

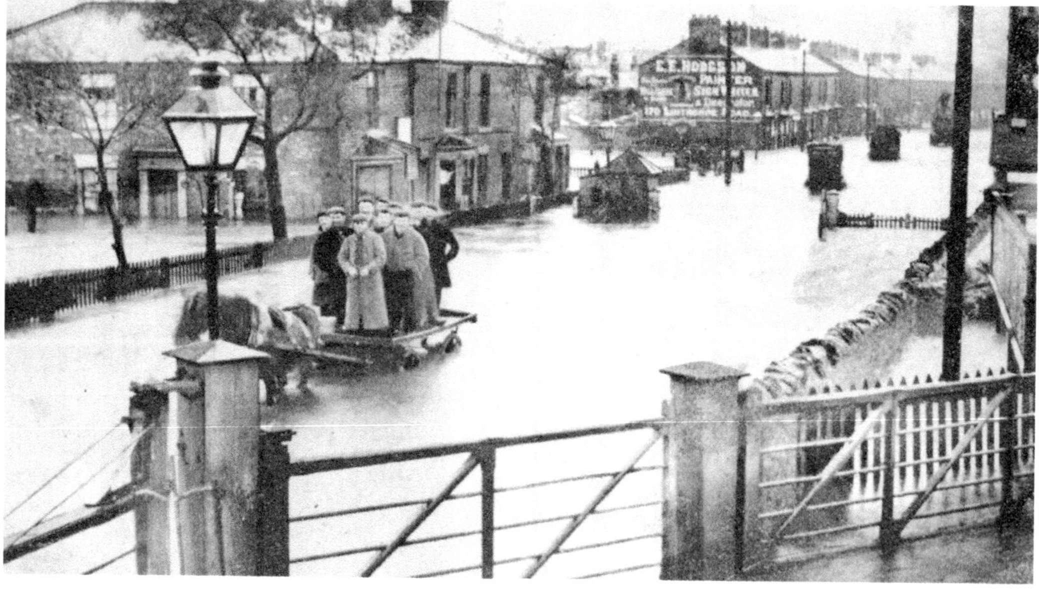

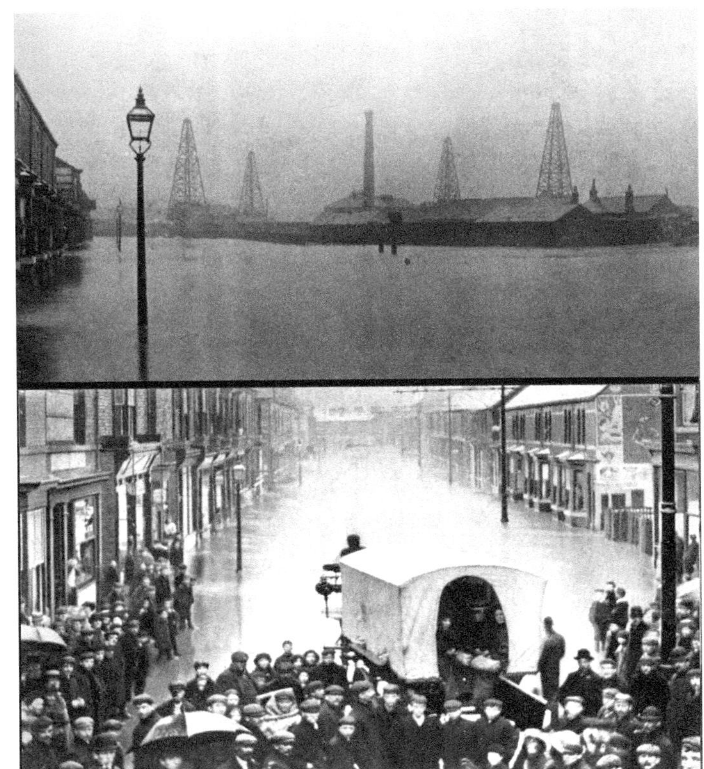

Further evidence of the flooding in North Ormesby is shown here, as are the derricks from the salt wells which were a feature of the skyline for many years.

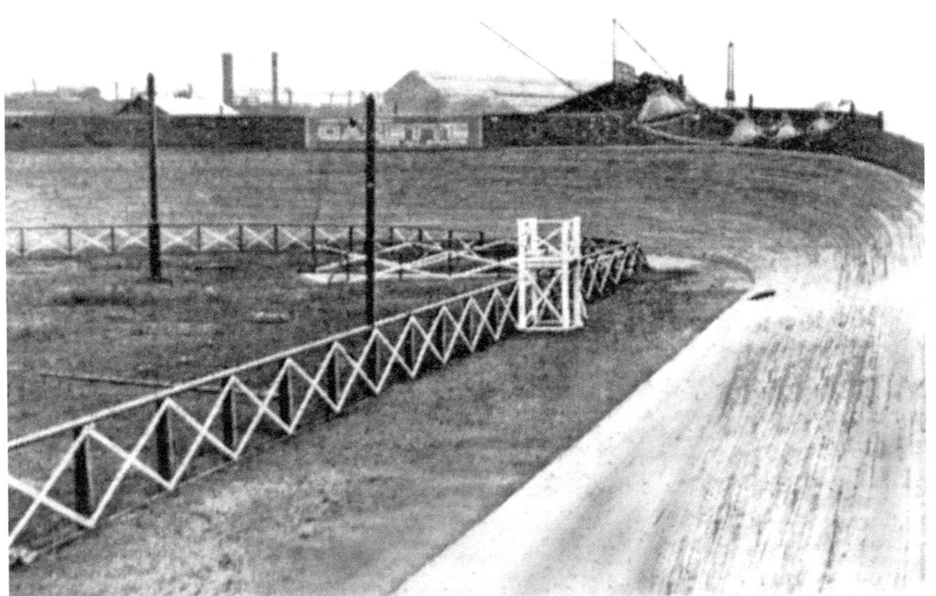

Middlesbrough's new Velodrome opened in July 1937 when more than 3,500 people watched an exciting programme of cycle races held there. These featured Syd Cozens, the famous English professional sprint champion, against Eddie Smith, one of Australia's top riders. Cozens was the overall winner.

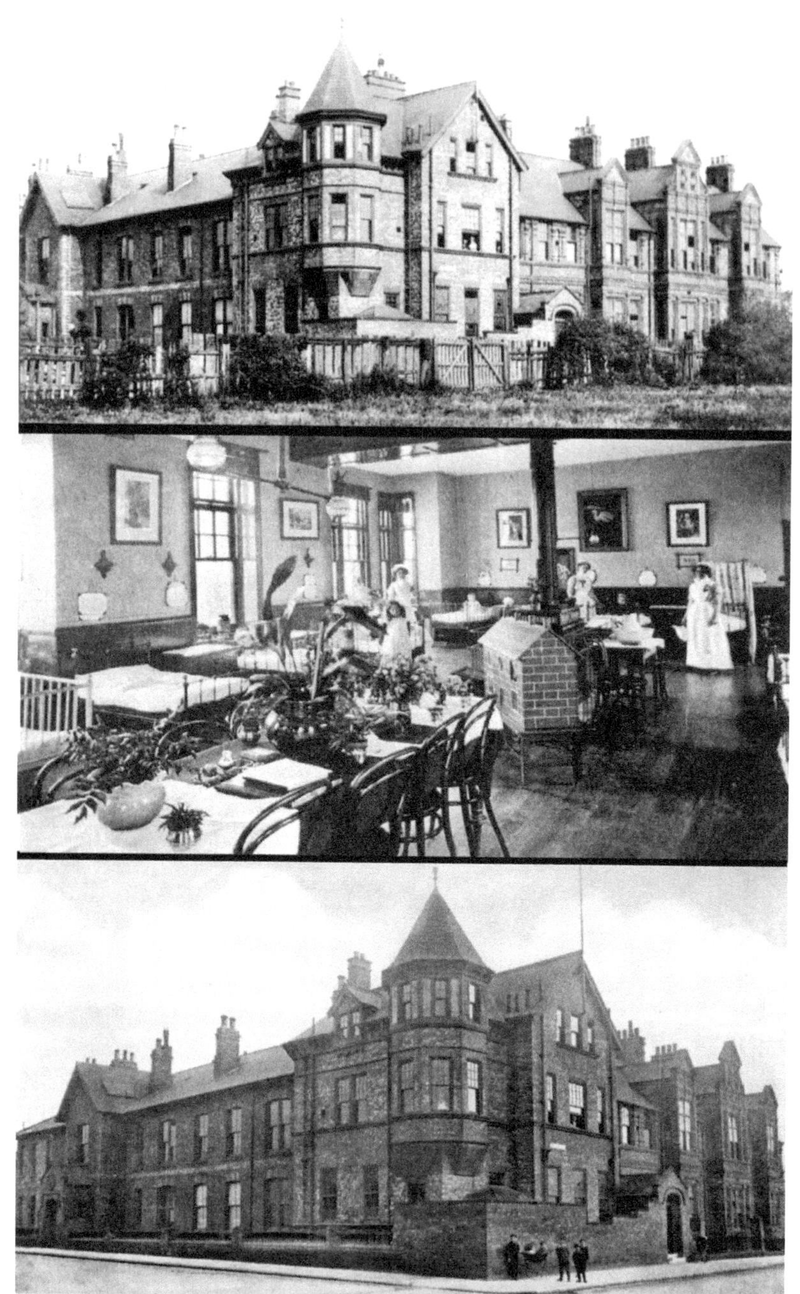

North Ormesby Hospital, or the Cottage Hospital (as it was then known due to its association with the Cottage Hospital in Middlesbrough), opened on 23 May 1861 and was the first purpose-built hospital in the area. It cost £2,646 to build and much of this was met by public subscription. Initially there was only accommodation for twenty-five patients. When North Ormesby Market began in 1875, the tolls from the stallholders were given to the hospital by Mr Pennyman.

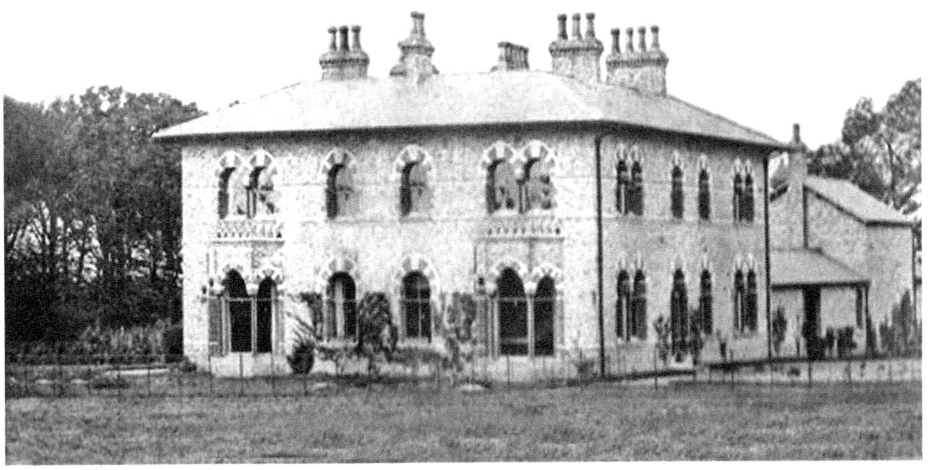

Park End House was situated at the southern end of Ormesby Road in grounds which faced Ormesby Hall. This image is from around 1890, when the area was open countryside and Ormesby Road was a narrow country lane.

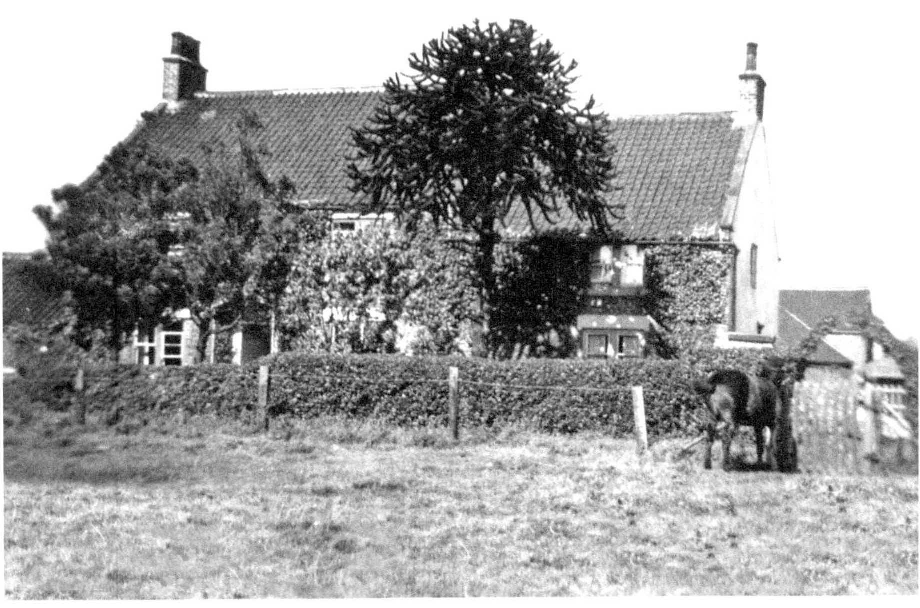

Berwick Hills Farm is shown here in 1951, in its final years before it was demolished as part of the post-war housing programme. Fortunately, a number of images of life on the farm have survived, having been retained by Jeff Wilkinson, son of the last farmer to farm there. The Wilkinsons moved to Berwick Hills in 1944 from White House Farm which stood close to North Ormesby, where they had farmed since the early 1900s.

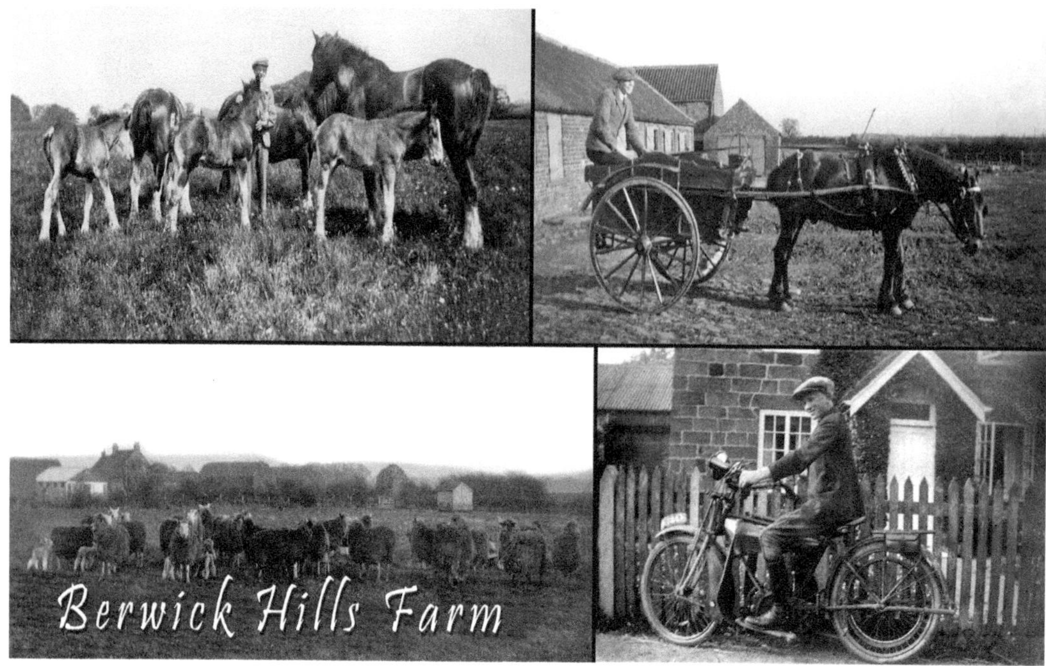

These unique images provide an excellent idea of life on Berwick Hills Farm in its final years. While it is tempting to see life there as idyllic, it clearly was hard, demanding work for the Wilkinson family. It is fascinating, as well as slightly poignant however, to consider that these views are now consigned to history with the green fields replaced by housing estates. The farm is seen both at a distance and close up behind the image of Jeff on his motorcycle.

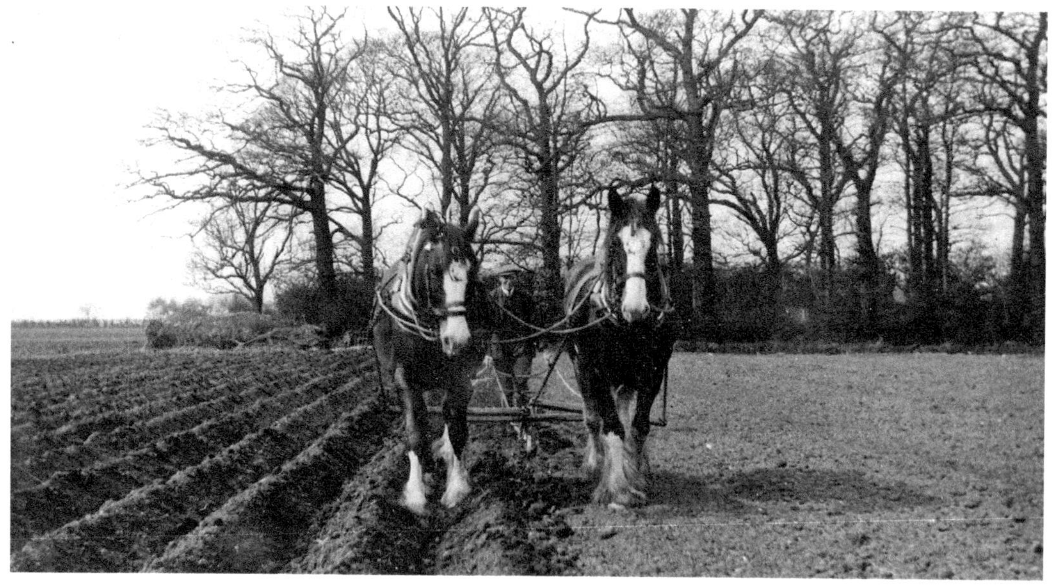

Raymond Wilkinson ploughing in the spring of 1947. The distant clump of trees was located east of the farm, close to Ormesby Road. One or two of these trees still remain today as a natural feature of the housing estate.

7

THOSE 1920S AND '30S

The town of Middlesbrough achieved its century during these two decades ...

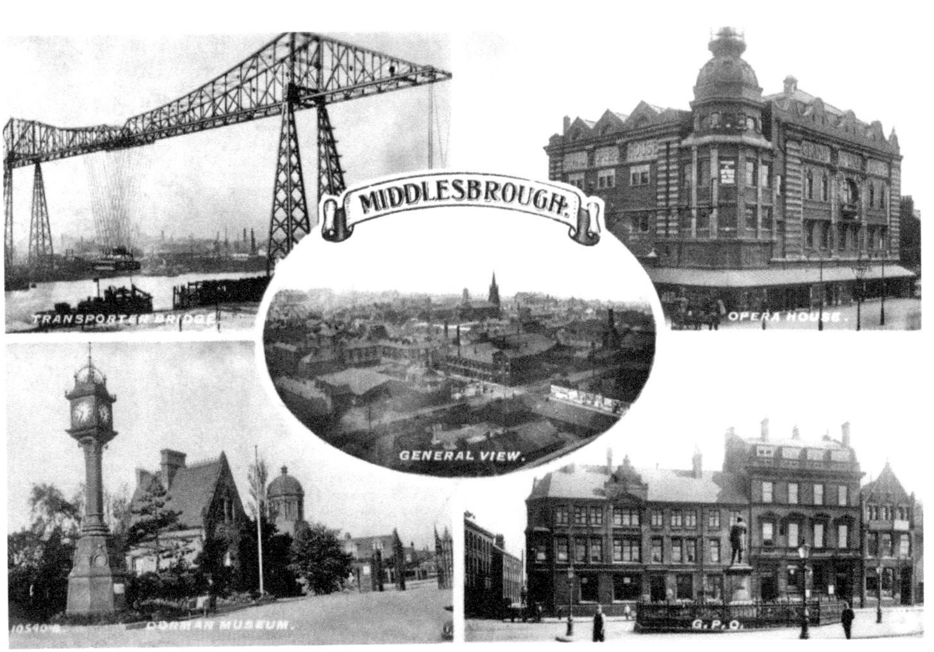

This image is a multi-view of Middlesbrough from the early 1920s. It shows some highlights of the town including a view in the middle of the old town taken from the top of the Transporter Bridge, showing St Hilda's Church and the old Town Hall.

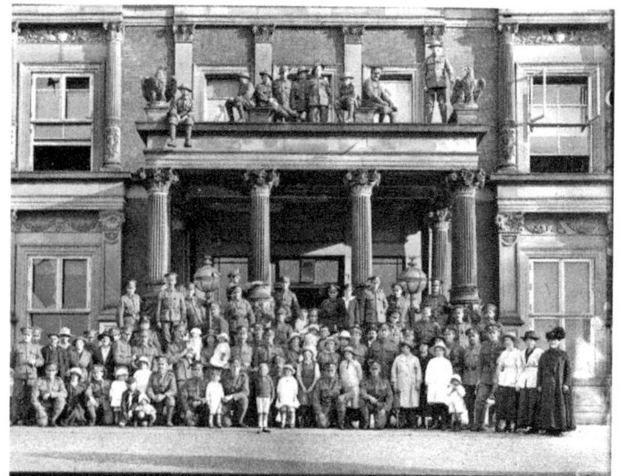

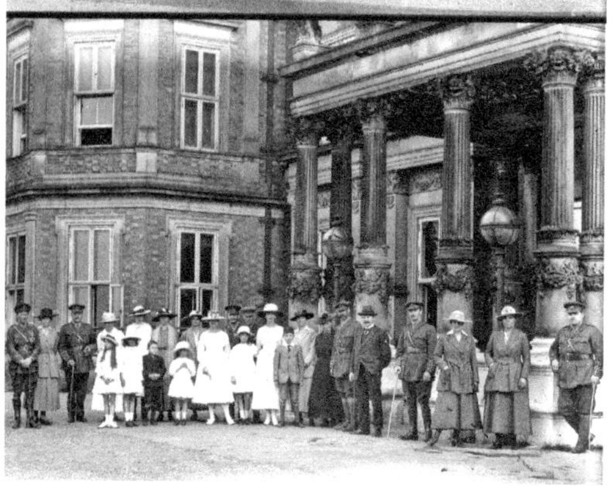

Left: An appeal went out from the Mayor of Middlesbrough on 7 December 1914 for more men to serve in the army. Following an enthusiastic meeting on 6 January 1915, 200 soldiers of the 12th Battalion Yorkshire Regiment went to Marton Hall for preliminary training. These images show soldiers gathered at the Hall along with their families. At this time the Hall, once a residence of some grandeur, had been unoccupied for some years and the outer fabric at least seems to have been in need of some attention.

Below: Like many other communities across the country, Middlesbrough joined in the official 'Peace Celebration' held over the weekend of 18, 19 and 20 July 1919, led by the mayor, Councillor J.S. Calvert. A commemorative programme produced at the time gives full details of the celebration. The first day was for children, while the Saturday was 'Peace Day' when events included the presentation of a tank by Brigadier General Blair to the mayor, who received it on behalf of the Corporation, as seen here.

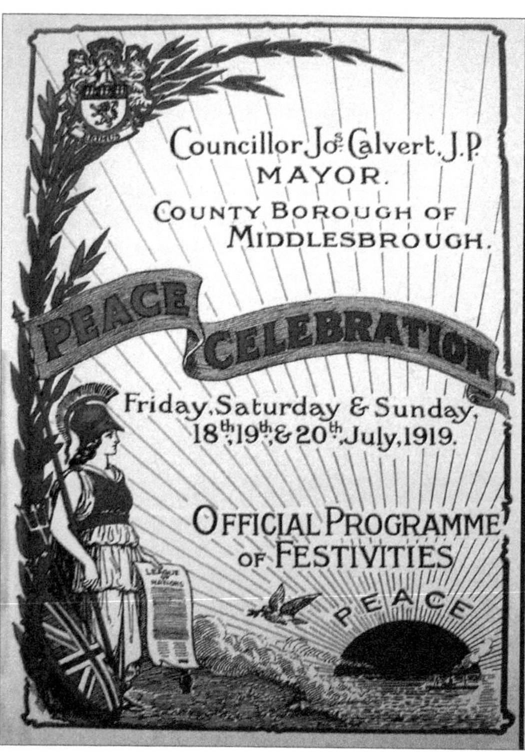

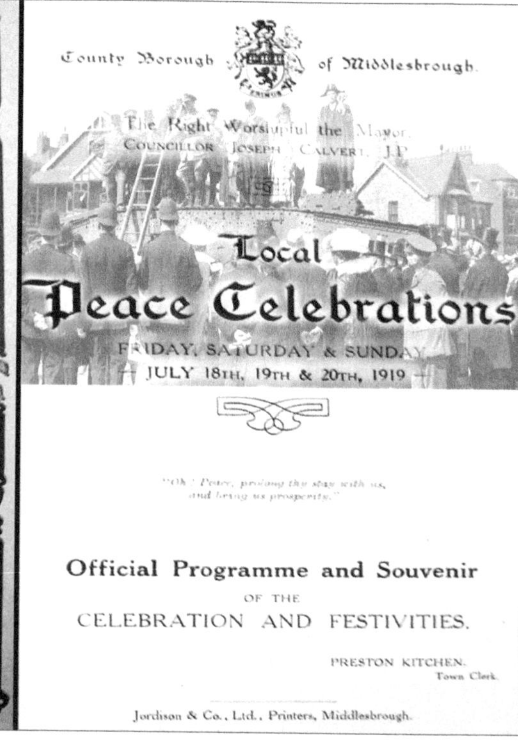

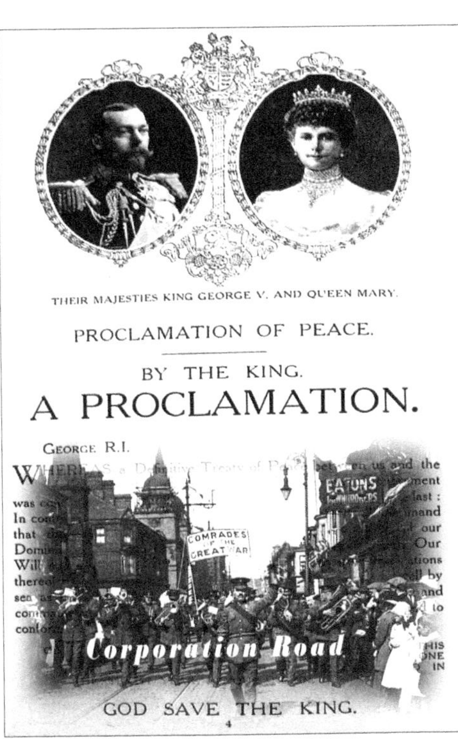

THEIR MAJESTIES KING GEORGE V. AND QUEEN MARY.

PROCLAMATION OF PEACE.

BY THE KING.

A PROCLAMATION.

GEORGE R.I.

WHEREAS a Definitive Treaty of Peace between us and the [...]

GOD SAVE THE KING.

4

COPY OF RESOLUTION

Passed at a Meeting of the Middlesbrough Town Council, held on
Tuesday, the 8th day of July, 1919.

The Right Worshipful the Mayor of Middlesbrough
(Councillor Joseph Calvert, J.P.)
in the Chair.

SIGNING OF PEACE TREATY —Ordered unanimously
that We, the Mayor, Aldermen and Burgesses of the County
Borough of Middlesbrough, in Council assembled, desire to place on
record our deep sense of satisfaction that the World-wide War, in
which the British Empire has been engaged along with her Allies
against Germany and her Allies since August, 1914, was brought to
a victorious conclusion by the Treaty of Peace, which was signed at
Versailles on the 28th of June, 1919.

We greatly rejoice at the triumph of Arms of the Sons of our
Empire at home and from overseas, and those of our Allies, in this
unparalleled struggle for Freedom and Liberty.

We are deeply conscious of the inestimable sacrifice made
by those who have given their lives [...]

We [...] Right Hon.
D. Lloyd George [...] and of
those associated [...] a just
and lasting [...]

Town Clerk.

5

Above: Also included in the programme
was a Proclamation of Peace from King
George V and a resolution passed by
Middlesbrough Town Council on 5 July
1919. Highlights on Saturday included
the march of the regimental band of the
9th Battalion of the Yorkshire Regiment,
seen here marching along Corporation
Road. At 10 a.m. Lieutenant Colonel R.S.
Hart presented the regiment's colours to
the mayor at the Town Hall, watched by a
large crowd.

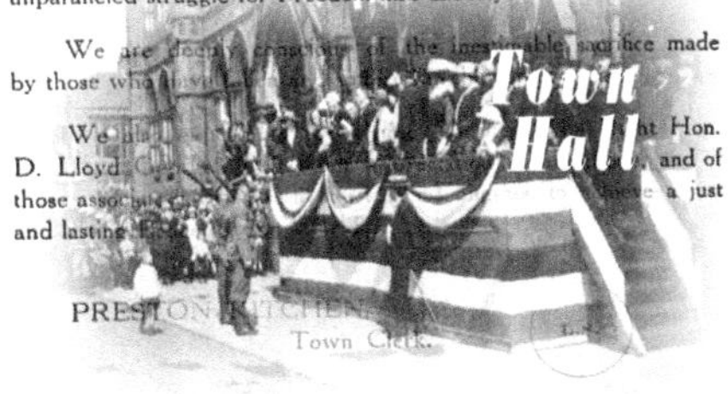

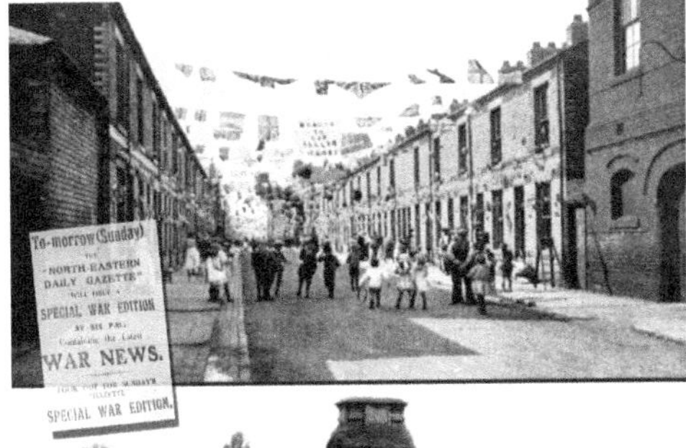

Right: Many streets in the town held
their own celebrations, including Beech
Street, as shown in the upper image. In
contrast to the celebration of peace, the
remembrance of the dead culminated
in the unveiling of the town's official,
permanent war memorial on land opposite
the Dorman Museum on 11 November
1922. These images show the dedication
of the 34ft-high cenotaph memorial and
the placing of the flags. Over 3,000 names
were recorded on the bronze name plates
seen close to the park gates.

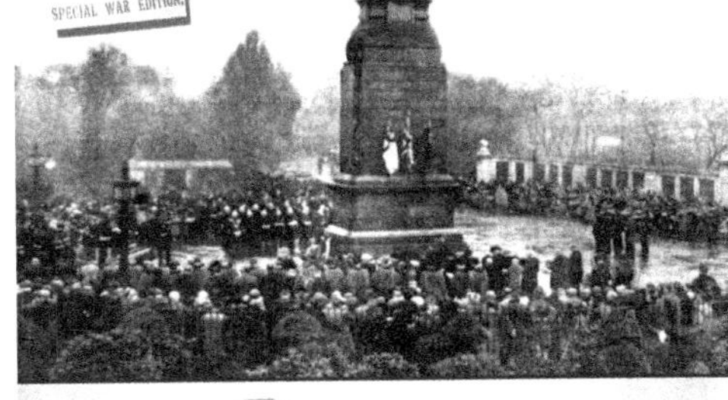

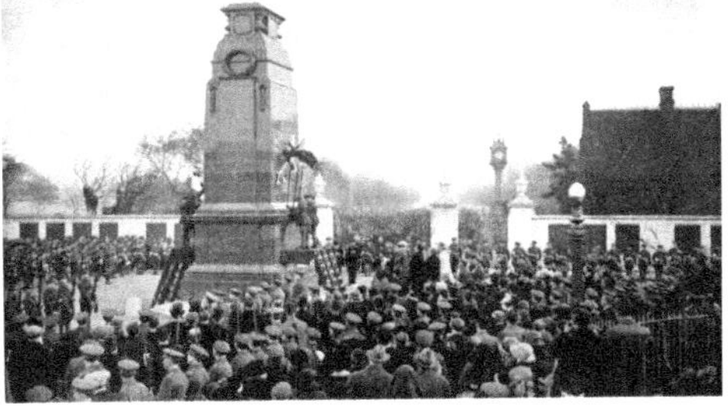

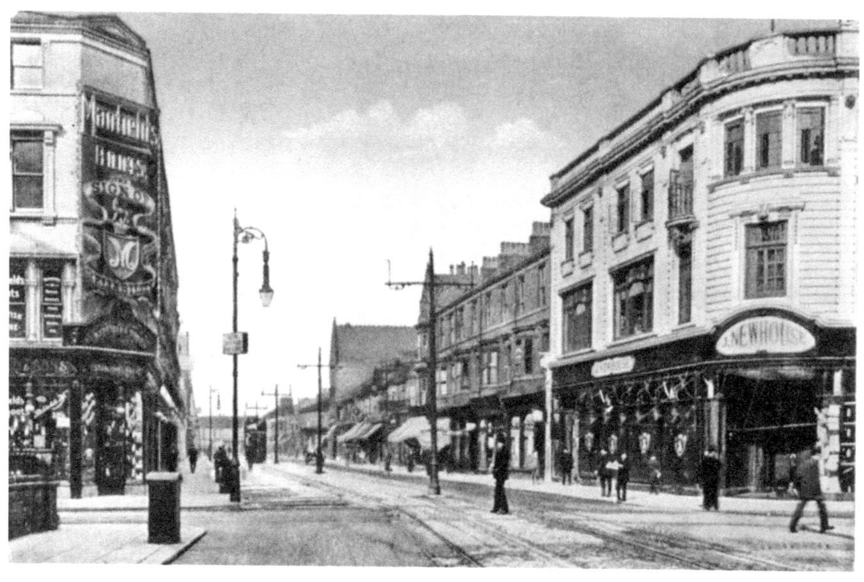

John Newhouse's Department Store in 1923. This building replaced the King's Head Hotel in 1912 when the store moved from Albert Road. On the left is Manfield's Boots Store, which closed in 1923 to make way for Binns. Beyond Newhouse's is the United Presbyterian Church on the corner of Hill Street. Built in 1865, the final service in the church was held on 27 July 1919. It then became the Scala Cinema, eventually closing on 8 April 1961. A distant tram travels down Newport Road on its route to Norton Green.

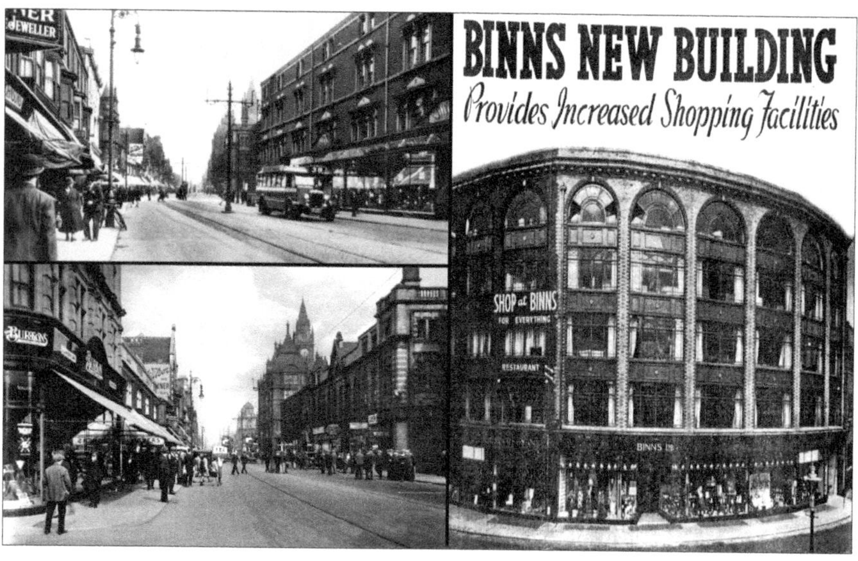

These views show the corner of Corporation Road and Linthorpe Road in the early 1930s. Binns has become one of Middlesbrough's flagship stores since its opening in 1923 on the site of Manfield's Boots Store. The premises were greatly extended in 1937, as seen here. The building was burnt down in a spectacular blaze on 27 March 1942, leaving only the outer shell. The left upper image shows a bus passing the store, while the lower image is from outside Binns store looking down towards the Town Hall and the Empire Theatre.

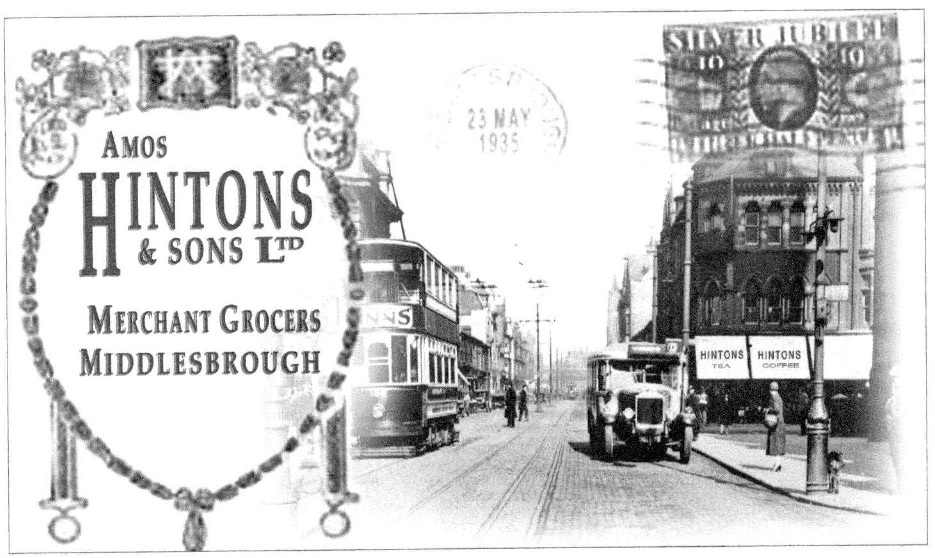

A commemorative envelope from 1935 reflects the esteem in which Hintons & Sons Ltd were held. The image shows the flagship store in the group on the corner of Albert Road and Corporation Road, where they had been since the 1890s. Amos Hinton had died in 1919 but his name lived on through the shops until the latter years of the twentieth century when the business was sold.

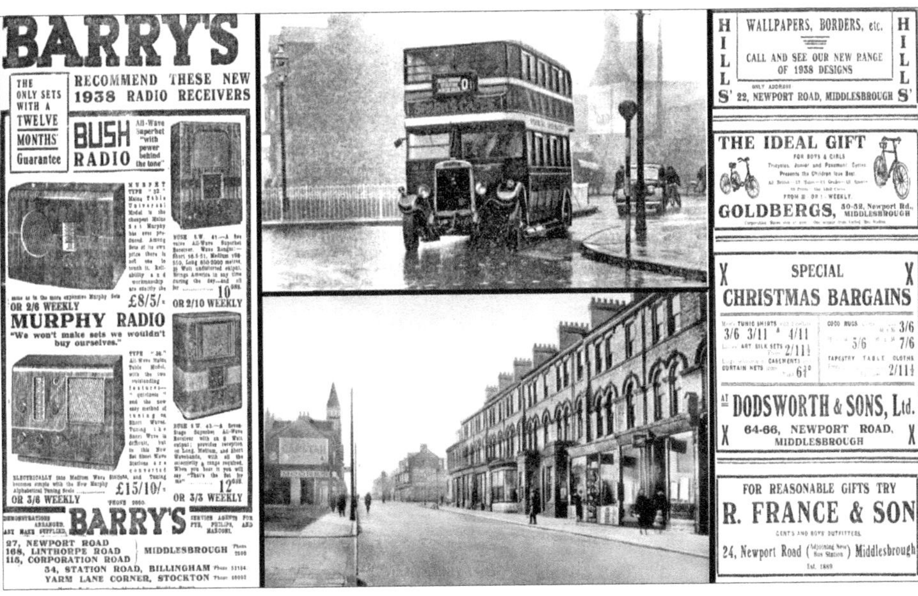

Newport Road, seen here in the late 1930s, remained part of the main routes west to Stockton. The upper image shows a Middlesbrough Corporation bus, the 'O' service, on its way to North Ormesby from Norton Green. It is passing what was then a new roundabout at the approach to Newport Bridge. This roundabout had caused a lot of controversy as it was considered too big! Cecil Gorman, Borough Engineer at that time, maintained that the roundabout was there to stop overtaking and slow down traffic and so he was 'more than satisfied with it'. The advertisements are from a promotion advertising some of the shops based in Newport Road in the mid-1930s.

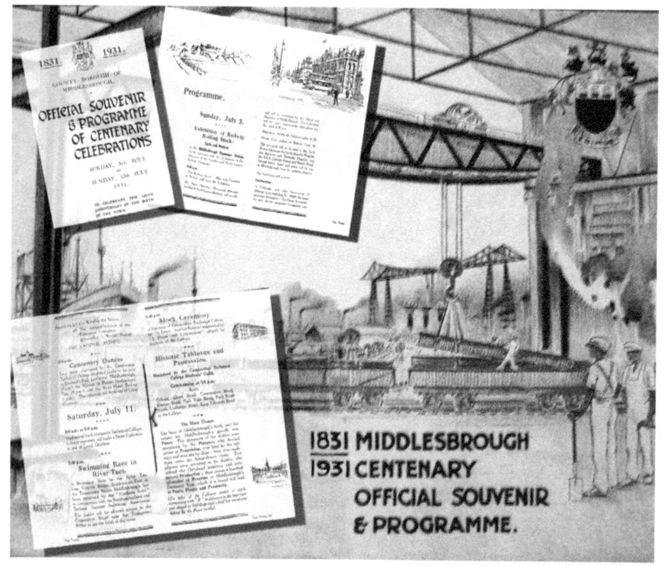

The official centenary of the town took place in 1931 and this is the commemorative programme produced to mark the event. The Centenary Celebrations were held from 5-12 July and were a mixture of reflections on the town's history and pure entertainment. Events included an exhibition of rolling stock from the NER, another of material relating to the history of the town in the Central Library, a 'Sports for Children' event, Garden Party and a swimming race in the River Tees. The week culminated in a 'Historic Tableaux and Procession' and a 'Grand Air Pageant'.

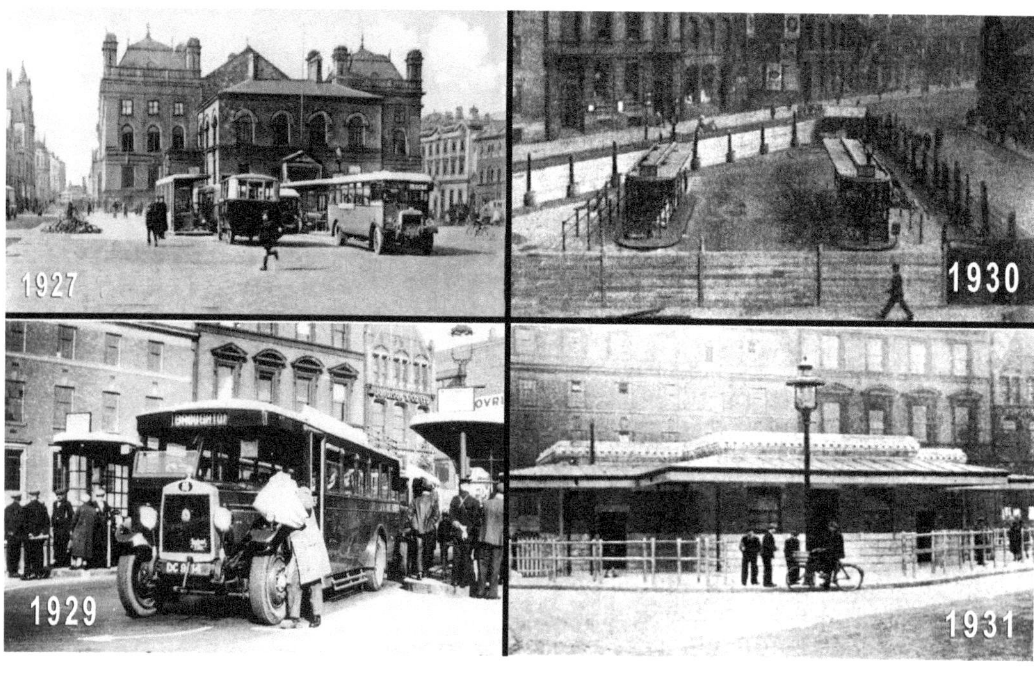

A bus station first opened at the Exchange in 1925. After Middlesbrough Tramways Committee took control of the bus station on 21 January 1930 they quickly decided that the site required further development which would require demolishing the previous facilities. The original bus station is shown here in 1927 and 1929; the other images show the site surrounded by hoardings ready to be knocked down and the new bus station, which was completed on 6 March 1931. As new housing was now being built some distance from the town, the Corporation services, which operated from the Exchange, became increasingly important.

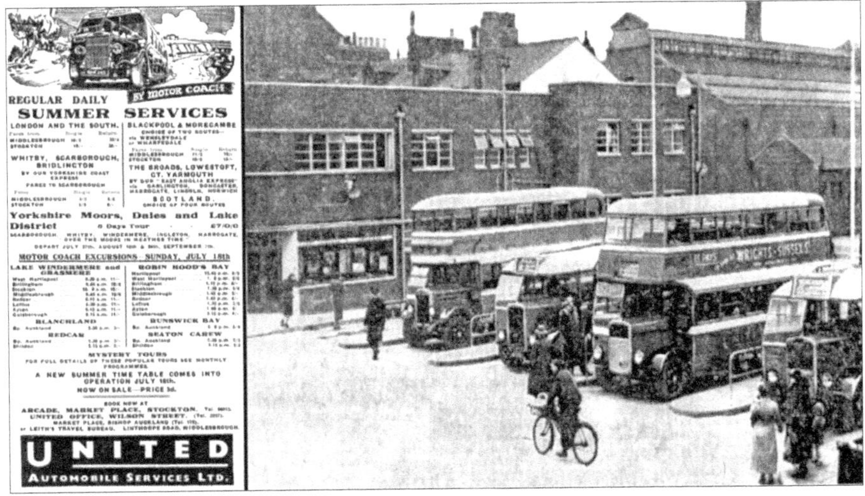

The new United Bus Station shortly after it opened in 1937. Building the terminus had meant the demolition of several properties which had been there since the 1860s, but contemporary newspaper reports approved of the new terminus, calling it a great asset for the community, bringing more people into this part of the town and brightening up a 'very gloomy area'. Previously the United buses had operated from the Exchange Bus Station.

This aerial view of Middlesbrough in 1934 shows the main centre of the town with some important features marked in the annotation. The pattern of the streets is shown along with the density of the housing in this area – although it is a great improvement upon that found in the old town. This was still an era when many people lived close to the centre of the town, although some were already moving away from the town centre to new estates like Brambles Farm built in 1929.

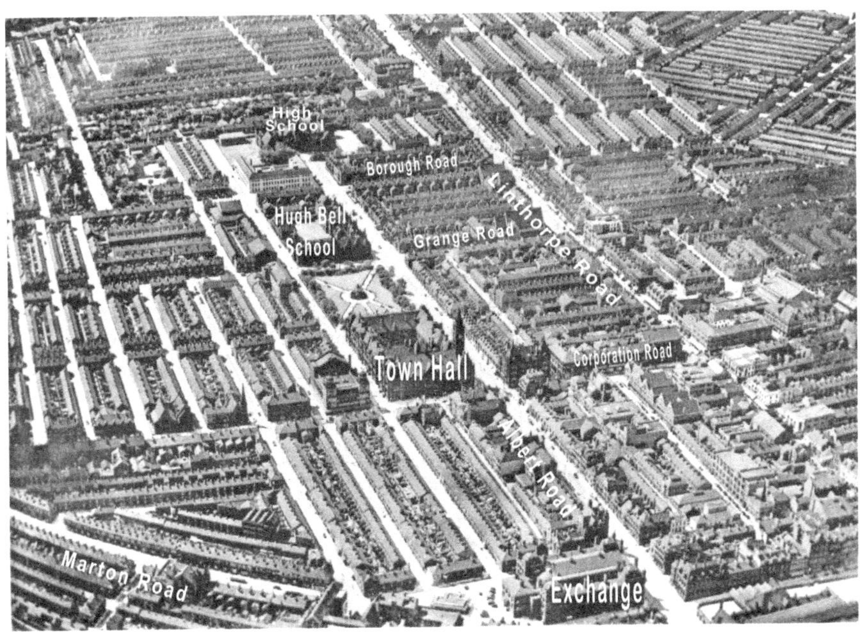

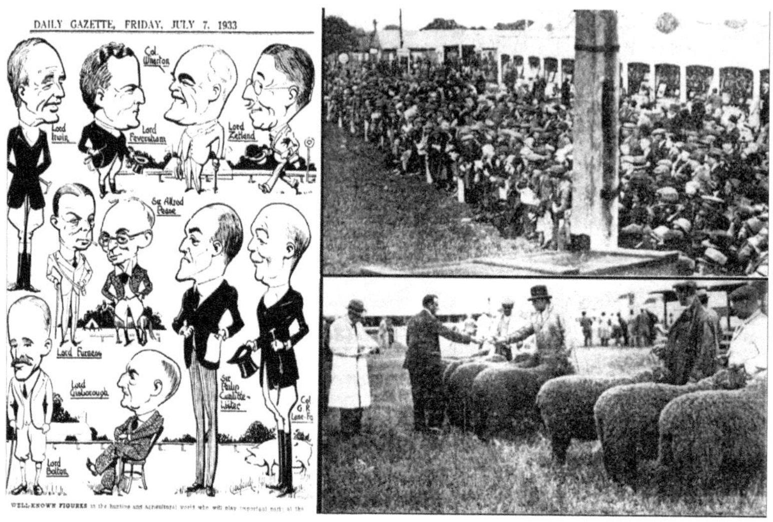

The ninety-third Great Yorkshire Show was held from 11-13 July 1933, on a 100-acre field at Prissick Base – only the third time Middlesbrough had hosted the event, the other occasions being 1892 and 1906. Caricatures of some of the leading figures behind the event are shown here, as are crowds at the show watching the sheep judging. Hosting the Great Yorkshire Show proved to be a coup for the town especially as they won a Gold Cup for setting a new record attendance; 52,232 people attended, beating the previous record, set at Leeds, by over 3,000 people. The Show Secretary, A.S. Cavers, said that despite an image of smoke and grime, the show at Middlesbrough had been held in one of the finest settings in its history, on a 'marvellous site ... framed by nearby hills bathed in sunshine'.

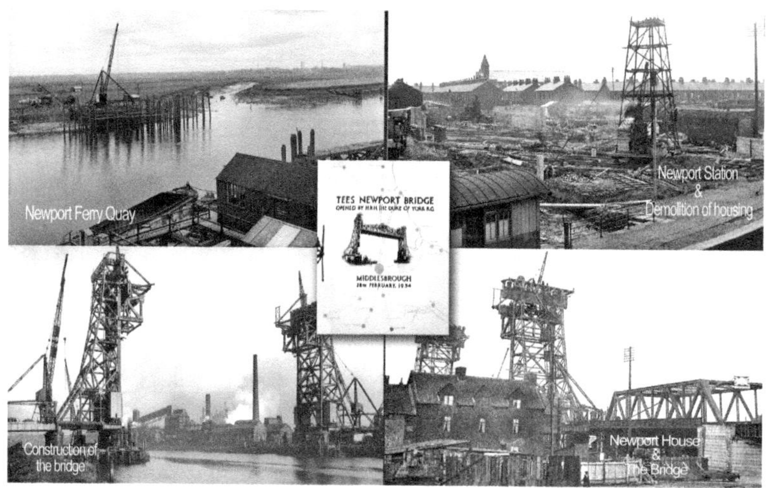

The need for a bridge linking the town with the rapidly developing industrial area north of the river had been recognised in the early 1920s. Having decided upon a bridge at Newport, the Tees Bridge Act was given Royal Assent on 4 June 1930. These images show the construction of the bridge at various stages together with the commemorative programme marking the opening in 1934. Building the bridge meant the demolition of several houses in Calvert Street and Samuelson Street as well as the buildings at Newport Station. It is interesting to see old Newport House, the granaries built by the Hustler family in the seventeenth century and now private residences, although soon after this they were demolished. The images also provide an excellent view of the Ironmasters District.

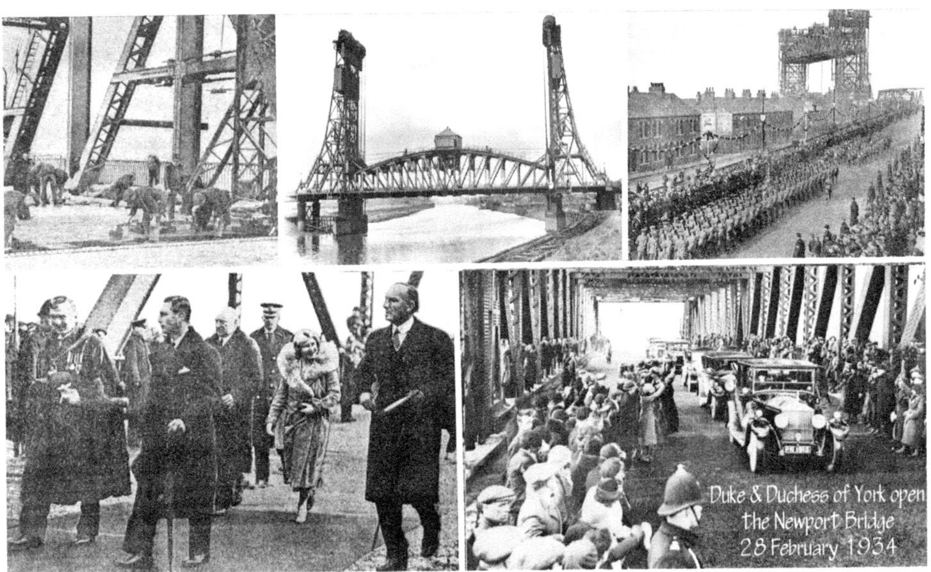

The Duke and Duchess of York came to open Newport Bridge on 28 February 1934. The upper images show workmen finishing preparations for the visit, the completed bridge and the Durham Light Infantry marching up the approach road to the bridge to be presented to the royal party. The Duke, accompanied by Alfred Cooper, Mayor of Middlesbrough, is shown lower left walking across the bridge after the civic and religious proceedings. Lower right is the royal car travelling over the new bridge taking the royal party back to Wynyard Park, where they were guests of the Marquess of Londonderry. This was a popular visit with large crowds throughout the day as the royal party travelled through Stockton, Thornaby and Acklam onto Linthorpe Road. A sign of the times is that the only problem faced by police was the over-enthusiastic cheering of the girls from Kirby Grammar School.

By the 1920s Middlesbrough Town Hall was well known as an entertainment venue. One memorable performance given there was by Rachmaninoff on 23 November 1933, when he played some of his own works as well as works by Beethoven, Schumann and Schubert. He was given rapturous applause and a standing ovation at the end of the recital. At an interview afterwards he admitted to being very pleased at the warmth shown to him by the Middlesbrough audience. A very different style of entertainment came with the opening of the Gaumont Cinema in Linthorpe Road on 30 March 1931. This was performed by the Mayor and Mayoress of Middlesbrough watched by large crowds. The opening programme of films is shown here.

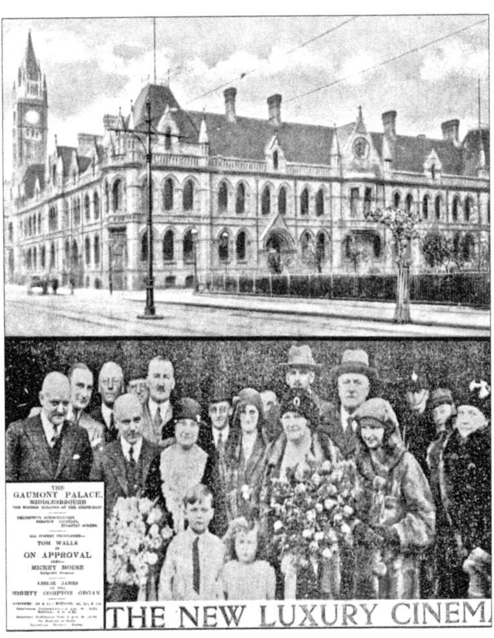

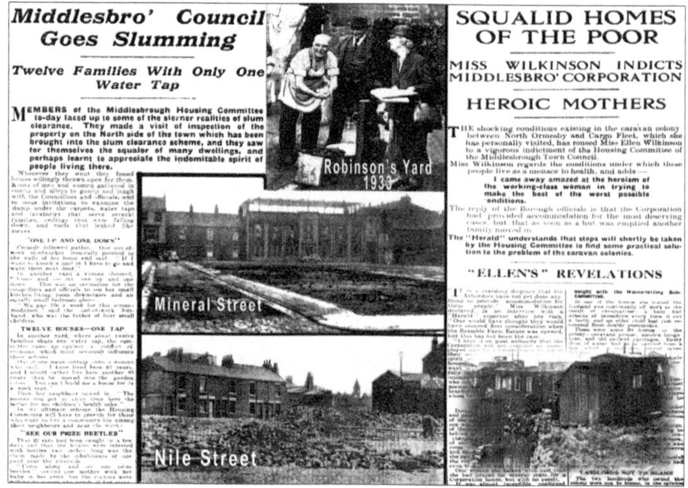

Above: Slum clearances continued with the Nile Street clearance in the early 1930s, work first suggested nearly thirty years previously. The clearance is shown here together with similar work in Mineral Street. Property owners argued that the clearance was destroying good property as well as bad and that the compensation was inadequate. However, medical evidence overwhelmingly supported the work; the death rate in the old town exceeded that of the rest of the borough by 50 per cent and deaths from TB were double. The top image shows two councillors observing a resident of Robinson's Yard, off Lower East Street, using a communal water tap in 1933. Ellen Wilkinson (Labour MP for Middlesbrough 1923-31) continually fought for improvements. It was Ellen who highlighted the plight of the 'caravan colony' at Cargo Fleet, where those unable to obtain housing were forced to live in caravans on a muddy site often in horrendous conditions.

Below: During the 1920s and '30s changes continued across the town as old lanes were brought into service as modern roads, old buildings were demolished and new ones erected. The widening of Green Lane dates from this period as does the building of a well designed new property at Netherby Farm close to Slip Inn Bank, shown here on 17 February 1932. Blue Hall, on the corner of Burlam Road, was demolished. It had been built in 1870 on the site of an earlier building and had been used as a hostel for women before becoming a private residence again. Some of the large Victorian residences were also being demolished. 'Ravenscroft', built in 1873 on Marton Road close to the junction with Clairville Road, is shown here during demolition in January 1936.

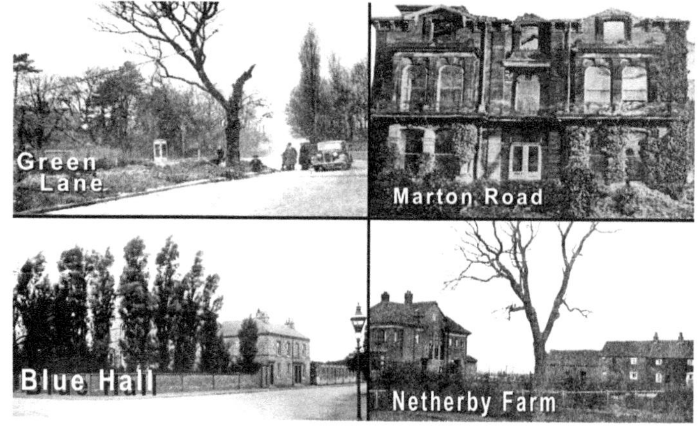

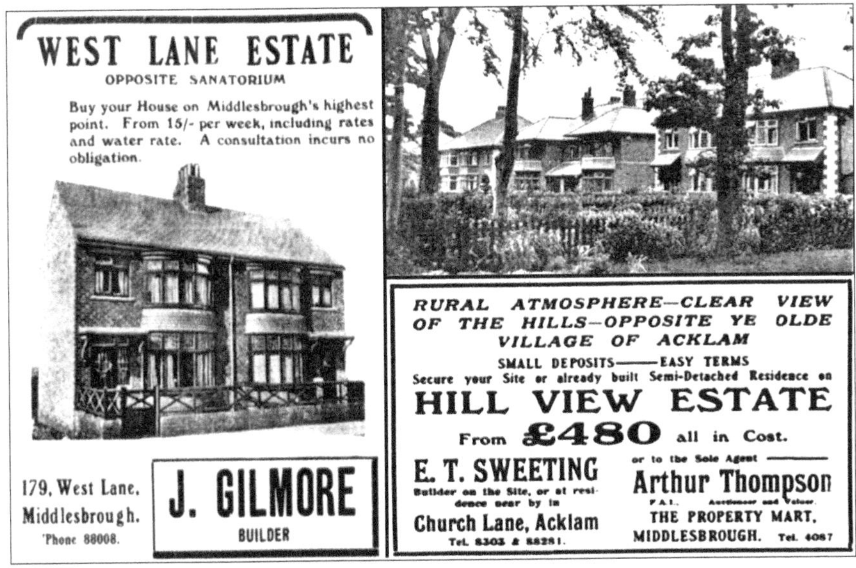

Inspired to a degree by the Garden City Movement, Middlesbrough's first council estate, Acklam Garden City was built in 1919 as part of the Corporation's efforts to redress a lack of suitable housing. Other estates followed, including Whinney Banks in 1929, despite some local opposition from people in private residences in the Cambridge Road area. By the 1930s building was ongoing south of the old village, much of it by builders eager to cash in on an increasingly mobile middle-class who wanted to own property. As is evident in the advertisements, builders emphasised the rural nature of the location when marketing their properties.

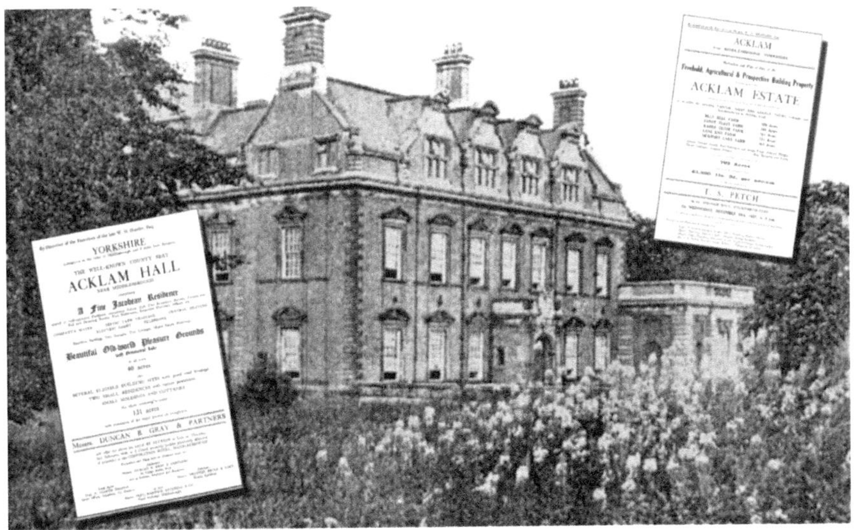

When William Hustler died in the 1920s the Acklam Hall Estate was put up for sale. This took place on 14 December 1927, with the sale of Acklam Hall following on 2 February 1928; the insets show the catalogues for the sales. The Hall was acquired by Middlesbrough Corporation for £11,500, and after some modifications, opened as a grammar school for boys, taking in its first pupils in September 1935. Today the building is no longer used as a school but remains the town's only Grade I listed building.

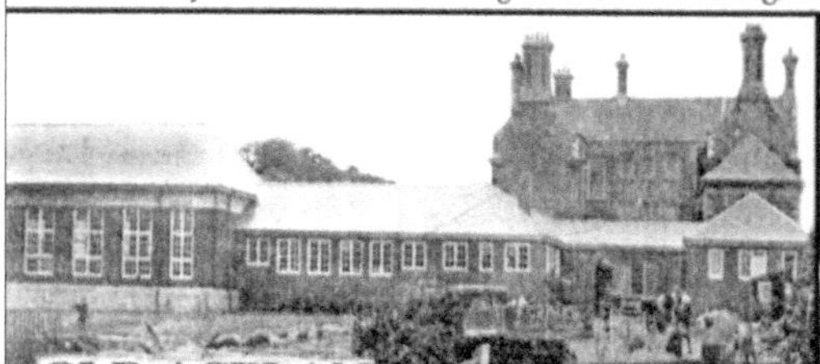

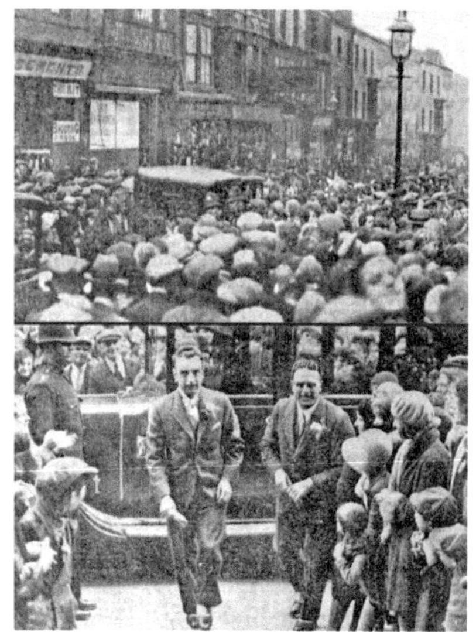

OLD ACKLAM BELL

TO BE USED IN NEW SCHOOL

CONVERTED HALL

The quaint old bell at Acklam Hall, Middlesbrough, which in the old days of the Hustler family used to summon those living on the estate to work and which rang again when labour was over, will very shortly now call schoolboys to their lessons.

In the work of reconstructing this large and handsome red brick mansion into a school for higher education, the bell was found and has been cleaned up and restored near to the position on one of the outer walls of the building.

A little of the history of this old bell was told to a "Herald" representative on Wednesday by Mr. P. B. Haswell, the architect to the Middlesbrough Education Committee, who is superintending the conversion work at Acklam Hall.

BEAUTIFUL TONE

He said that when the bell was found and the part it had played in the life of the Acklam estate became known, it was agreed that it would be appropriate to use it as a school bell.

" The bell has the date, 1815, stamped

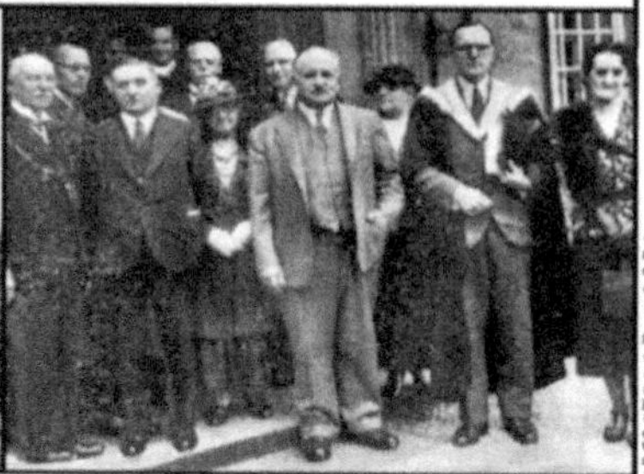

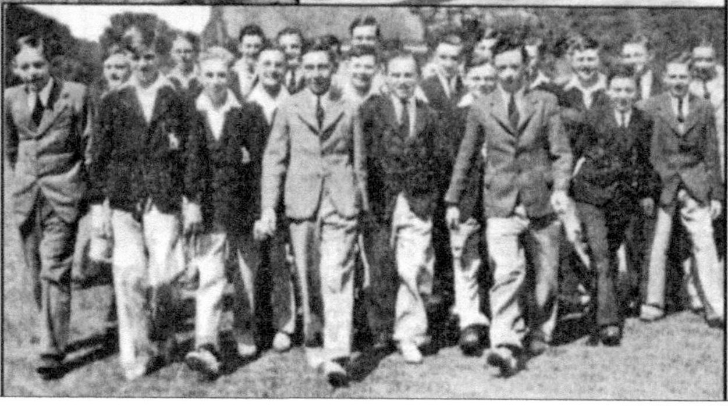

ACKLAM HALL SCHOOL

OFFICIAL OPENING

TO-MORROW

HISTORICAL LINK

Middlesbrough's newest secondary school, Acklam Hall, which has had already one year of school life, was officially opened on Thursday by the chairman of the Education Committee (Councillor J. W. Brown).

The Mayor (Councillor A. Elstrop) presided over the ceremony, and after a description of the building by Alderman A. Weatherhead and a dedicatory prayer by Canon W. T. Lawson, Councillor Brown declared the school officially open. An inspection of this former seat of the Hustlers took place by the invited guests, and was followed by a display of physical training by the boys.

A beautifully illustrated brochure issued by the Education Committee, which indicates the delightful surroundings under which the scholars are taught here, states that the story of Acklam goes back to a time before the Norman Conquest. Although there is scant record of events in those early days, it is known that in the reign of Edward the Confessor, the manor of Acklam, tended by descendants of former Danish invaders, was of great worth. Acklam appears five times in Domesday Book.

HUSTLER FAMILY'S HOME

The manor of Acklam had many owners until 1812, when the Hustler family began a connection which lasted until 1928. The present Acklam Hall was built by Sir William Hustler, and the ceiling at the head of the beautiful stairs bears the date 1683.

Giving details of the history of the manor, the brochure states: " With the death of the late Mr. and Mrs. Hustler the hall ceased to be a family seat. But though the name of the owner has gone into history, it is a happy circumstance that their grand old home will not suffer the lot which has befallen so many stately houses, even in Cleveland, to fall into disrepair and decay. As a secondary school it will receive a new life to foster within its walls a spirit of learning."

The hall and 56 acres of ground were purchased by the Middlesbrough Education Committee, in 1928, for £11,500. The contract price for the adaptation and extensions was £17,473. Furniture and equipment have cost approximately £1,500.

In 1929, when the intake at Middlesbrough Boys High School rose to 570 pupils, it was so cramped that classes had to be taught in the assembly hall. As a solution it was decided that Acklam Hall would be converted into a grammar school for boys. The necessary alterations, including some new buildings (see top image), were completed only weeks before the first intake of 231 pupils were due to start. Twelve rooms were large enough for classrooms but some of the smaller bedrooms had to have partition walls removed. The old dining room became the art room while a gymnasium was built in the Hall's old garage and the stables were converted into science rooms. The old bell from the Acklam Estate was retained as a link with the Hustler family. The official opening took place on 23 July 1936. The other images here show the headteacher, Mr R. Gill, with guests at Speech Day in 1937 and pupils arriving for the same event in 1939.

Footballers have always received a lot of adulation and media attention, as shown in these images from June 1931 when Middlesbrough's England international player, Billy Pease, was married at St Mary's Cathedral in Sussex Street. Large crowds gathered to watch the bridegroom's car arrive and to cheer as Pease left his car accompanied by his best man, international swimmer Jack Hatfield, who was himself regarded as one of the town's sporting heroes.

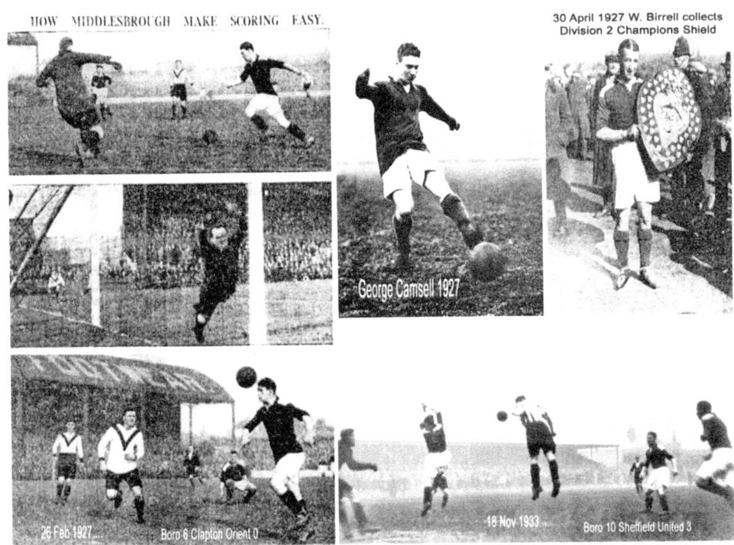

The legendary footballer George Camsell dominated the inter-war years, especially the 1920s, when Middlesbrough was involved in two relegations and promotions. Older fans will remember Camsell scoring a record fifty-nine league goals in 1926/27 as Middlesbrough won the Division Two championship. These images include scenes from that season including Camsell in action and Billy Birrell collecting the championship shield after defeating Reading 5-0 at Ayresome Park on 30 April 1927. Another club record is commemorated here with an image from 18 November 1933 when Middlesbrough beat Sheffield United 10-3, still their highest ever win! Camsell scored four goals that day.

Ayresome Park underwent considerable rebuilding in the 1920s and '30s. Having been promoted back to the First Division, several ground improvements were made, mainly to the West Stand, known then as the 'Workhouse End'. Old wooden railway sleepers were replaced by concrete terracing complete with crash barriers – the stand is shown in 1929 prior to the redevelopment and later when the work was ongoing. The image top right, is remarkable not only because of the amazing score line but because the small stand in the background was the former Main Stand at the previous ground in Linthorpe Road. It was replaced in the mid-1930s by the new South Stand, able to seat 9,000 fans. A roof was also put on the West Stand (Workhouse End) at this time.

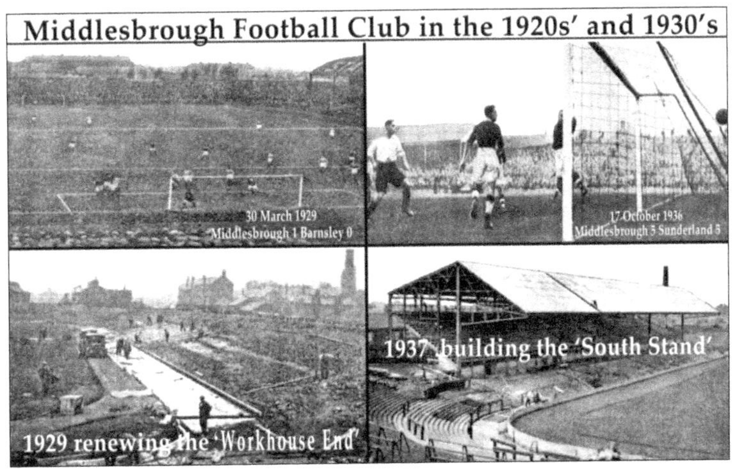

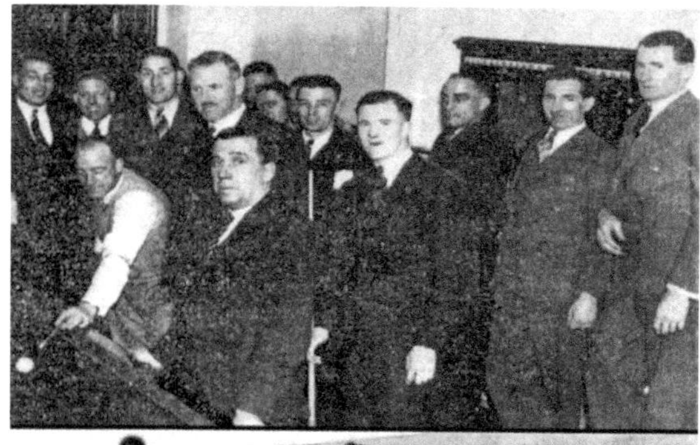

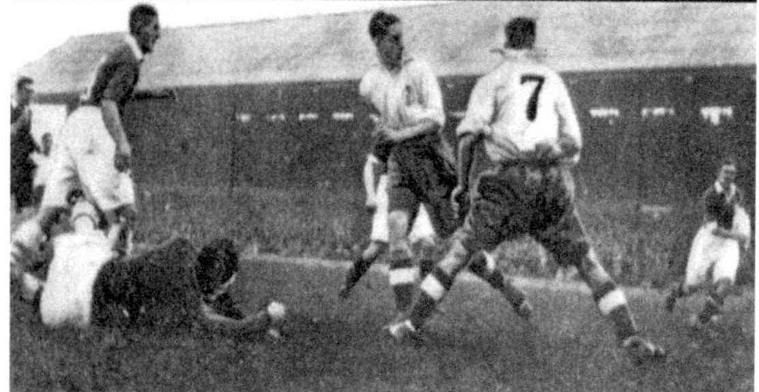

Recognition of the ground improvements at Ayresome Park came in 1937 when, for the first time in twenty-five years, the club hosted an England international. On 17 November they played Wales. The England squad stayed at the Zetland Hotel in Saltburn and are shown on the evening before the game. In the centre is a young Stanley Mathews; while at the front is Charlie Cole, who was also the Middlesbrough trainer at this time. Behind him is Stanley Rous. The game was played on a damp afternoon with England winning 2-1 in front of 30,000 spectators. This is Mathews about to score the winning goal at the Workhouse End. It was to be sixty-five years before another England game was held in Middlesbrough.

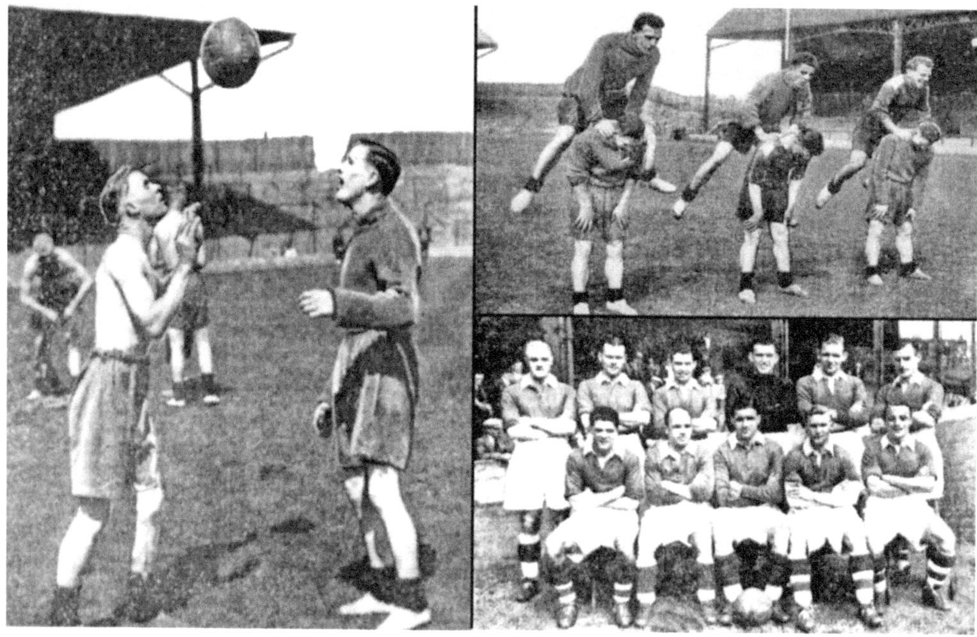

Middlesbrough had a strong team in the late 1930s helped by a young, blonde eighteen-year-old from South Bank St Peter's, Wilf Mannion. Over seventy years later his statue outside the Riverside ground testifies to his status in the club's history. He is seen here in pre-season training with George Wardle. The team photograph was taken in August 1939 before a pre-season friendly with Sunderland. It was to be the last one for over six years. Having lost the opening two games, Middlesbrough drew 2-2 on 2 September before 12,000 fans. When war began the next morning the League was cancelled, and on 23 September the club announced that they were returning season tickets to fans.

April 1939 ...Middlesbrough prepares for war

Preparations for war centred very much on the provision of shelter in the anticipation of the mass bombing of the town. Public air-raid shelters had sprung up all over the town, including these two at Clairville and in Victoria Square, where it had been decided that seven air-raid shelters would be erected for employees from the municipal buildings. In the background is the Town Hall complete with sandbags. Mrs J.C. Williams of 1 Hutton Road was the first person in the town to receive an air-raid shelter when they were issued to householders in April 1939. Councillor Sir W.H. Crosthwaite, Alderman E. Spence and Councillor H. French – as members of the ARP Committee – toured the town on a fire-engine to check on the black-out, ending up on top of Ormesby Bank where they declared it a great success. The shelter images demonstrate the indomitable British spirit; a family pose having decorated their shelter with Union Jack flags while above, Mrs Banks and her neighbour are vacuuming and dusting their street shelter so it would be clean for the next air-raid.

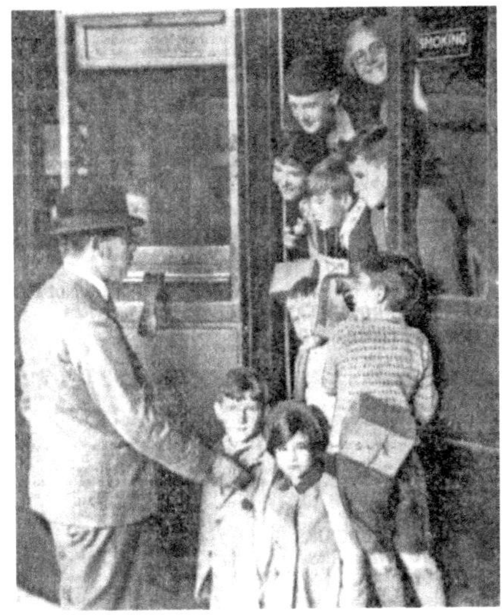

This group of evacuees are being packed off at Middlesbrough railway station for destinations then unknown but which we now know were probably some of the farms and small villages in North Yorkshire. As is usually the case, the experiences of evacuees from Middlesbrough varied. Many people were homesick while others are still in touch, seventy years later, with the family who took them in.

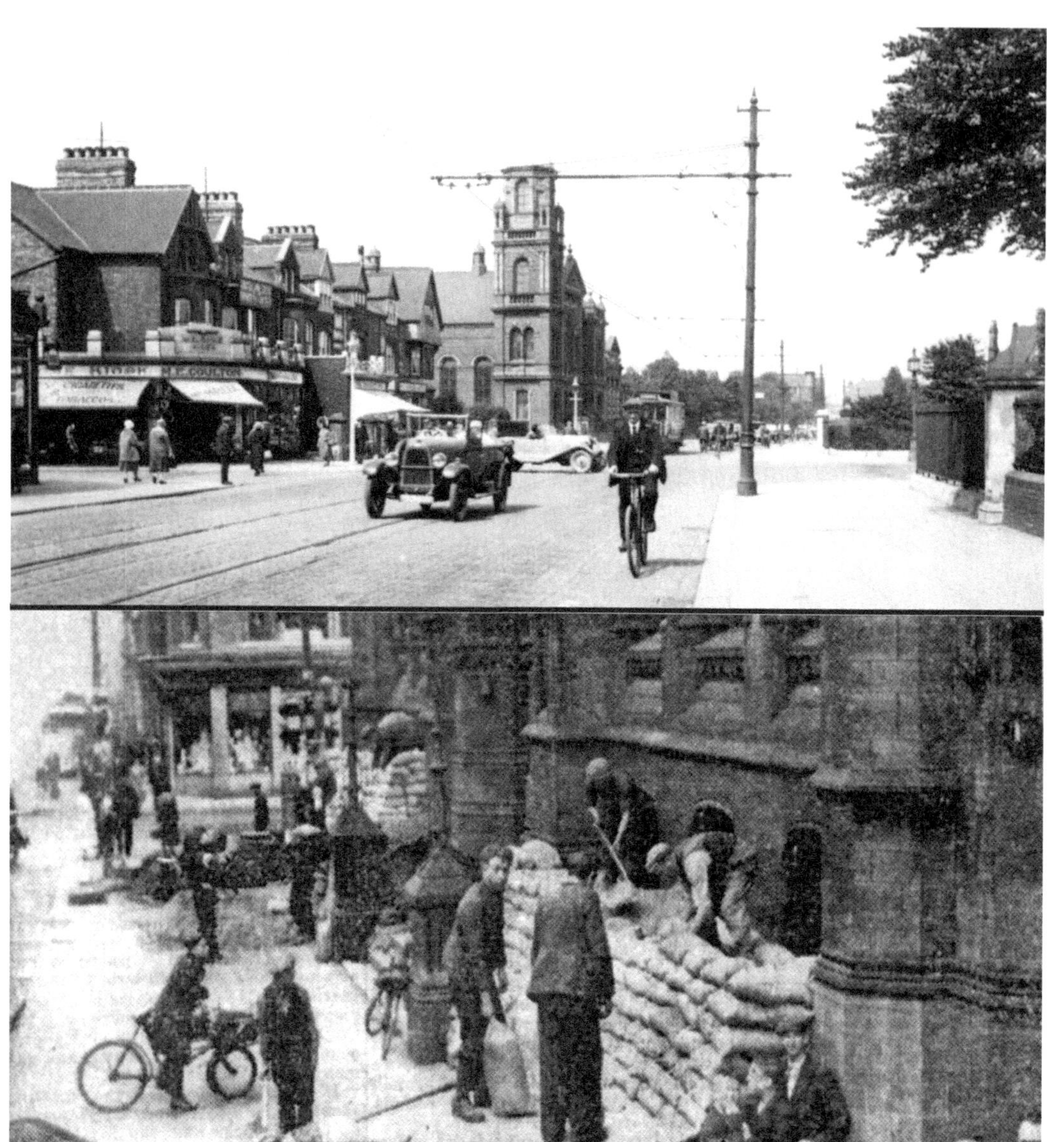

These two images demonstrate the contrast of life in Middlesbrough during the 1930s. The upper image is a peaceful scene showing Linthorpe Road close to the Dorman Museum and the Park Wesleyan Chapel while the image below is from 1938 when, during the Munich Crisis, when there was a general feeling in the town that war was imminent. Local newspapers reported that when volunteers and the ARP Committee had finished assembling 132,000 gas masks at 11 p.m. on 28 September 1938, they burst into cheering and spontaneous singing of the National Anthem. Sandbags were placed around key buildings including the Town Hall Crypt, shown here, as this was to act as the 'nerve-centre' controlling the town's resources in case of any arising emergencies. This view is taken in Albert Road looking towards Hinton's store on Corporation Road.

A CHANGING SCENE

Inspired by the Max Lock survey, a progressive Middlesbrough Council dealt vigorously with the pressing need for housing. Post-war Middlesbrough was all about change. These dramatic images provide a small insight into that world.

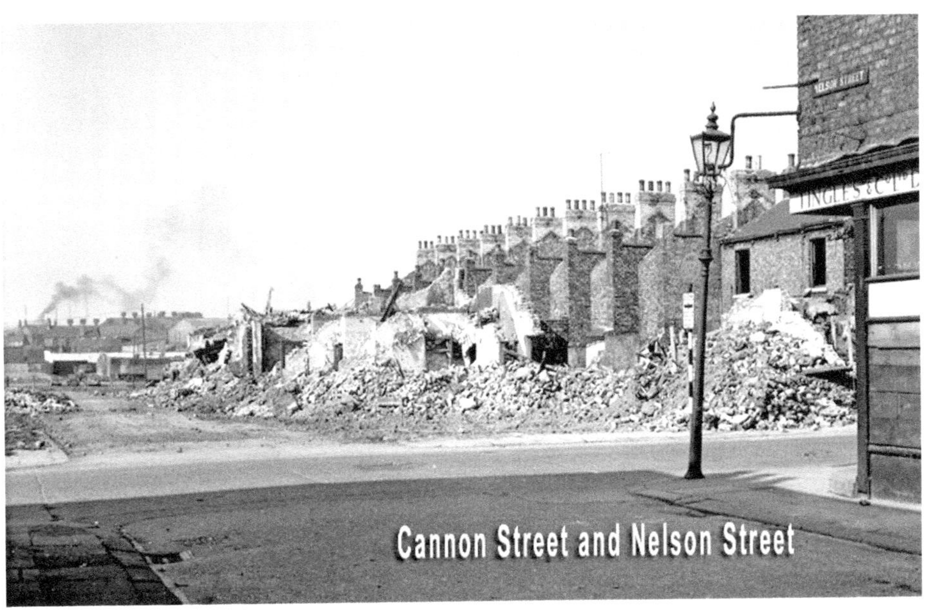

One of the best known streets in the town, Cannon Street, succumbed to the bulldozers in the 1960s, an event which for many took away the heart and soul of their community.

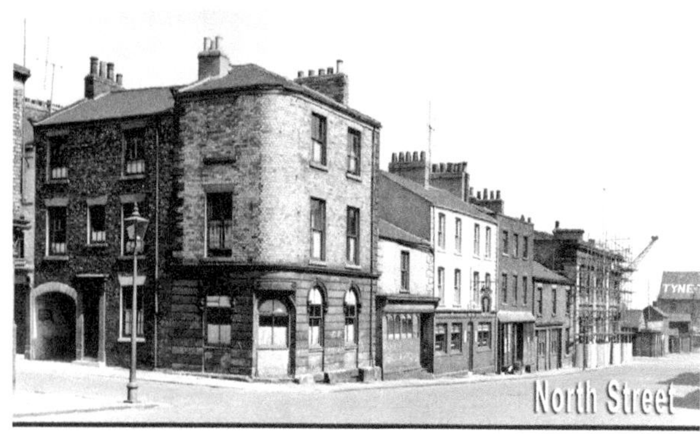

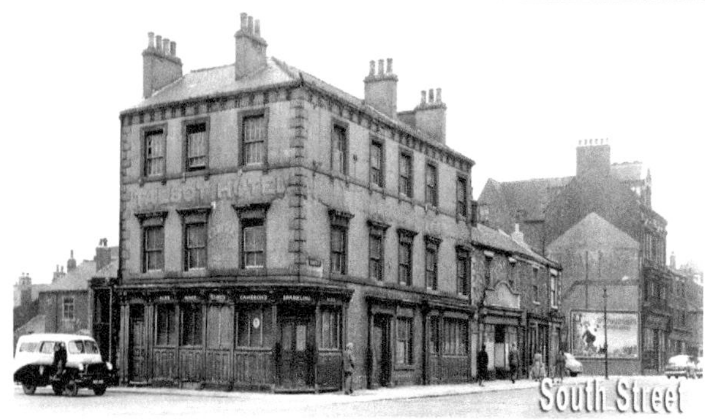

After the Second World War a massive programme of slum clearance began, one which would go on for over two decades. In the old town alone over 4,000 houses would be demolished and new programmes of rebuilding started. As with the clearance of Cannon Street in the 1960s, not everyone would welcome this wholesale demolition. The upper view is from the corner of Dacre Street and North Street looking towards the river, while below across the old Market Square is the Talbot Hotel on the corner of South Street with the site of Amos Hinton's first shop in the distance. Once the hub of the old town, these tumble-down buildings are a poignant reminder of Middlesbrough's early years.

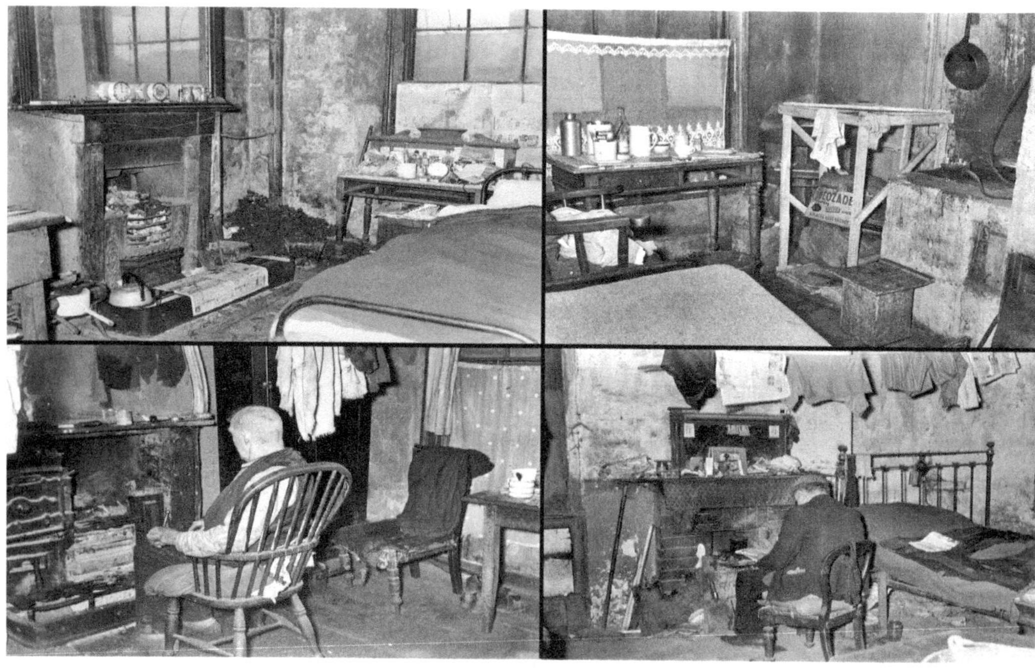

These images from February 1957 show men in their rooms in a large lodging house on the corner of Durham Street and Lower East Street. It is perhaps shocking to see that people were living in conditions more reminiscent of the Victorian era than post-war England but these images show vividly the problems that Middlesbrough Council were fighting hard to eradicate.

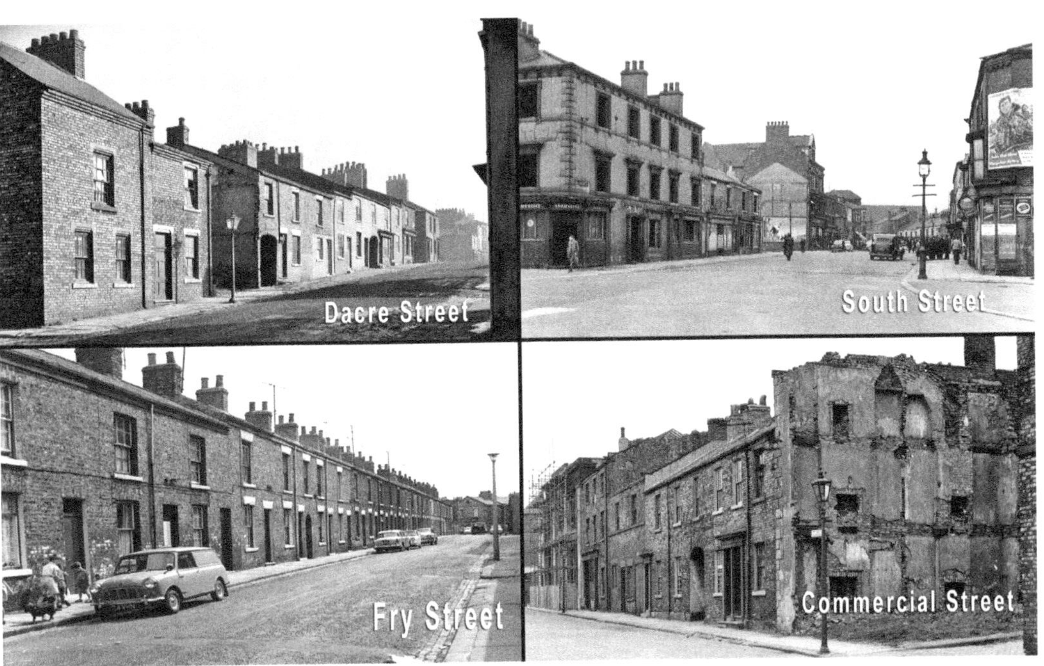

Many of these streets have been featured earlier in this book and it is interesting to compare those images with the views here as they await the arrival of the bulldozers. Fry Street, incidentally, stood on the site of the current Thistle Hotel.

Taken from outside the Steam Packet public house on Stockton Street, this view looks towards West Street, with the corner of Dacre Street visible in the distance. Some small children play outside the corner shop, hardly noticing the cameraman. The demolition is ongoing all around as street by street the area is cleared.

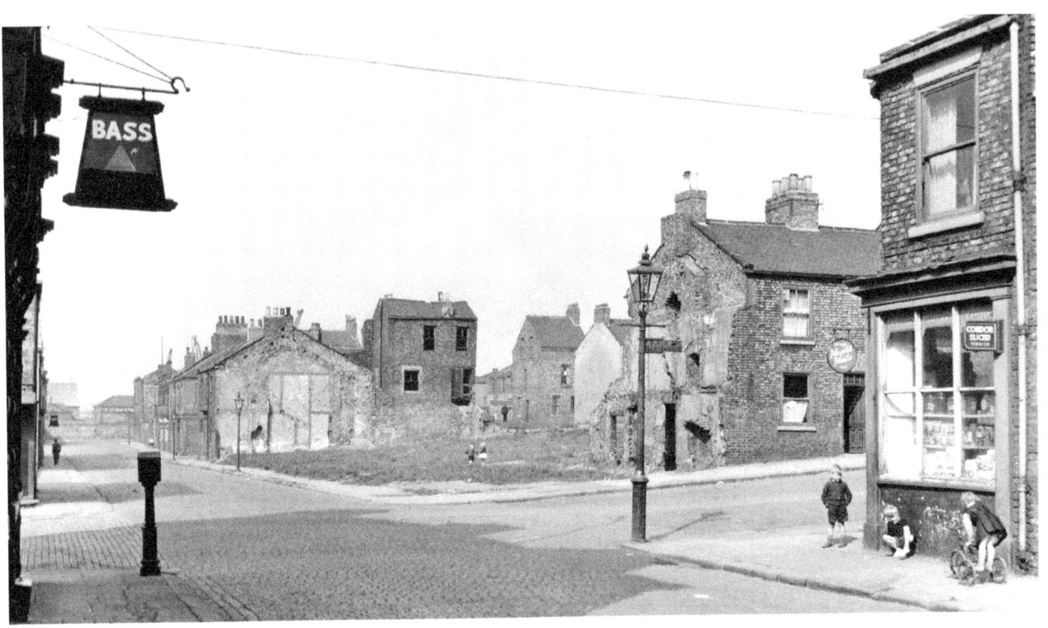

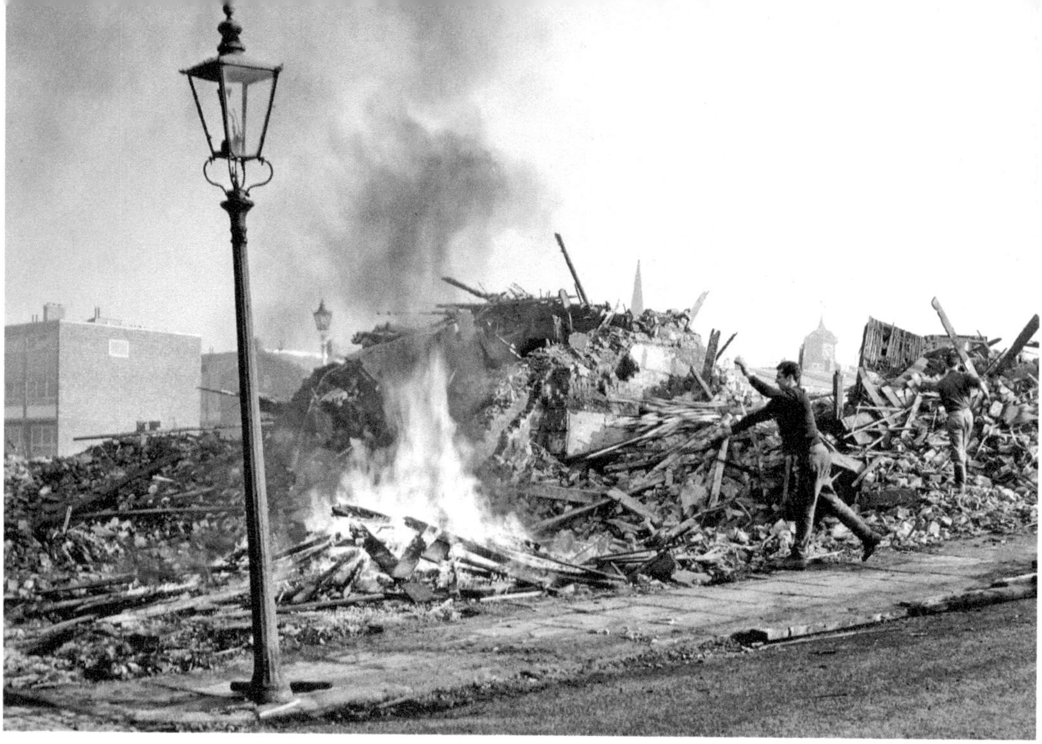

The past is being burnt away on this huge fire of demolished material on Richmond Street. In the distance the top of the old Town Hall is visible as is the spire of St Hilda's Church. In front of these one of the new blocks of housing can be seen.

These houses in Commercial Street had for many years been considered as slum properties: residential housing in very close proximity to commercial premises, built on land close to the river and unable to be properly drained.

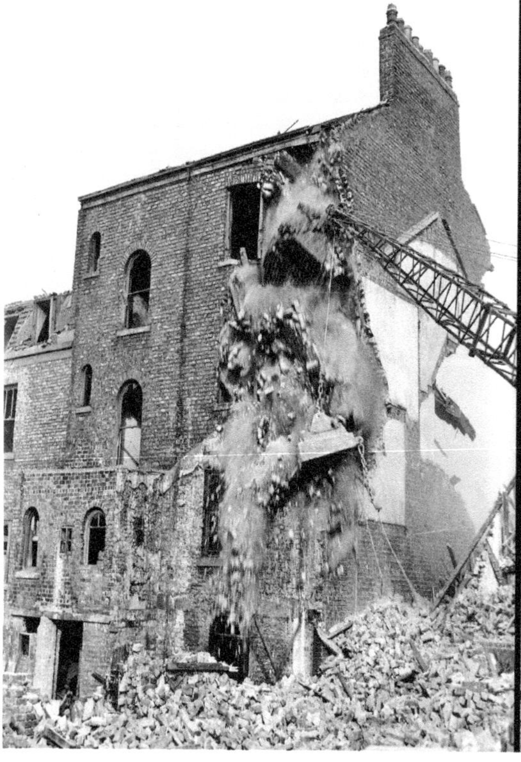

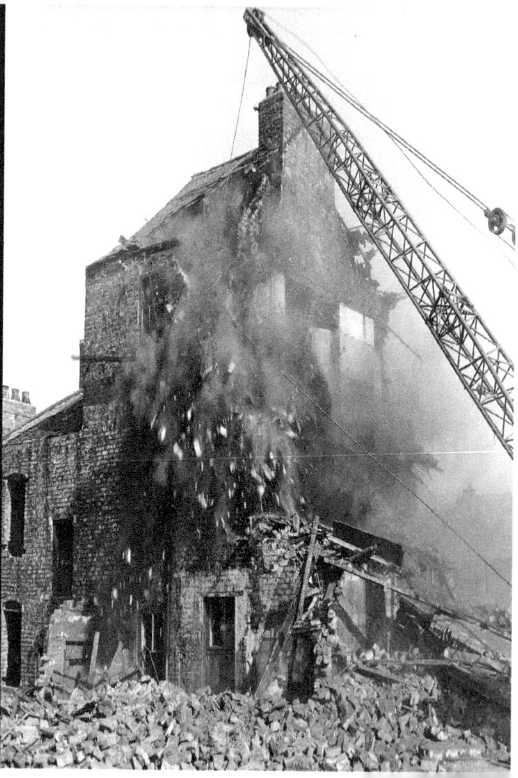

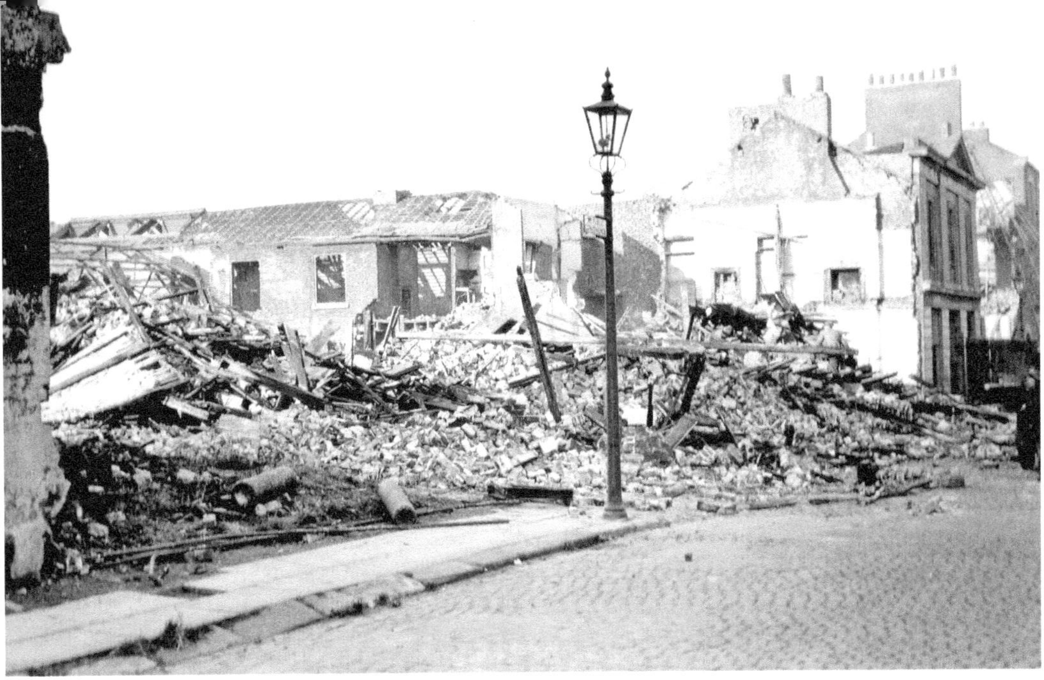

As each property is destroyed bulldozers move in and sweep the debris away. With the previous images still in mind, the sheer scale of the clearances becomes clear as we look at this heap of material piled up in Commercial Street.

By the mid-1960s the demolition of Cannon Street was in full swing, as shown by the following images. This view, dated 15 February 1964, looks towards Boundary Road with Milbank Street on the right – today this would be close to the site of the Sainsbury's store.

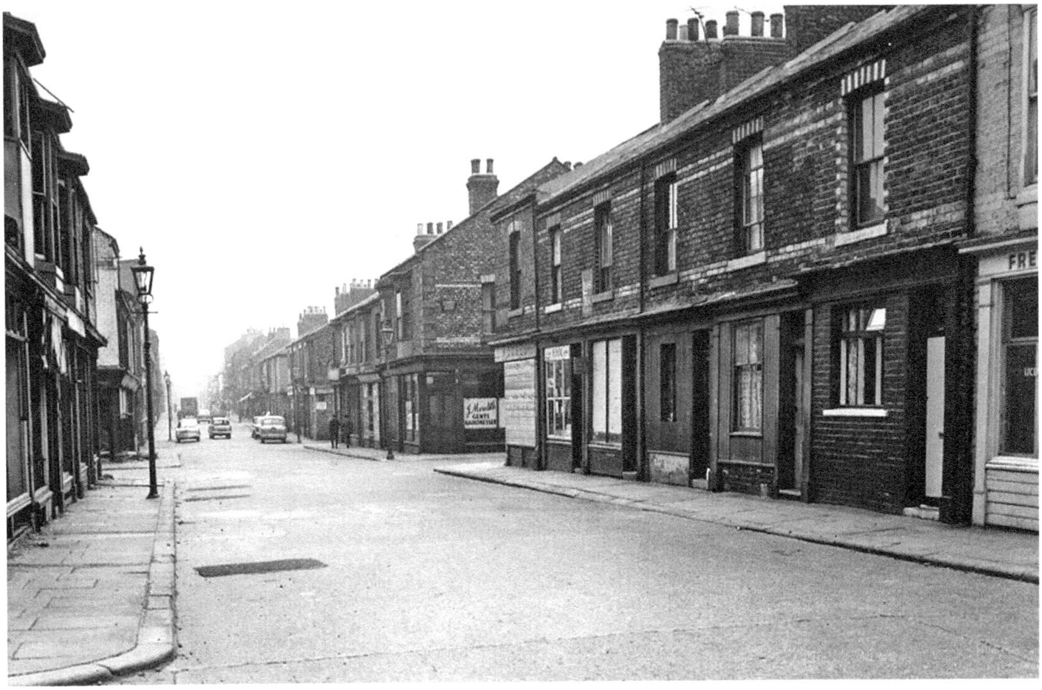

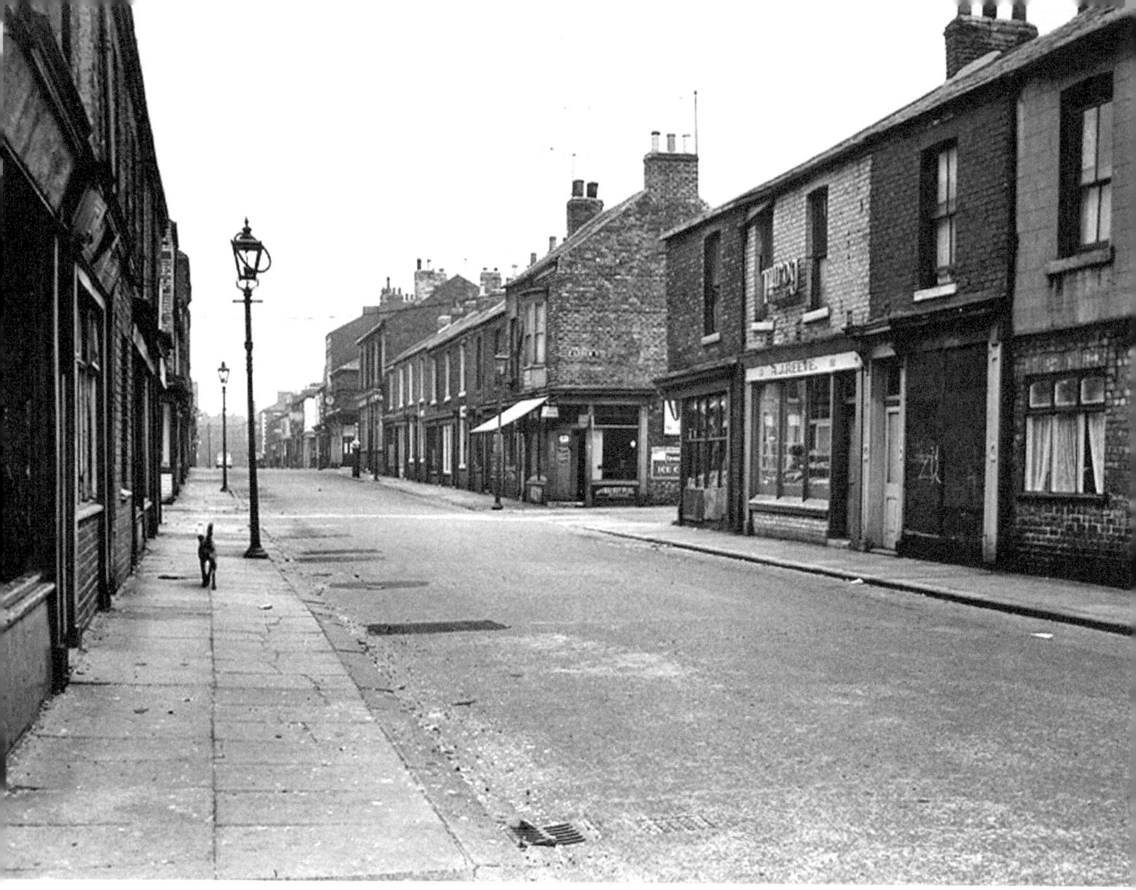

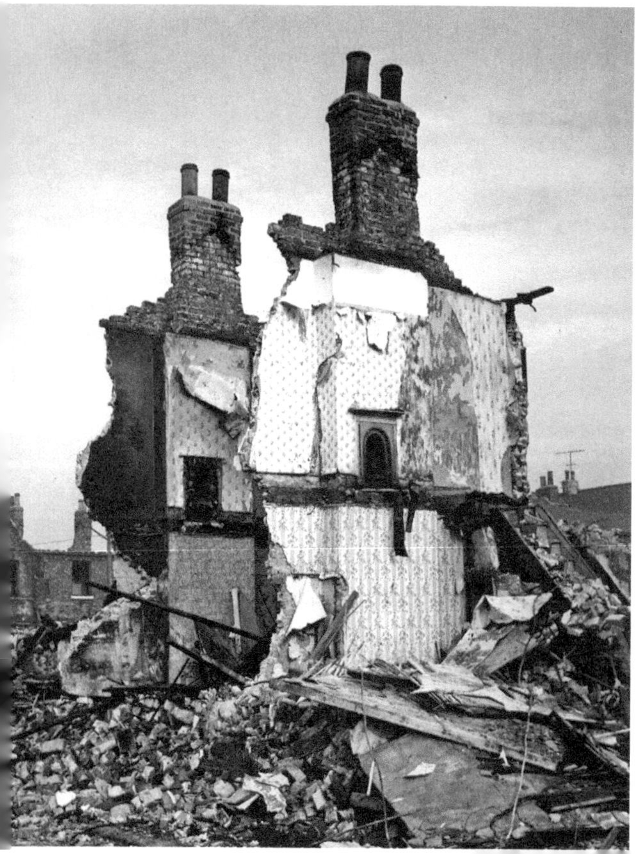

A dog wanders down the pavement of Cannon Street in this view from 17 July 1964. The image is further down towards Boundary Road when compared with the previous image. Lime Street is on the right.

A stark view from the clearance of Cannon Street as only the final shell of this property remains. The bedroom fireplaces and strips of wallpaper, left hanging from broken walls, paint a bleak picture of progress.

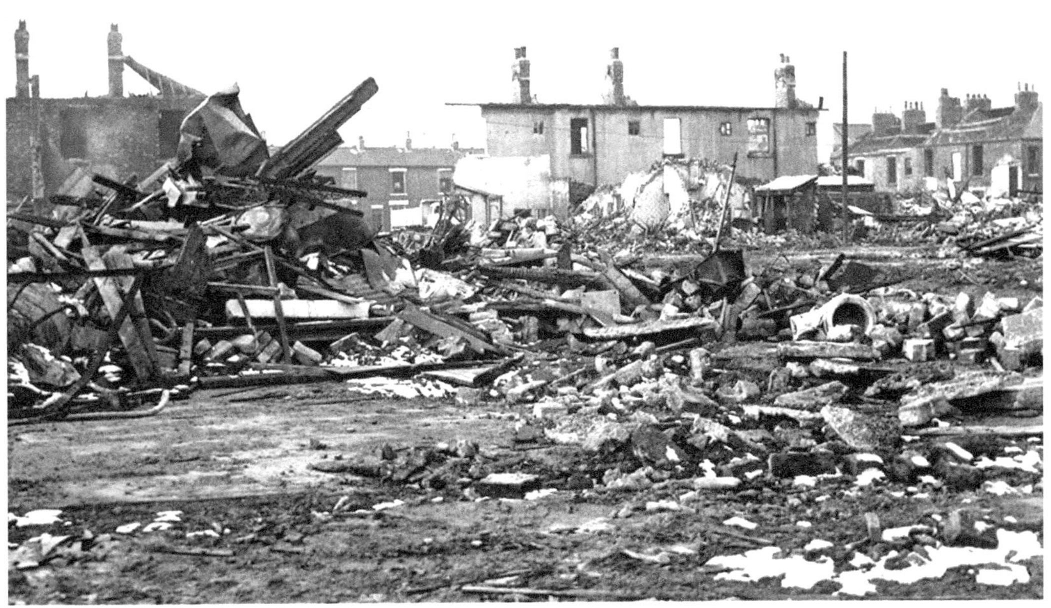

This picture is dated 15 February 1966 and the clearance has almost reached Newport. Today, standing amidst the industrial estates that cover the site, it is difficult to believe that this myriad of streets and terraced houses ever existed.

With hindsight we now know that the replacement of the Victorian slums with these new properties in the late 1950s and early 1960s provided no permanent solution, for the properties shown here have, only fifty years later, also been demolished. Visually the properties are very much of their time with a relatively simple, modern design. Two of the structures from the old town that still survive today, the Transporter Bridge and the old Town Hall, are visible in the background.

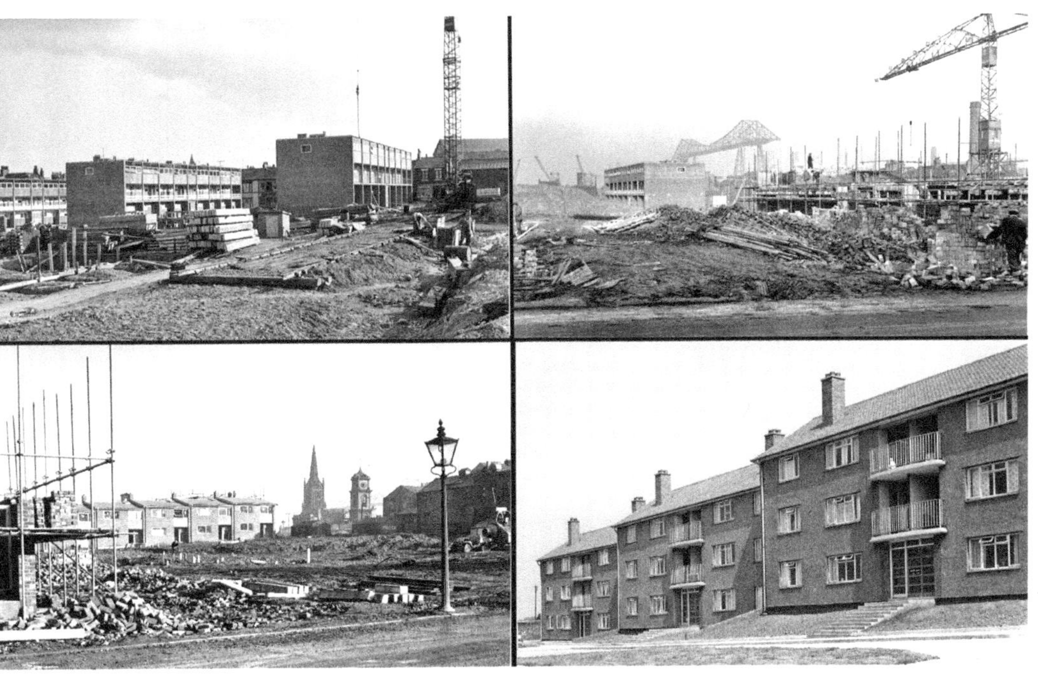

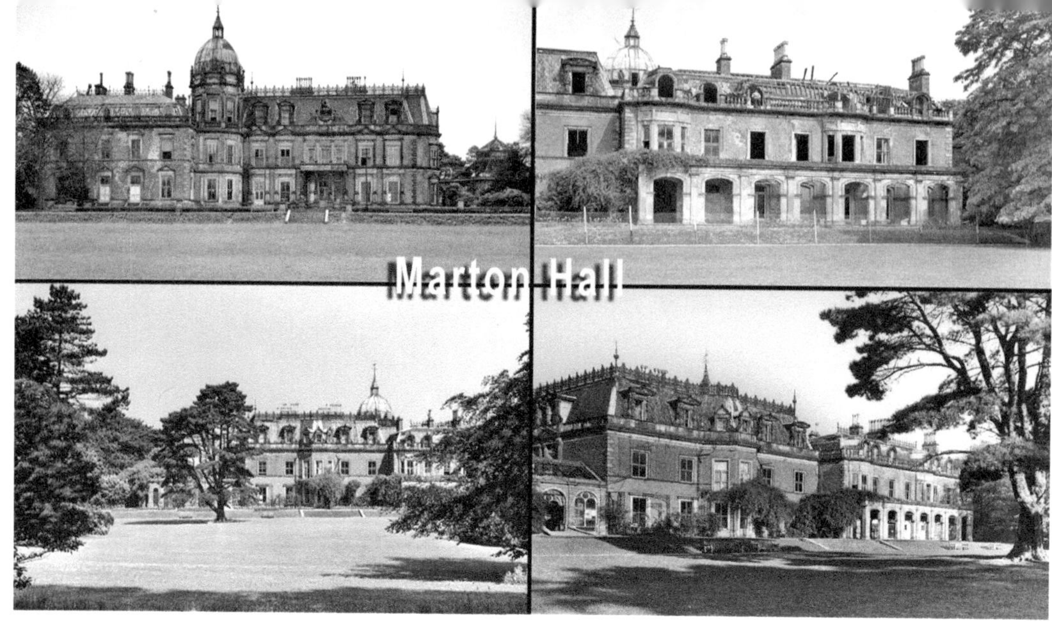

The demolition of buildings in the early 1960s was not confined to the old town. Marton Hall, regarded by many as one of Middlesbrough's most elegant buildings, was demolished in 1960, an event which even today, fifty years later, is still hotly debated by those who believe that it should have been saved. Whatever your views are, it is sad to see so much elegance destroyed. The Council had taken the decision to demolish the Hall in 1959 but on 4 June 1960, soon after work began, the building caught fire and a large part was destroyed. The images show the Hall in its final days.

A series of images taken during the demolition process. Many people argued that some of the more decorative features of the Hall could have been saved. An example is the elegant marble fireplace, shown here. The image of the tower and the bulldozer close by is especially poignant.

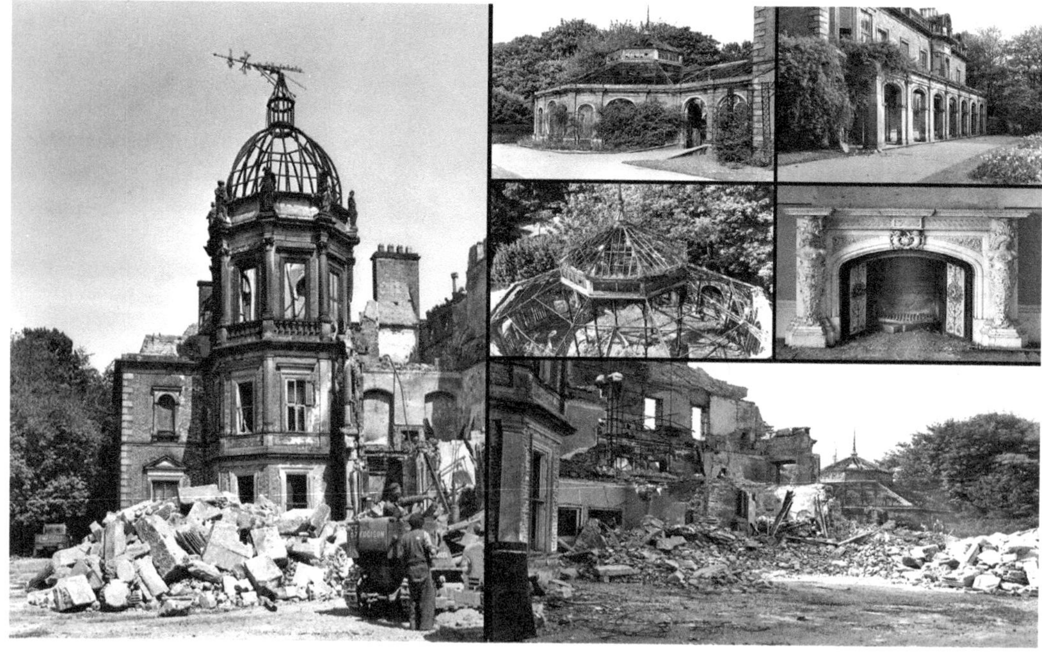

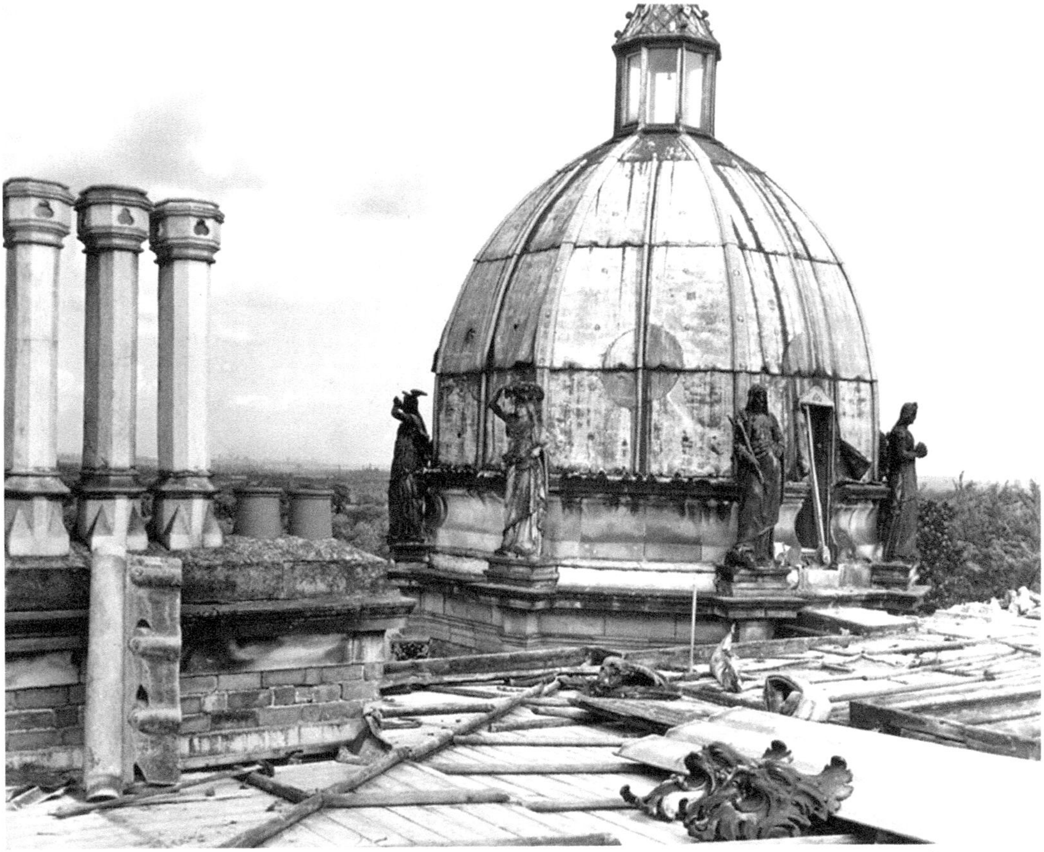

Perhaps the most stunning image in this series is this one of the Dome and the statues as we look north across to the industrial skyline of Middlesbrough. Note in the foreground the two gargoyles laid on the roof.

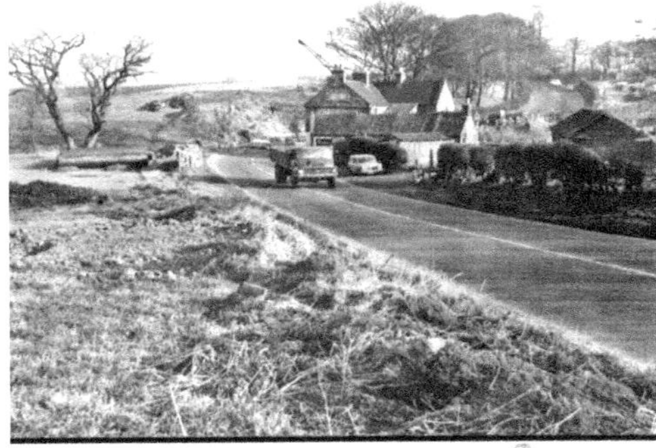

These images show the realignment of the road at Slip Inn Bank in 1962. The old road is still there today although few people are even aware that the Slip Inn pub ever existed. Many of the roads in the outer areas of the town had to be improved in the 1960s as traffic increased with more people moving to areas like Marton and Nunthorpe.

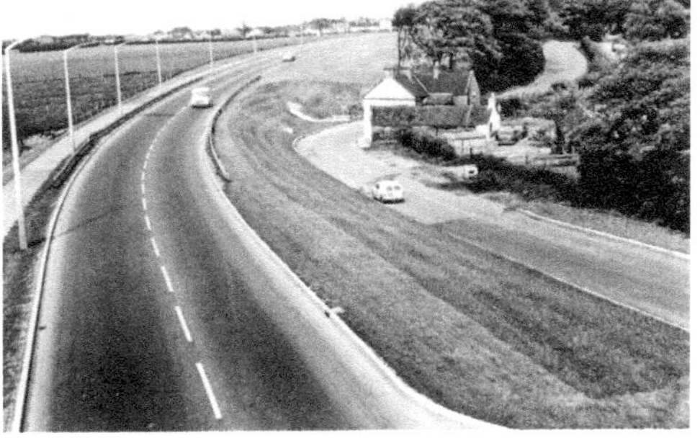

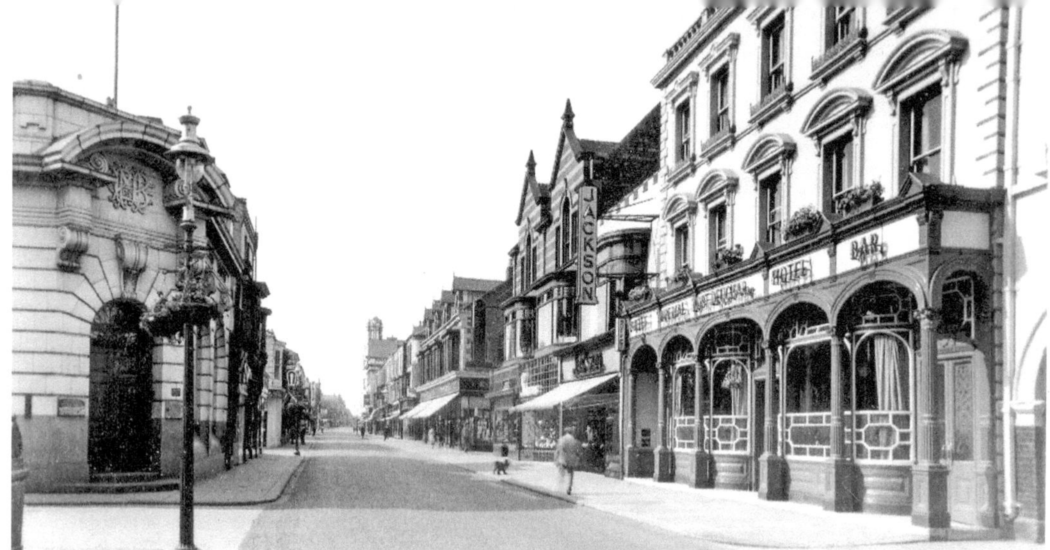

Linthorpe Road in the early 1960s. The picture was obviously taken at a quiet time as usually this was a very busy route. Soon this area would be pedestrianised as the buildings on the left were swept away by the Cleveland Centre. In the distance Wright's Tower House can be seen, while the buildings in the foreground include the Imperial Hotel (right) and the National Provincial Bank premises on the left.

This image, taken from the corner of Corporation Road and Albert Road, shows the Corporation Hotel, still one of the largest hotels in the town at this time. Newport Road can be seen in the distance – today this area is also pedestrianised while the Corporation Hotel is a distant memory for most people.

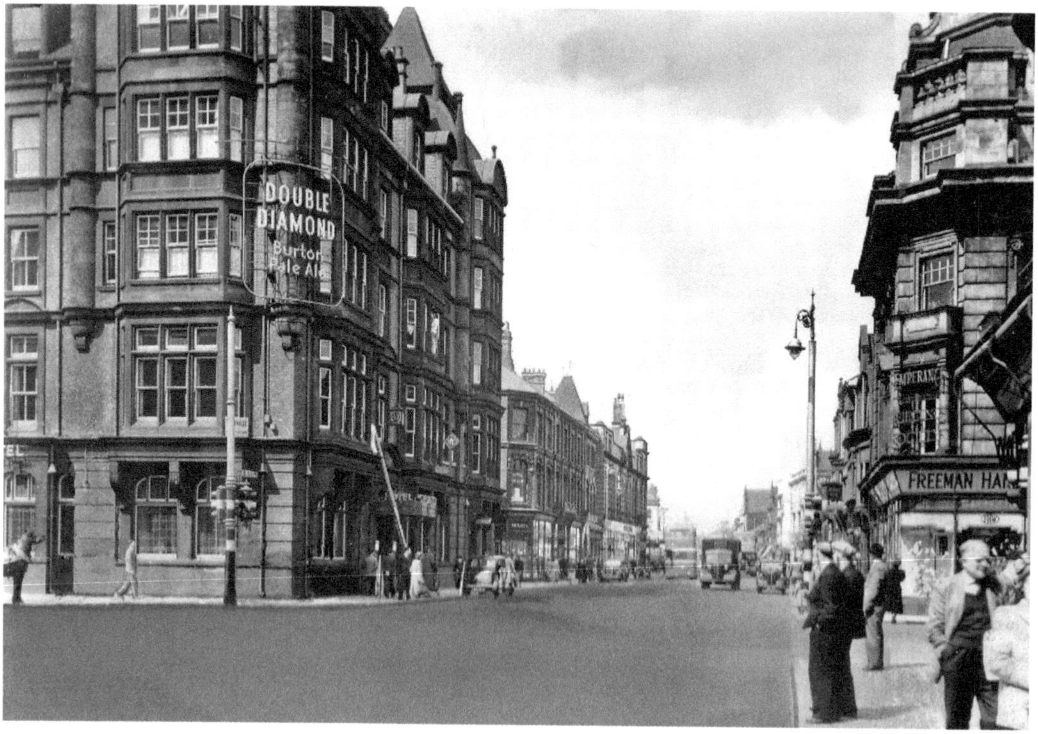

Two different views of Linthorpe Road. The upper image is from the corner of Bolckow Street with Marks and Spencer's store just visible on the right, while below is Wright's Tower House and the corner of Grange Road. Today the buildings on the right have been replaced by the Cleveland Centre and the Tower House is a McDonald's restaurant. Note that Linthorpe Road is not yet pedestrianised – many shoppers will recall a busy shopping day in Linthorpe Road trying to avoid the traffic as they walked along!

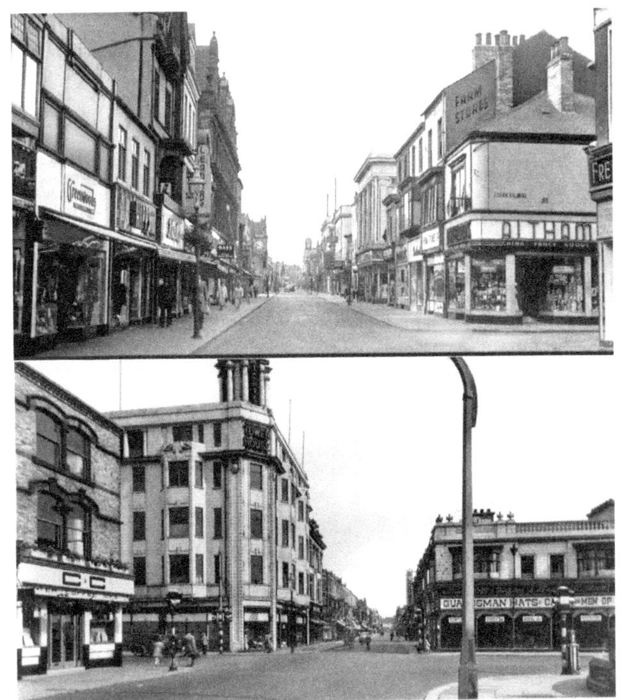

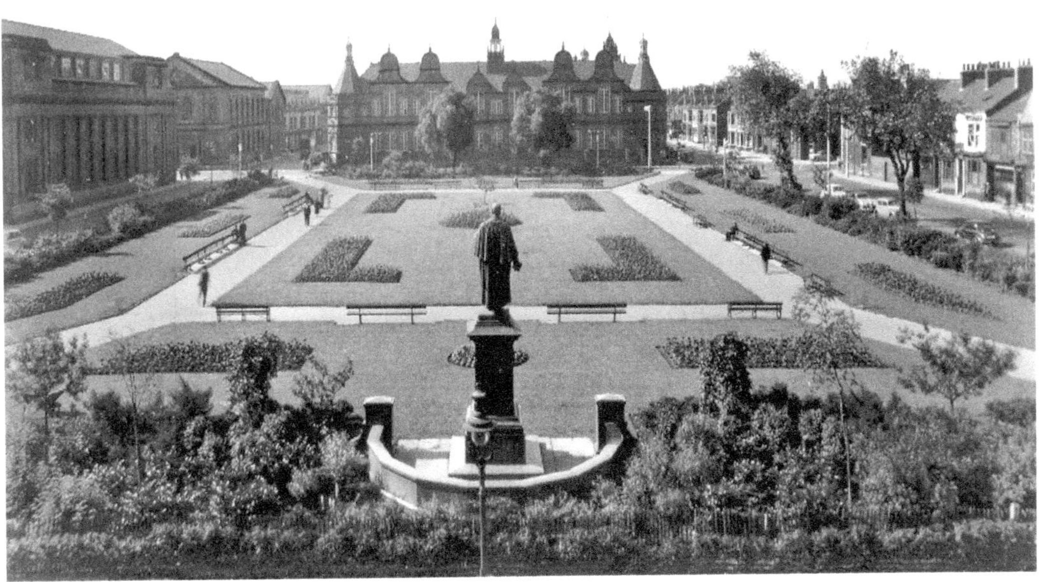

The theme of this chapter has been change, exemplified by this scene from fifty years ago. As it has done since its unveiling on 21 June 1913, the statue of Sir Samuel Sadler faces across Victoria Square to Hugh Bell School and the Central Library. Today only the library remains unchanged and many of the other buildings have gone. Change has always come quickly to Middlesbrough, making it appropriate to finish with an image of Victoria Square, an oasis of calm amidst the hustle of town life for over a hundred years.

BIBLIOGRAPHY

BOOKS

Bass, B. *Rudds of Marton* (Earth-Net Communications, 2001)
Bell, Lady Florence, DBE *At the Works* (Arnold; London, 1907)
Graves, Revd J. *History of Cleveland* (Jollie, 1808)
Harrison, J.K. *Eight Centuries of Milling in N. E. Yorkshire* (North York Moors National Parks Authority, 2008)
Harrison, J.W.H. *A Survey of the Lower Tees Marshes* (publisher unknown, 1916)
Hempstead, C.A. *Cleveland Iron and Steel Industry* (British Steel, 1979)
Horton, M. *Story of Cleveland* (Cleveland County Libraries, 1979)
Kirby, R.L. *Ancient Middlesbrough* (Woolston; Middlesbrough, 1899}
Lillie, W. *History of Middlesbrough* (Eyre & Spottiswood, 1968)
Mathews, A.D. *Acklam Hall: House and History* (1987)
Menzies, P. *Cleveland in Times Past* (Countryside; Chorley, 1987), *Around Cleveland* (History Press, 2009)
Moorsom, N. *Middlesbrough as it Was* (Hendon, 1983), *Book of Middlesbrough* (Barracuda Books, 1986)
Ord, J.W. *History and Antiquities of Cleveland* (London, 1846, reprinted Shotton, 1982)
Pollard, A.J.(ed.) *Middlesbrough Town & Community 1830-1950* (Sutton; Stroud, 1996)
Polley, L. *The Other Middlesbrough* (University of Teesside, 1993)
Roberston, W. *Middlesbrough's Effort in the Great War* (Jordison; Middlesbrough, 1924)
Stephenson, P. *Central Middlesbrough Vols. 1-3*, (1999-2003), *Linthorpe Road & Village* (2000)
Tomlin, D.M. *Past Industry along the Tees* (A.A. Sotheran, 1980), *South Bank to Eston* (Countryside, 1987)
Waterson, E. and Meadows, P., *Lost Houses of Yorkshire and the North Riding* (Raines, 1990)
Woodhouse, R. *Empire Theatre 1897-1987* (Middlesbrough, 1988), *Middlesbrough A Pictorial History* (Phillimore, 1989), *Stockton A Pictorial History* (Phillimore, 1990)

OTHER SOURCES

Ancestry website, ancestry.co.uk, Births, Marriages and Deaths Index, Census Records 1841-1901
Billingham Express, various editions 1952-66, *Billingham Press*, various editions 1946-52, *Evening Gazette Teesside*, various editions 1899-1968, *Stockton and Teesside Herald*, various editions 1919-40, all available on microfiche at Middlesbrough Reference Library
Cleveland and Teesside Local History Society: *History of Middlesbrough in Maps* (1980), *History of Stockton in Maps* (1982), *History of River Tees in Maps* (1990)
Jeffrys Thomas, Map of North Yorkshire 1771
Middlesbrough Extension map 1856 held at Teesside Archives
Middlesbrough Jubilee, *Illustrated London News*, 8 October 1881
Middlesbrough Football Club, *Lantern Magazine*, April 1895
North Ormesby History Group, 1999-2001, Windows on the Past
Ordnance Survey, 6 inch & 25 inch series, 1857, 1893, 1897, 1916)
Pease Joseph, Diary Extracts August 1828, unpublished
Smallwood Album US742, held at Teesside Archives
Stockton Local History Journal, Notes on Teesside Rail Stations (April 2006)
The Times, Online Archive 1785-1985, (Times Newspapers, 2008)
Tweddle G.W. Notes of the History of Middlesbrough 1881, unpublished
The Diaries of Ralph Jackson 1749-90 - consulted 1982-92 at Middlesbrough Reference Library.
Various oral interviews conducted between 1978 and 2008, typed up as statements of individual memories
In addition a large number of Trade Directories for County Durham and North Yorkshire, covering the period 1828 to 1939 have been consulted and used to provide and verify information.